The British Party System

Third Edition

The British Party System

Third Edition

Stephen Ingle

PINTER
London and New York

Pinter
A Cassell Imprint
Wellington House, 125 Strand, London WC2R 0BB
370 Lexington Avenue, New York, NY 10017-6550

First and second editions published 1987 and 1989 by Blackwell
Third edition published 2000

British Library Cataloguing in Publication Data
A catalogue record for this book is available from the British Library.

ISBN   1-85567-472-6 (hardback)
       1-85567-473-4 (paperback)

Library of Congress Cataloging-in-Publication Data
Ingle, Stephen.
    The British party system / Stephen Ingle. - 3rd ed.
    p. cm.
    Includes bibliographical references and index.
    ISBN 1-85567-472-6 (hc.)
    ISBN 1-85567-473-4 (pbk.)
    1. Political parties–Great Britain–History. I. Title.
    JN1117 154 1999
    324.241'009–dc21   99-34500
                                                            CIP

Typeset by BookEns Ltd, Royston, Herts
Printed and bound in Great Britain by T J International Ltd, Padstow, Cornwall

Contents

Acknowledgements

I should like first to record my thanks to those at Cassell who assisted me in the publication of this third edition of *The British Party System* for their encouragement and forbearance. It was a mistake to leave such a gap between the second and third editions (though this was not through choice) and as a consequence this edition has been substantially rewritten. This task would have been much more difficult had I not benefited from my wife's help in typing up, filing and cataloguing substantial numbers of newspaper and periodical articles. She is also a better proofreader than I. I have enjoyed, too, the advantage of working in a Department in which a number of colleagues research and write in the field of political parties. I should also like specifically to thank one of our excellent departmental secretaries, Nicola Jeffress, for her help in typing, scanning and photo-copying material.

Finally I should like to record my thanks to a former departmental secretary, Mrs Betty Skinner, who was always protective of my time and hugely helpful in typing and retyping chapters amidst her many other duties. Sadly Mrs Skinner died before this edition was published. She will be sorely missed, and I should like to dedicate this third edition to the memory of a loyal colleague and a good friend.

Stephen Ingle
Stirling, 1999

CHAPTER ONE

Parties and Party Systems in Britain

> "We MUST have a bit of a fight, but I don't much care about going on long", said Tweedledum. "What's the time now?" Tweedledee looked at his watch and said "Half-past four." "Let's fight till six, and then have some dinner," said Tweedledee.
>
> Lewis Carroll, *Alice Through the Looking Glass.*

Defining political parties generally or simply discovering where and when they originated in the United Kingdom, is no easy task. In his book *Political Parties and Party Systems*[1] Alan Ware suggests that parties are as easy to recognise but as difficult to define as elephants. This simile seems to suggest either some confusion about large animals or a rather strange understanding of politics: most of us would feel rather happier identifying elephants than parties. We need a much better understanding of the nature of the beast that is the subject of this study – British political parties, that is, and not elephants – before we can even attempt a definition.

Parties and how to recognise them

Ware begins his analysis of political parties by pointing out that although they are an essential part of the modern democratic framework, parties are nonetheless not a universal feature of all polities; indeed the political philosopher Rousseau saw them as a badge of failure. Some systems are governed by monarchical or dynastic families, some by military élites. In the British Isles, the self-governing Isle of Man possesses one of the oldest parliaments in the world but it has no political parties. In a number of the states of the US laws were introduced banning parties from contesting local elections at the beginning of the twentieth century and when Poland abolished political parties altogether in the late 1920s the socialist playwright Bernard Shaw welcomed the move as setting the Polish people free. Most democrats, however, believe that parties bring clear advantages to the running of polities by fulfilling certain essential functions and these may be identified as follows:

Popular involvement in government

Most parties seek to control the machinery of government and organise themselves to win elections and form governments (or participate at least in their formation). It is true that some parties seek to destroy and not administer the government. This was the traditional claim of the various Western European Communist parties, for example, and today in the UK the Scottish National Party (SNP) or Plaid Cymru (PC) seek power in order to dismember, not to run the British state. Sinn Fein has contested United Kingdom elections though it refuses to recognise the legitimacy of Westminster and does not take up its seats. Some parties seek not power itself but influence over those who wield power. In the 1997 UK general election the Referendum Party sought primarily to put pressure on the government-to-be to hold a referendum on the issue of British participation in a single European currency. Some parties do not seek even to influence but simply to make a statement: the Monster Raving Loony party in the United Kingdom has been contesting elections for over twenty years with no intention of forming or influencing a government; so too the Magillicudy Serious party in New Zealand.

Legitimacy

Most parties, however, seek power and they do so through the electoral process; they accept, or at least claim to accept, the legitimacy of that process whatever its outcome. Some may have good grounds to question the legitimacy of the outcome but not the process. In some developing countries for example the United Nations will provide teams of observers to ensure the fairness of elections, so that the outcome is seen to be legitimate. The traditional Irish electoral advice – vote early and vote often – suggests that electoral outcomes even in these islands may not always have been completely legitimate. As recently as the general election of 1997 the Labour MP for Glasgow Govan, Mohammed Sarwar, was the subject of claims of electoral malpractice though the courts eventually found in his favour. Moreover, the Liberal Democrats have often complained bitterly about the distorting nature of the British first-past-the-post electoral system, which has consistently caused them and their predecessors to be grossly under-represented in the House of Commons. Yet they have continued to contest general elections with great vigour. Though they seek to change the electoral system they do not contest its legitimacy.

Ideology

Ware speaks of parties as representing 'organised opinion'[2] and suggests that it is the range of that opinion which distinguishes even small parties from pressure groups. He goes on to point out, though, that the larger the party the wider the range of opinion it is likely to embrace, and that the need to win the votes of the non-committed has tended to make all major parties to some extent 'catch-all' parties: that is, parties which abandon or minimise ideological commitment (organised opinion) in order to win elections.[3] Ware goes on to suggest that some parties organised around a charismatic leader, such as the Argentine Peronist party, may lack any ideological commitment. There are also parties whose primary identification is with a social class or group rather than with an ideology, the Country (now National) party in Australia for example. Nevertheless, class or group-based parties, charismatic and even catch-all parties tend to fight elections on the basis of ideology, even if it is mostly symbolic, and that ideology will give rise to voter expectations in terms of which account will have to be given if that party gains power. It is true that some parties, especially charismatic ones, may seek to break the mould of traditional ideological confrontation but only to replace it with their own mould. Thus Peron's party could accommodate traditional leftists and rightists but in a new nationalist agenda. The British Liberal/Social Democrat (SDP) Alliance sought to bring together disillusioned activists and voters from the left and right of centre so as to 'break the mould' of British party politics; but only to recast it in a more suitable shape.

These are the chief characteristics of political parties in general. They apply to parties in the UK just as elsewhere. There is no doubt that parties seek to involve people and groups in the quest for political power, that they seek to do so legitimately through the electoral process and that they claim to represent an organised opinion – an ideology – and some have claimed to represent a class too. British parties are committed to the 'rules of the game', while recognising that these rules may change, perhaps substantially, over time. A defining characteristic of British parties is the fact that they have been prepared, like Tweedledum and Tweedledee, to stop fighting 'at dinner time' whoever is winning.

Parties and how to define them

In the newly-established USA Madison was not well disposed to parties, seeing them simply as factions 'actuated by some common impulse of passion, or of interest, adverse to the rights of other citizens, or indeed to the permanent and aggregate interests of the community'.[4] While by no means a defining characteristic of parties it is salutary to remember that party interests may not equate with the common interest. It was this possibility that concerned Rousseau among others. Downs sees parties as teams (that is, coalitions whose members are agreed on a spectrum of policies) 'seeking to control the government apparatus by gaining office in a duly constitutional election'.[5] But there is a sting in the tail as far as Downs is concerned, for he argued famously that 'parties formulate policies in order to win elections, rather than win elections in order to formulate policies'.[6] Although this has Orwellian overtones it does highlight another aspect of party activities which Maor believes is characteristic; their attempt to influence the public in addition to the policy-makers.[7] More positively, Ware defines a party as 'an institution that (a) seeks influence in a state, often by attempting to occupy positions in government, and (b) usually consists of more than a single interest in society and to some degree attempts to "aggregate interests"'.[8] Ball insists on the following characteristics: a degree of permanence, a commitment to fighting elections and gaining influence on the legislature, a commitment to gaining executive power (or to influencing those who have done so) through strength in the legislature, a distinct identity.[9]

Although each of these definitions adds something to our understanding of what political parties are, none captures the compelling simplicity of Burke's classical encompassing definition: 'A party is a body of men united for promoting by their joint endeavours the national interest upon some particular principle in which they are all agreed.'[10] Yet even Burke does not achieve the economy of Epstein's seemingly disingenuous but probably realistic definition: 'Almost everything that is called a party in any Western democratic nation can be so regarded ...'[11] But Epstein's definition invites the question: what kinds of group would be likely to call themselves parties? A working definition culled from the above might be as follows. Parties are principally groups of people organised to seek to wield or influence political power through agreed constitutional means in the name of some 'organised opinion' which binds them together and which distinguishes them from other groups. That organised opinion may represent, for example, religious, ethnic, geographical, ideological or economic opinion, or more likely some combination of these. Parties may seek to wield that influence directly through control of policy but they may also seek to wield influence indirectly through electoral pressure on those who do control policy.

Parties in Britain

To understand the historical development of British political parties we should seek their origins in the time when political disputes began to be settled not by recourse to violence but by constitutional means; to a time when a commitment to the principle that conflict should be confined within mutually accepted rules became common enough to be relied upon (i.e. legitimate). Clearly a precondition of such a commitment is the possibility of victory for competing groups either individually or in combination, and on a reasonably regular basis; an expectation somewhat optimistically represented in modern electoral times by the well-known 'swing of the pendulum' theory. Precisely because the credentials of a party system tend to be judged largely by the absence of overt violence and intimidation, it is taken for granted that such systems will operate optimally in a constitutional framework, best of all in a constitutional democracy. But let us be clear: the essential function of political parties is not to avoid conflict but to canalise it into constitutional waters. Party structures and strategies may change to meet changing circumstances – in nineteenth-century Britain, for example, the advent of mass democracy – but their basic functions will remain largely unchanged. So, bearing these notions in mind, we should be able to recognise British political parties when we see them. But recognising is not defining.

Origins

Is it proper to accept the 'Whig interpretation' of history and begin our story at the time of the constitutional settlement of 1688–89?[12] Certainly the two-party myth begins with the Whigs and the Tories of those days, but Samuel Johnson, who ought to have known, insisted that the first Whig was the Devil himself. Going back to the Fall of the Angels for the origins of parties might lead to an excessively long book. Indications of nascent political parties, however, might be discerned as early as the fourteenth century, in the struggle between the king and his supporters – the 'court party' – on the one hand, and the baronial opposition on the other. More specifically, when they were out of power, the Lancastrians sought consistently to limit monarchical power during the period, and even when the Lancastrian Henry IV gained the throne he felt obliged to institutional-ise the influence of the Council.[13] But the ferocity of the Wars of the Roses gives the lie to any notion of the emergence of genuine political parties at that time. When writing about the seventeenth century, however, historians commonly refer to the existence of parties. In the great debate in the House of Commons on 8 February 1641, for example, on the continuance of the episcopacy, Gardiner speaks of two parties standing opposed to each other 'not merely on some incidental question, but on a great principle of action which constituted a permanent bond between those who took one side or the other'.[14] Similarly in 1680 the division over the extent of the legitimate powers of the crown was essentially a division between parties, and the bloodless Revolution of 1688 resulted in the permanent decline in the powers of the crown and its supporters (the Tories) and in the triumph of those who sought to restrict royal power (the Whigs). Now parties would contest power within parliament, and already the seventeenth century 'had given them a myth and a martyrology and the name of two gangs of ruffians, Whig and Tory'.[15] The emergence of something recognisably like parties at Westminster should not obscure the fact that no such divisions were considered important by the population at large; even at Westminster, 'party' was not always a decisive consideration thereafter. Yet the positions adopted in the Glorious Revolution demarcated two sides. As David Hume wrote: 'Factions were indeed extremely animated against each other. The very names, by which each party denominated its antagonist, discover the virulence and rancour which prevailed ... The court party reproached their antagonists with their affinity to the fanatical conventiclers of Scotland who were known by the name of Whigs; the country party found a resemblance between the courtiers and the popish banditti in Ireland, to whom the appellation Tory was affixed.'[16].

It would be reasonable to conclude that by the end of the seventeenth century, according to our definition, two parties existed. They did not operate in a clearly structured party 'system', however, and there was no general recognition by constitutional writers of the benefits to be gained by two parties competing for power; simply, the Tories desired to dominate the Whigs and the Whigs the Tories.

Eighteenth-century parties: parliamentary factions

Throughout the eighteenth century the great parliamentary protagonists or parties tended to be powerful aristocratic families and their political dependants, with neither programmes nor organisations but simply the hierarchical ties of patron and client. Elections, especially for county seats, were notoriously expensive during the eighteenth century. When Wilberforce stood for Yorkshire in 1784, he and his running mate had to put together £18,000. Not surprisingly only about 15 per cent of county seats were contested. Borough elections, too, were expensive. Voters in Hull, for example, were awarded a token for the promise of their vote which they would exchange for substantial amounts of ale. Moreover, the demands on members did not end at election time. Sir Charles Hotham, having been hounded for favours of all sorts by his East Yorkshire constituents, wrote: 'I cannot help offering it as my most serious and earnest advice to those who shall succeed me to suffer no consideration to induce them to become representatives of Beverley or Scarborough ... If they will be in parliament it should be much further from home.' For those who accepted the poisoned chalice, membership of the House was a sign of social eminence and members were generally wealthy and independent-minded. There were, it is true, numbers of young members enjoying the patronage of a landed gentleman, but when his interests were not at stake they had the freedom to act much as they chose.

In 'party terms', as the eighteenth century wore on, fewer than half the members of either House would have been, or have wanted to be, categorised as Whigs or Tories. Certainly these 'parties' might federate to form governments but they lacked both the sanctions and the rewards – the sticks and the carrots – to encourage any permanent loyalty in the Commons. These prerogatives belonged either to the king or to the great magnates like the Duke of Newcastle who had considerable numbers of parliamentary seats at their disposal. Nothing more formal than an elementary whipping-in of known supporters on particular issues took place, together with informal gatherings at the great houses or clubs and some cursory canvassing. Whig and Tory could usually be identified among the members of George III's Houses of Parliament but what made a man what he was, in Plucknett's words, was 'not what he proposed to do in the future, but what he thought about the past'[17] – by which he meant that every Tory saw himself as a latter-day cavalier and every Whig a latter-day roundhead[18] – and the parties to which they belonged were characterised by the historian Feiling as possessing little more than 'a continuous tradition and some elementary framework … and a descent of political ideas'.[19]

Toward the end of the eighteenth century, however, three major issues were to have a profound effect upon British politics: parliamentary reform, the American War and above all the French Revolution. 'The Whig rhetoric', according to one commentator, 'spoke of reform, parliament and the people', though within their own ranks they were divided as to the definitions and implications of these terms, from the radical Wilkes to the Whig Grey. The Tories were for 'King, Church and Constitution', but the varieties of interpretations they gave their causes was illustrated by their divisions over Catholic emancipation and the reform of parliament.[20] Numbers of influential Whigs were favourably disposed to the American colonists in their struggle for political rights which those Whigs felt to be no more than the birthright of the British (despite the fact that the overwhelming majority of the British did not enjoy them). The Tory government was opposed to the colonists' claims and sought to deny them by force. There was, moreover – initially at least – support among the more radically-minded Whigs for the principles of the French revolution, whereas the Tories almost to a man were staunchly opposed (as indeed were many Whig magnates). Within this new quasi-ideological framework the idea of governments resigning when they had lost the confidence of the House began to take shape, thus encouraging a greater degree of permanence and sense of cohesion among the groupings. A more formal party system was beginning to emerge in parliament.[21]

Party politics at this time did not concern the vast bulk of the population. Prior to the Great Reform Act of 1832 the entire British electorate comprised only approximately 435,000. Moreover, those who contended for power came exclusively from the same class. On the eve of its transformation by the Great Reform Act, British politics could be summed up, according to Ostrogorski, in a single sentence. 'It was the absolute domination of the aristocratic class.'[22] Ostrogorski went on to make the point that the power and social homogeneity of the ruling class were buttressed by the notion of gentlemanly behaviour which was an 'unwritten charter' like the constitution of the realm. According to a table prepared about 1815, the House of Commons contained no fewer than 471 members who owed their seats to the goodwill of peers and landed gentlemen and it was certainly considered ungentlemanly not to support one's patron. In Disraeli's *Coningsby*, Lord Monmouth says to his grandson: 'You go along with your family, sir, like a gentleman; you are not to consider your opinions like a philosopher or political adventurer.' It is an interesting but not often remarked feature of the pre-reformed House of Commons that, at much the same time that Burke wrote to his several thousand Bristol constituents explaining that he owed them not his vote but his judgement, most members in the House thought it gentlemanly to follow the instructions of one individual patron. The great Whig parliamentarian Charles James Fox remarked in 1797 upon the paradox that members representing large towns debated whether they ought to follow their own judgement or the interests of their constituents but that those representing a noble lord entertained no such doubt, 'and he is not considered a man of honour who does not implicitly obey the orders of a single constituent.'

The party system which grew up during the period from the Glorious Revolution to the 1832 Reform Act was not always dominated by two parties and, even when it was, they performed quite different functions from modern parties. Moreover, calculations of party support in the House indicate a substantial fraction – as much as a third – who could not be given a party label at all. Nevertheless, that system accommodated the rehabilitation of the former Jacobite Tories within the constitutional framework and regularised disputes between aristocratic factions without jeopardising the monopoly of power of the class as a whole. Divisions in the unreformed House, as Ostrogorski pointed out, 'in no way impaired the homogeneousness of the single united ruling class.'[23] G.K. Chesterton's description of the developments prior to 1832 was more colourful. 'It was the very soul of the old aristocratic polity', he wrote, 'that even a tyrant must never appear as a tyrant. He may break down everybody's fences and steal everybody's land, but he must do it by Act of Parliament and not with a two-handed sword. And if he meets the people he's dispossessed, he must be very polite to them and enquire after their rheumatism. That's what's kept the British constitution going – enquiry after rheumatism.'[24] What Ostrogorski and indeed Chesterton omit, however, is the potential for growth and development within the unreformed system when parties, even within the same class, compete for power. For to be victorious and gain power within a constitutional system they must appeal to some constituency beyond themselves and their opponents, and as royal power waned an appeal to other social classes was to become inevitable.

Nineteenth-century parties: the growth of democracy

The early nineteenth century was to see the advent of a new social class with wealth and influence and, to some extent, a distinctive ideology. The energy and ambition of this new class are well captured by Sir Thomas Throgmorton about whom the *Quarterly Review* of 1825 reported that he would appear at dinner wearing a suit of cloth which had been on the backs of his own sheep that very morning. These thrusting radicals represented the break-up of the social homogeneity of the ruling class and were to cause the House of Commons to cease to be an arena in which the factions within the ruling class contended for power. They were able to use the party system of 'we' and 'they', Whig and Tory, to their own advantage and eventually, with Whig support, they were able to forge a party of their own and to challenge the dominance of the landed aristocracy.

What was the radicalism that so many of these men supported? According to John Stuart Mill it represented a frontal attack on 'the wretched supposition that the English institutions were models of excellence'. Certainly radicalism, with its belief that democratic suffrage constituted, in Mill's words, 'the most essential of securities for good government', was one of the driving forces behind the Great Reform Act. For the radicals 1832 was the first step on the path to full male suffrage; to their Whig allies, whom they regarded as 'squeezable material', the Reform Act represented pretty much the opposite: simply the perfecting of existing constitutional arrangements. The last step, not the first.

Meanwhile Wellington and others were not so much dismayed at the advent of parties such as the ones we might recognise, but instead prematurely mourning the death of parties as they knew them. Indeed after the election of 1830 there was no agreement even as to who had won, the government claiming gains of twenty-two seats and the opposition declaring that the government had lost fifty! This is perhaps more easy to understand when we remember that prior to 1918 general elections were not held on a single day but usually spread out over two, three and even four weeks. If parties in Wellington's sense were dying, other kinds of party were taking their place. The House of Commons was regularly dividing into two camps on major issues. Governments were beginning to pursue policies with more consistency than hitherto and, as royal patronage declined after 1832, it was not long before governments were 'going to the people', still only about five per cent of the population, with specific measures which they promised to implement if elected. This happened most notably in 1834, when Sir Robert Peel beguiled his electors at Tamworth with a platform of policy commitments. These were later incorporated into the famous Tamworth Manifesto, though in truth it was to be another forty years before the manifesto came to play its modern role. To speak of a party system at this time then requires us to understand that although there were identifiable groups with what might be described as rudimentary ideological positions on the major issues of the day, they were by no means effectively disciplined in the House of Commons, and there was almost nothing in the way of extra-parliamentary organisation.

This is not to imply that the concept of party as it developed during the nineteenth century was an unreal one. According to Barker the essence of party in the British context is not so much ideology or organisation as simply the emergence of a leadership which could retain allegiance.[25] This allegiance would in turn promote continuity, and as Gilmour points out the continuity, 'was of power and opposition, not of names and parties.'[26] Barker argues that party signifies something much less and yet also much more than is suggested by the definitions which we used earlier; he believes it to represent a response to deep human instincts – the stimulus of leadership and the warmth of personal contact. From a different perspective Katz and Mair stress the importance of individual actors: the interaction between them 'is the driving force of party life'.[27] Most men (women's feelings on the matter must wait) have a natural desire for some system of sides or teams to which they can pledge their loyalty. It was natural enough, given the traditional division of 'ins' and 'outs', power and opposition, for some kind of two-party system to emerge: not an ideological division, though, but one based on 'bodies of common sentiment' for a 'side and its colour'. That such partisanship existed and was a feature not only of the late eighteenth but also of the nineteenth and even twentieth centuries, suggests that it might indeed have been natural. There are countless examples in literature of the emotions evoked, especially at the hustings, by this 'common sentiment', as Dickens's description of Eatanswill in *The Pickwick Papers* shows:

> It appears then that … every man in Eatanswill, conscious of the weight that attached to his example, felt himself bound to unite heart and soul, with one of the two great parties that divided the town – the Blues and the Buffs.… There were Blue shops and Buff shops. Blue inns and Buff inns – there was a Blue aisle and a Buff aisle in the very church itself.

Descriptions of the partisanship of nineteenth-century elections are to be found in a number of novels, for example in George Eliot's *Felix Holt*. This account was based upon Miss Eliot's personal experiences at the Nuneaton hustings in 1832 when the Riot Act was read out and a detachment of Scots Greys ordered in. Later in the century Disraeli and George Meredith were also to give descriptions of 'robust' election campaigns based upon personal experience. Anthony Trollope, later still, described his fortnight's canvassing in the East Yorkshire borough of Beverley as 'the most wretched fortnight of my manhood'. Fictionalised, his experiences were offered to posterity in the novel *Ralph the Heir*. Most of the participants in the earlier electoral excitement, though, would not even have had the right to vote and virtually none could reasonably have felt that either party represented their interests. The loyalty and commitment were obviously self-generating, evidence for Barker's 'deep human instinct' theory. On the other hand, it is unlikely that these emotions had no ideological substance at all – Dickens' description suggests the opposite. Moreover, Barker's socio-psychological characterisation of parties could equally well apply to other kinds of groups – for example rival football teams. Perhaps Barker has drawn our attention to another dimension of parties but not surely an alternative characterisation.

But to return to the plot, if something vaguely resembling a modern two-party system was emerging by the late 1830s, it was not destined to last long for in 1846 the Prime Minister, Sir Robert Peel, in repealing the Corn Laws which his government had been pledged to maintain, smashed the historic Tory party, sending some of the more progressive Conservatives, on his untimely death four years later, into the newly emerging Liberal party. In the shorter term this measure destroyed not only his own party but also that coalition of Whigs and radical and middle-class representatives who had defeated the Tories, for these had no need to stay together any longer and did not in fact do so. 'Parliament', according to Ostrogorski, 'ceased to exhibit its old consistency because society had lost it. The constant multiplication of degrees in the social scale, the variety of new aspirations, the change of social relations from the concrete to a generalised standard, all found their way into the House, narrow as the entrance to it was at that time.'[28] If Ostrogorski was right, then this suggests that Barker's thesis of the naturalness of the two-party structure needs to be re-examined. Barker might be persuaded to modify it to incorporate some idea of temporary breakdown, indicating that from time to time there will be a dealignment of social classes and political power, but he might still insist that the 'natural' divide will reassert itself, as indeed it appeared to do by the 1860s. Nevertheless we might argue that it is the process of social change itself which is natural and that parties will respond accordingly. Changes in society and in political representation were clearly afoot as the century wore on and the middle class – Macaulay's 'brave, honest, and stout-hearted class ... anxious for the security of society and ... hostile to corruption and oppression'[29] – was able to challenge aristocratic political eminence by commandeering its own party and helping to create what was increasingly to become a two-party system based largely upon social class. The Liberals were, however, more than simply a party for the middle class. They represented a wide variety of single-issue group activists, campaigning on issues such as temperance and education reform. Such groups were almost invariably associated with Nonconformist sects and considered themselves, rightly, as 'outsiders'. Hence their radicalism.

There are other aspects of the 1832 Act to be considered. At the time the duty of preparing lists of voters belonged to the overseers of the poor in every parish and any qualified elector could have his name included in the register (and indeed object to names already on the list). Shortly after the Act was passed registration societies began to be formed with the purpose of ensuring that all known supporters of the party were registered to vote. Sir Robert Peel quickly appreciated the significance of registration, describing it as an element more powerful than king or Commons. 'The registration', he said, 'will govern the disposal of offices, and determine the policy of party attack; and the power of this new element will go on increasing as its secret strength becomes better known and is more fully developed.'[30] Peel prophetically predicted the 'systematic organisation' of registration, because he grasped the new reality that, in order to win, candidates would have to gain the votes of a large number of people to whom they were not personally known. They could do this best by outlining what they proposed to do if elected. This is what he himself did in the Tamworth Manifesto, which may be regarded as both the first modern election address and the first party manifesto – though it is a nice historical irony that the document appeared after the election.

Peel's prediction was justified: registration societies multiplied over the next quarter of a century and by 1861 the Liberals had established the Liberal Registration Association which had the principal task of coordinating constituency registration and establishing societies or associations where none existed. The name of this body was later changed to the Liberal Association. Characteristically the registration societies formed after 1832 were not in any sense representative but self-elected and self-perpetuating, and it was only with the passage of time that pressures towards greater representativeness made themselves felt. Conservatives in Liverpool, for example, organised originally in 1832, reorganised themselves in 1848 into a representative constitutional association based upon wards with elected officials, each holding positions on the associations. These local Conservative clubs fulfilled a number of social functions, providing reading rooms and educational facilities, sickness benefits, seaside excursions and so on. They helped to integrate into politics a body of men most of whom, until 1867, did not posses the vote.[31] Ostrogorski referred to registration as 'a gap through which the parties ... made their way into the constituencies and gradually covered the whole country with their network of organisations'.[32] In 1867, however, the second major electoral reform of the century was to transform the franchise and to require parties to organise their supporters. The electorate had more than doubled (to approximately 1,365,000); and organising the party vote was becoming a full-time responsibility. Parties began to appoint agents, to encourage the growth of 'clubs' which would cement voter loyalty by providing a centre in which the faithful could drink, organise lectures and generally socialise.[33] Parties also began to set up constituency organisations to such an extent that within twenty years very few candidates indeed would stand for election without the support of an agent, a constituency association and a number of local clubs.[34]

The 1867 Act also stimulated organisation at the national level. Within a year the National Union of Conservative and Constitutional Associations (NUCCA) had been formed to maximise Conservative support from its working-men's clubs and local associations already in existence, and annual conferences were established. These became important when at the Crystal Palace in 1872 the party leader Disraeli chose the occasion to make a major speech, signalling in many respects the opening of an epoch of truly national general elections. By 1878 the National Union had grown sufficiently to establish provincial bodies. The Conservatives had also established a Central Office in 1870, pretty much under the control of the party whips, to stimulate the growth of new constituency associations and to draw up lists of prospective candidates. No doubt the party leadership wished to keep a paternal eye on the activities of NUCCA, but the new arrangement led to some duplication and friction.[35] However, these problems remained manageable owing to the influence in both bodies of John Gorst, who headed the Central Office and was honorary secretary of NUCCA. Central Office was to grow to the extent that in 1911 the post of party chairman was created to coordinate the organisation and provide liaison with NUCCA. All in all, Conservative party organisation was 'in advance of anything the Liberal had and must have greatly helped the Tories towards their first parliamentary majority in thirty years.'[36] Equally important for the future development of the party in the country was Disraeli's Primrose League, founded in 1883 to promote Conservative values. Its membership had exceeded one million by 1890.[37] As Fisher rightly points out, one of the most important contributions the League made to the development of the Conservative party was to involve numbers of women – long before they enjoyed the vote – in party organisational affairs.

The Liberals, who had generally been somewhat slower off the mark than their opponents, were to respond to the changes ushered in by the Second Reform Act in a spectacularly successful fashion. The 1867 Act created four three-member constituencies, Leeds, Manchester, Liverpool and Birmingham. During the passage of the bill, the House of Lords had successfully added an amendment to the effect that voters in these cities would be allowed only two votes. Now, the Liberals of Birmingham believed that there were enough Liberals in their city, if properly organised, to ensure the election of three Liberal MPs. In order to achieve the necessary organisation the Birmingham Liberal Association reformed itself on a democratic basis at ward and city level. The number of Liberal voters in each ward was ascertained and each was advised how he should use his two votes. The upshot was that three Liberals were returned for Birmingham in the following election, thereby thwarting their Lordships' intentions. In 1873 the association appointed as its secretary Francis Schnadhorst who, together with Birmingham's favourite-son-to-be, Joseph Chamberlain, sought to gain control of municipal government for the Liberals. That year Chamberlain was elected mayor and the party was massively successful in the council elections. The Birmingham association was clearly a shining example for municipal political associations throughout the country, an example which the Conservatives would ignore at their peril. Moreover the three-member constituencies enabled Liberals more easily to preserve the electoral alliance between the Whigs and the radicals; they could select candidates from both camps.

It is generally considered that the Conservatives' electoral success of 1874 was attributable in some measure to the activities of the National Union and the Central Office, and the lesson was not lost on the Liberals, including those irregulars in the Liberal army, the single-issue groups. At a conference held, appropriately, in Birmingham the National Liberal Federation was formed, with Chamberlain as its president and Schnadhorst its secretary. There was an important difference, though, between the Liberal Federation and the Conservative National Union. The Federation sought to take on the mantle, to use Chamberlain's words, of being a 'Liberal parliament', formulating by open democratic debate the policies to be followed by future Liberal administrations. It was this aspiration which earned for the Federation Disraeli's dismissive description, 'the Birmingham caucus'. But the value of the caucus was undeniable: it was instrumental in the party's triumph in 1880. All the same, its overwhelmingly radical character put it at odds with the parliamentary leadership. Hanham quotes a member of the Leeds Liberal Association awakening, at a local meeting, to the changing nature of party organisation: 'As I listened to that debate ... I realized the fact that a great revolution had been suddenly and silently wrought, and that the control of the Liberal party had ... passed out of the hands of its old leaders into those of the men who managed the new "machine"'.[38] The deadlock was not broken until an open breach formed between Gladstone and Chamberlain over the issue of Home Rule for Ireland in 1886, after which Chamberlain and the Liberal Unionists left the party and formed a separate association. Thereafter, with the fear of Birmingham-inspired radicalism removed, the great majority of local associations affiliated to the National Federation.

Another feature of the 1880 election had been the national tour undertaken by the Liberal party leader, William Gladstone. Hitherto party leaders had satisfied themselves with campaigning in their own constituencies. This development was said to have filled Queen Victoria with some alarm, but it was to become a standard feature of subsequent election campaigns and in a sense only built on the national role assumed by Disraeli earlier. Equally important for the development of modern parties, especially the Liberals, was the increasing reliance on central funds for constituency campaigning. We have seen already how expensive eighteenth-century campaigns could be but, with the growth of the electorate to over five millions in 1884, the prospect of 'persuading' electors to support a candidate had become prohibitively expensive. However, the Secret Ballot Act of 1872 made it impossible to judge the effectiveness of persuasion and anyway the Corrupt and Illegal Practices Act of 1883 made it illegal! Pinto Duschinsky has shown that the percentage of Liberal candidates' expenses provided by central party funds was to grow from four per cent in 1880 to twenty-seven per cent by 1906.[39]

Other major changes, too, were taking place in parliamentary procedure in the House of Commons during the 1880s. In order to combat the disruptive tactics of Irish members, Gladstone began to end debates on a majority vote, thus requiring party cohesion. These changes, largely designed to ease the passage of his Irish legislation, tended to favour the government and hence set up a reaction among the opposition. Alpheus Todd, writing in 1887, was moved to declare that the job of the opposition had become to attack '... every measure, act or word, of every member of the ministry, in short to constitute a standard censorship of the government'.[40] Similar to the present system, then, but not the same, and Hanham is right to conclude that 'cartoonists who showed Disraeli and Gladstone as two pugilists were nearer to the mark than those who emphasised the overriding importance of ideas and lofty moral aspirations'.[41] In that decisive sense, late nineteenth-century parties, even at their most combative, remained different from modern parties. Nevertheless fewer than 60 per cent of divisons were 'whipped' in the 1860s; by 1906 that figure was nearer 90 per cent.

One major development in nineteenth-century party history still remained, the displacing of the Liberal party by Labour. By the 1880s it was becoming clear to an increasing number of labour leaders that the existing party framework was not taking sufficient account of the interests of labour. Working-class males had been enfranchised in 1867 or in 1884 (the Third Reform Act) but only a few were able to become parliamentary candidates because some measure of personal wealth or patronage was still generally necessary to enter politics. For example, the Liberals supported only eleven successful working-class candidates in the 1880s, the so-called Lib-Labs, though miners' candidates also secured election and these too took the Liberal whip. Moreover, the Liberal leader, Gladstone, 'the people's William', was focusing his party's attention more on Ireland than on domestic reforms. During the last twenty years of the century the Liberal party took insufficient note of the rise of two phenomena related in the modern mind but not in the Victorian mind: working-class politics and socialism. They came together officially only in 1893 at a conference in Bradford which included representatives of trade unions and socialist societies and which established the Independent Labour party to secure the better representations of the interests of labour. Little followed directly but in 1899 the Trades Union Congress called a meeting in London to which representatives of seventy trade unions, the Independent Labour party and socialist societies were invited. This conference established a Labour Representation Committee (LRC) with the declared purpose of creating a Labour group in parliament with its own whips and its own policies, ready to co-operate with any party which showed itself interested in promoting legislation in the direct interest of labour. The LRC's first secretary was later to become Britain's first Labour Prime Minister, James Ramsay MacDonald. Shortly the LRC fought its first election, putting forward fifteen candidates of whom two were successfully elected. More important, though, was a decision taken in 1903 that successful parliamentary candidates should sign a pledge restraining them from identifying with any section or interest within the major parties. To be independent, however, was to be independently financed, and the same conference took a decision to make a levy on all members of affiliated bodies to provide MPs with £200 per annum. (In 1911 all MPs were to receive an official salary.)

Once again, then, a major change in the British socio-political structure would be accommodated within the constitutional framework. Like the bourgeoisie in the first half of the nineteenth century the working class managed not merely to articulate its own interests within the party framework but to shape a political party in its own image capable of winning power on the back of the majority working-class vote. It was entirely fortuitous that Labour's constituency was large enough for the party to aspire to win power but not too large to drive the owning class to consider extra-constitutional means to hang on to power.

Twentieth-century parties: class politics

The rise of the Labour party, in parenthesis, indicated as well a major change in the nature of party politics. We observed that the fierce inter-party competition of the earlier part of the nineteenth century, exemplified by the hustings, did not represent a pattern of expectations among the people, most of whom did not have the vote. As the century wore on, though, parties began to strive for power on the basis of appeals to the growing electorate that they and not their opponents could better manage the interests of the nation. At much the same time, those interests became more diverse and yet more interdependent, and managing them became a much more complex task. Indeed, it became increasingly difficult finally to state what those interests were, though they became more or less synonymous with managing the economy. The original purpose of parties, of canalising conflict into constitutional channels – agreeing to stop fighting at dinner time – had become transformed by the complexities of the modern economy and the expectations aroused by democracy into a purpose far more positive and sophisticated. Socialism flourished in and indeed contributed to this atmosphere of expectation and confidence.

For their part, there can be little doubt that the Liberals, severely weakened by the loss of Chamberlain and his radical Unionists in 1886, exhausted by their attempts to solve 'the Irish problem', had not responded to this new challenge on the left. It was also damaging for a Liberal party to find itself, at the outbreak of hostilities in 1914, in government at a time of war when, almost by definition, illiberal measures would be essential. Worst of all for the party, though, was the split occasioned by the leadership crisis in 1916 when Lloyd George replaced his party leader Asquith as Prime Minister and head of the war-time coalition. The split between the 'Squiffites' and the Lloyd George Liberals was never to be effectively healed. It is an amazing paradox, addressed by a number of studies,[42] that the Liberal party won the general election of 1906 with a majority over its Conservative opponents of 243 seats, yet this was the last working majority the Liberal party was to win.

The struggle between the Liberal and Labour parties as to which was to be the major opponent of the Conservatives continued for most of the inter-war period. The first battle occurred in 1922 when the Conservatives withdrew from the post-war coalition and forced Lloyd George to fight an election which the Conservatives easily won. More significantly perhaps, Labour overtook the Liberals as second party, to the extent of forming a minority government in 1924 (Labour had 151 seats to the Liberals' 40, but the Conservatives held 412 seats). Though MacDonald's ministry was short-lived his party's achievement in gaining power in so short a time was remarkable. In 1929 the party again came to office, this time as the largest single party (287 seats to the Conservatives' 260). The Liberals by contrast, unified superficially by Asquith's death the previous year, managed to win only fifty-nine seats. The battle for the centre left was effectively over, at least until the modern era.

Success over the Liberals, however, was not matched by success in managing the economy, for in 1931 Prime Minister MacDonald found it necessary to establish a national coalition government with himself at the head, and as a consequence the bulk of his party left him to his new friends. The depleted Liberals split once more when the National government introduced protectionist measures in 1932, thereby losing the support of the Liberal free-traders. The Coalition or National Liberals continued in what was to become a permanent alliance with the Conservatives and eventually they lost their separate identity during the 1950s. The independent Liberals managed to survive but only with a handful of seats. The Labour party, on the other hand, went on to achieve an historic success in 1945, forming the government with one of the largest non-coalition majorities of the century. A period of over twenty years of Conservative party dominance, either independently or as the major partner in a coalition, had come to an abrupt and unexpected end.

If the distinctive feature of the post-war party system was overwhelming domination by two parties, an equally important if less immediately obvious feature was the considerable amount of agreement that existed between the parties over a wide variety of policy issues for approximately a quarter of a century. The framework of the party system seemed to have acquired a stability, not to say rigidity: between 1945 and 1959 only thirteen seats (including two university seats and two Northern Ireland seats) changed hands at by-elections out of a total of 168, and five of these were in the pre-election year of 1958. One of the reasons for the 'me too-ist' character of British politics during these years was the attempt made by the Conservative party to acclimatise itself to the aspirations of a post-war electorate. By the 1950 election the party had undertaken a series of organisational and policy reforms which revitalised the party machine and 'modernised' its politics, principally by emphasising the party's commitment to interventionist politics.[43] Although the Labour government contrived to win the 1950 election, it did so with a majority of only six and managed to survive for just eighteen months. In the 1951 election, although gaining more votes than the Conservatives, Labour lost and their opponents began thirteen years in power.

By the early 1960s, however, Britain's economy began to falter and the Conservative government became increasingly unpopular: in 1962, it suffered a startling by-electoral defeat in the safe seat of Orpington at the hands of the Liberal party. This event was very harmful to the government but more significantly proved to be a turning-point in the history of the post-war Liberal party, ushering in the 'Liberal revival'. In 1964 Labour took office under Harold Wilson, though with only a slender majority and so in 1966 Wilson went to the country again. For only the second time in its history the Labour party came to power with a substantial majority. By this time, however, the economy was in serious decline and Labour's inability either to manage the economy successfully or to convince socialist supporters of its ideological good faith led to a series of confidence-sapping by-electoral defeats. In 1967, for example, of eight by-elections in constituencies held by Labour no fewer than five were lost. A pattern rapidly became established of the electorate's moving decisively against a government it had elected only a year or so before: this was quite new.

In 1970, somewhat against the odds, Labour was defeated at the general election and Edward Heath became Prime Minister and inaugurated a legislative programme which moved decisively away from the consensus politics of the post-war period. Heath initiated a reform of industrial relations, the aim of which was to restrict the power of the trade unions, and he pursued an industry policy designed to eliminate government intervention in industrial affairs; 'lame ducks' would no longer be supported by public funding. Heath's abrasive style of leadership offended many within and without the party and his mid-term conversion to interventionism, some said to a form of corporatism (including a statutory incomes policy), offended many more. In 1972 and 1973, of eight by-elections in constituencies held by the Conservatives four were lost. Significantly each of the four was won by the Liberals who also won a seat from the Labour party.

The Heath administration had also to contend with major industrial disputes, notably with the power workers and the miners. In 1974, in the face of a miners' strike which resulted in power cuts and industries working a three-day week, the Conservatives decided to hold a general election to strengthen their hand. The election was lost, though in fact the Conservatives polled more votes than Labour. Heath sought to hold on to power by offering a coalition to the Liberal party, which had returned fourteen members, but no agreement was possible and Labour eventually came to office with a majority of four. Eight months later Wilson turned to the electorate once again but his position was not greatly improved. A substantial increase in the Liberal vote in the February election seemed to have been largely responsible for ensuring the stalemate, and although the 'wasted vote' argument was deployed by the major parties subsequently, the Liberal vote stood up surprisingly well, ensuring another hung parliament.

The Labour government of 1974–79 was beset by a number of major problems among which rampant inflation and a poor and worsening economic performance were the most important. The government sought support for its economic and industrial strategies through a concordat with the Trades Union Congress (TUC) and for a time this approach was successful. But the small and diminishing parliamentary majority put a constant strain on ministers and this became particularly trying when the government felt obliged, in the face of the relative success of the Welsh and more especially the Scottish National parties, to pursue legislation to grant some measure of devolution of power to assemblies in Scotland and Wales. In the event referendums in both countries failed to produce a large enough majority in favour and the legislation was lost. Meanwhile the Labour government sought and obtained a pact with the Liberal party to sustain it in office. Sensing a general election in the autumn of 1978 the Liberals ended the pact (which seems to have given them little beyond some extra political visibility and some nearly disastrous by-election results), but in fact the election did not come until 1979 and the intervening winter witnessed the breakdown of the government's compact with the unions; the resultant so-called 'Winter of Discontent' produced a plethora of strikes which seemed to indicate that Labour's claim to be the natural party of government precisely because it could work with the unions was no longer tenable. In the spring of 1979 the Conservative party led by Mrs Thatcher won a clear victory and once more a Labour leader was borne down under a torrent of recrimination from the party's left wing to the effect that the government had reneged on its commitment to socialism.

It would be difficult to overestimate the change that took place in 1979. In many senses this was a traditional British election in which a conservative administration emphasising its managerial skills took on a radical opposition seeking to transform society; in this case, however, the conservative administration was Labour's and the radical would-be transformers were the Conservatives. Committed, like Heath in 1970, to rolling back the state, the new Conservative government initiated a policy designed to cut inflation, limit public expenditure and revitalise British industry. Apparent success with inflation together with Labour's internal divisions exacerbated by the departure of a number of right-wingers to found the Social Democratic Party, and with the kudos which Mrs Thatcher gained from the military successes of the Falklands War, enabled the Conservatives, despite high unemployment, failure to control public expenditure and an unexampled decline in the nation's manufacturing base, to gain a second and even more impressive electoral victory in 1983. The election of that year was also contested by a new political grouping, the Alliance, comprising the Liberal and Social Democratic parties fighting together on one manifesto. Alliance intervention helped to produce Labour's worst performance at a general election since 1935, arguably since 1918. Britain's party system, based upon two dominant parties since 1945, had changed, with the Alliance taking over 25 per cent of votes cast. In 1987 the Alliance was unable to improve upon its position. Nevertheless it remained a major electoral force, securing seven and a half million votes (23 per cent of the total) and thereby helping to secure a third successive defeat for Labour. The subsequent demise of the Alliance and the birth of the Liberal Democrats, together with the continuing inability of the Labour party convincingly to portray itself as a party of government was to keep it out of power until 1997. The Conservatives held office for eighteen years, having presided over a fundamental social and cultural change in Britain. From 1979, then, it would simply not be reasonable to describe the British politics as dominated by two more or less equal parties. The 1997 election, with the rout of the Conservative party, has done nothing to weaken the force of this argument: if Labour is able to hold on to office for a second or third term, there will still be no regular alternation of power and opposition. If, however, Labour were to be defeated after one period of office then British politics would clearly be dominated not merely by a single party but by the same single party. In fact, were we to measure back from 1997 to 1945 we should discover that in the very heyday of two-party politics the Conservatives would have been in office for over thirty-five years, for the great majority of which they enjoyed a good working majority, and the Labour party for only seventeen years, in eight of which their majority constituted a mere handful.

Parties and the two-party system

So far we have been talking about party politics and not specifically about party systems. Our historical survey indicates that the British political system has been dominated off and on over the past 300 years by two 'parties', but it also shows the nature of the domination and of the parties themselves to have been subject to constant change. The pattern of party politics, moreover, has changed just as dramatically, with long spells of dominance by one party, with parties constantly breaking up and regrouping, and with third (and indeed fourth) parties playing decisive parts from time to time. Given all this it comes as something of a surprise to find that most prominent British writers on British politics tended until recently to accept that Britain has traditionally been a two-party system, though none of them is convincingly clear as to what the phrase actually means.[44] Giovanni Sartori[45] offers a widely accepted working definition of such a system and we may safely use it to test whether Britain has or has had a two-party system. Before we do so, it is worth considering an essential precondition of its functioning at all: that the strength of the two major parties should reflect the major divisions of public opinion, not in any precise arithmetical or even proportional sense but roughly. In a two-party system, that is to say, we should expect that if party A wins an election it will have done so by virtue of having secured the support of the majority of voters. We must keep this precondition in mind.

Sartori's first criterion states that the two parties must be in a position to compete for the absolute majority of seats. True or false for Britain? Well, apart from the obvious exceptions when, at the beginning of our period party identities were weak, and when for long periods of time, third and fourth parties commanded substantial support, it is often forgotten how large a number of seats in the House were simply uncontested, constituting over 36 per cent of all seats as late as 1900 (indeed in 1918, 107 candidates were returned unopposed). Only partly true then.

His second criterion requires one party to win a workable majority. True or false? Jorgen Rasmussen has shown that about 30 per cent of elections in the twentieth century have failed to produce a majority in the House for one party. He concludes that 'Taking a very lenient definition of working majority – one party has twenty more seats than its combined opponents – only about half of the elections have produced such results'.[46] Continued

Conservative dominance, and now Labour's crushing 1997 victory may have blunted his arguments a little, but the system is simply not as decisive as is usually thought. Indeed one general election, that of 1964, when Labour came to power after thirteen years, produced an overall majority of precisely four. If a mere 350 voters in four particular constituencies had stayed at home on election day Labour would have had no majority at all. Once again, only partly true.

The third criterion is the willingness of a party with a majority of seats to govern alone, and this clearly has been a feature of the British system. So – true. The basis of this willingness might at first sight appear to have been the parties' ability to command the votes of their parliamentary supporters, but not necessarily so. Not until the early twentieth century were party votes the norm. For much of the nineteenth century, however, parties did not assume power in the belief that their supporters – if indeed they could infallibly identify them – would automatically sustain them, but rather that they could win support for their policies by persuasion and accommodation.

Arguably the most important feature of a two-party system, and Sartori's fourth criterion, is the regular rotation or alternation of power between the major parties. A party which has grounds for believing that it has no reasonable possibility of achieving power constitutionally is unlikely to be a strong supporter of the two-party system or indeed of the constitution. In the long run, we like to believe British parties share power more or less equally. This is simply a delusion. The parties of the left, that is, Liberal and Labour, have held power for much shorter periods than the Conservatives and have almost always secured smaller parliamentary majorities. In fact there have been only four occasions in this century when parties of the left have held substantial majorities and their years in office with such majorities have amounted to no more than thirteen (though the present administration seems likely to add significantly to that number). The Conservatives, by way of contrast, have enjoyed good working majorities on thirteen occasions and their years in office under such favourable conditions have amounted to sixty-three (including eighteen years when they were the dominant party in national coalitions). There has traditionally been a substantial disparity between the chances of power for the Liberal and Labour parties on the one hand and the Conservatives on the other. No need to ask for whom the pendulum has tended to swing; it has swung for the Conservatives.[47] So, number four is demonstrably false.

Of even greater interest perhaps are the results of a survey of electoral support for the major parties over the last hundred years. On only four occasions has an incoming government secured more than half of the votes cast at the preceding election. In the first two, 1886 and 1900, the Conservatives were in alliance with the Liberal Unionists and in the second two, 1931 and 1935, they were the major partners in a coalition. In only four elections in thirty was majority public opinion reflected in the choice of government. Moreover, not only were there extenuating circumstances in each (the two-party system clearly not operating) but in three of the four the majority was marginal anyway. In short, only once, in 1931, was a substantial majority of public opinion (61 per cent of those who voted) even nominally behind the government – and that government was a national coalition. Let me put this as plainly as I can: only once in more than a hundred years could a one-party government's claim to represent 'the people' or to have a popular mandate be taken seriously. So much for majority representation and the mandate theory; so much for the precondition of a two-party system.

It has been part of the British tradition, however, to claim that the two-party system has not only the imprimatur of history but also that of geography, so to speak. It has been argued by writers like L.S. Amery that the strongest democracies, the Anglo-Saxon ones, were two-party systems and that the deviant continental multi-party systems were somehow inferior and, in Henry Drucker's words, carried a certain opprobrium.[48] The evident success of most European systems, especially the German, seems to deal a hammer blow to traditional British amour propre, but so does a closer look at the Anglo-Saxon systems themselves. American parties, for example, bear a much closer resemblance to nineteenth-century British parties than to twentieth-century ones; they are organisationally weak and owe their periodic unity almost entirely to the personality and policy commitments of their leaders. For its part, Canadian government has been based on three or more parties and several minority administrations. (In fact nearly half of Canada's post-war administrations have been minorities.) Moreover, one major party, the Liberals, has been in power over three times as long as its major opponent the Conservatives. As for Australia, a two-and-a-half party system dominated by right-wing coalitions has been the norm. Until Hawke and then Keating won five consecutive elections for Labor between 1983 and 1996, the right had been in office three times as long as the ALP. Sartori claims that only New Zealand, with its three-and-a-half million population, could really be said to have operated a two-party system like the British. Indeed, Sartori, Lijphart and others claimed that New Zealand's was a far better claim than Britain's to two-party status[49] but even there the right-wing National party enjoyed office for twice as long as Labour after the war. Moreover in 1996 New Zealand exchanged its 'perfect' two-party system for a multi-party system following electoral reform. So, no geographical imprimatur then: all the world is out of step with Britain.

All this discussion begs a simple question: why are popular and even informed perceptions of British party history so mistaken? Perhaps the misconception originates in the work of that remarkable early psephologist Sergeant Willis whose research led him to expound, in *Iolanthe*, that:

> Every little boy and gal that's born into the world alive
> Is either a little Liberal or else a little Conservative.

Probably, though, it owed more to that seminal text, published in 1955, Robert McKenzie's *British Political Parties*,[50] in which 595 of 597 pages were devoted to the two major parties. McKenzie was especially influential as a result of his television journalism. Like Bagehot before him McKenzie believed that his times were typical whereas they were anything but. All the same the advent of radio and more especially television coverage of elections did much to cement the idea of two-party politics in the public mind. A simple 'for' and 'against' model of presentation has clear advantages for organising and treating material in what appears to be an unimpeachably fair and democratic manner and it scarcely occurred to producers and presenters that there might be more than two sides to an argument. What emerged as a consequence was a model of political behaviour which assumed the two-party system of the 1950s and 1960s to be fixed, permanent and rational, the final fruit of 300 years of slow maturation. From this false perspective the Whigs and Tories of the eighteenth century and the Liberals and Conservatives of the nineteenth century became simply part of the myth of a teleology developing towards the Labour/Conservative system of the 1950s and '60s. Such a picture confuses the essential with the accidental. To take the post-war two-party system as natural and – even worse – rational is to look at the present, the future, and the past through distorting lenses. We begin to see our system – post-war consensus politics with two more or less equally balanced parties – as the 'real' system, and to see everything which preceded it as somehow an anticipation of it, a working towards it. It is almost a perfect manifestation of George Orwell's precautionary dictum that to control the present is to control the past – and hence to control the future.

The truth of the matter is that the British party 'system' is, in Ian Gilmour's words, 'the result neither of the wishes of the British people nor the foresight of British statesmen. Like Tristram Shandy it was begotten in a fit of absence of mind.'[51] We could add that its subsequent development has been every bit as rhapsodic and undistinguished as that young man's and its future as full of uncertainties as ever his was. It could be said that the British party system has absorbed vast social and economic changes with a minimum of violence and disruption; cynics might want to describe it as an elaborate game designed to legitimise the power of the 'political establishment'. All might be prepared to agree that it has permitted the domination of United Kingdom politics by the predominantly wealthy south of England; perhaps that is one of the reasons why the Conservatives love the present constitution. Moreover, a stable two-party system has never applied with equal force across the United Kingdom; for over half a century neither Scotland nor Wales has had a two-party system and Northern Ireland has a quite different party system, facts which hardly rate a mention in textbooks on 'British' parties.

Conclusions

This historical review has painted in the background to the development of British political parties and put us in a good position to answer the original question: what are political parties? We have defined parties; we have discussed their functions in a democracy; we have considered their historical development in Britain; we have discovered that it is in adapting to changing circumstances that they fulfil their functions; we have found that history shows parties to be characteristically chameleon-like, changing to suit the social and economic environment. Marxists are not alone in appreciating the importance of class as environment, but the first half of our period indicates that political allegiances – the Buffs and the Blues – were just as strong before class competition became a major factor. We cannot dismiss the possibility that the socio-psychological function of parties, of giving voters and activists a cause and identity, may be as fundamental as any broadly socio-ideological functions they may perform. What is also clear, moreover, is that genuine two-party competition seems to require two party leaders of approximately equal stature, who can command the respect and loyalty of their supporters in parliament and who enjoy the support of approximately equal numbers of voters. There is no reason whatever to regard the simultaneous emergence of two such leaders as a natural, still less inevitable, phenomenon. Evenly matched two-party competition, therefore, is only one form that the 'system' may adopt and history shows it not to be the most prevalent. Common sense may lead us to conclude that a two-party system provides the most obvious and convenient check on abuse of government in a parliamentary system in which power is concentrated rather than constrained by constitutional checks and balances: it certainly is not the only one, however, nor necessarily the most efficacious.

Our historical picture tells us that Epstein's caveat is to be taken seriously: we cannot precisely define British political parties. But we can talk intelligibly about them. We can agree on their origins. More, we can agree that they fulfil certain crucial political functions in a democracy: by agreeing to stop fighting at dinner time whoever is winning, they endorse the legitimacy of the political system; they divert social and economic conflict into constitutional channels; they select priorities in the running of the state; they constitute a framework of accountability; they provide a non-violent outlet for people's natural propensity for taking sides and they provide a crucial link between the many and the few. But their shape, interrelationship and modus operandi have constantly changed and we can be fairly confident that they will continue to do so.

Notes

1. Alan Ware, *Political Parties and Party Systems*, Oxford University Press, 1996.
2. Ware, *Political parties and Party Systems*, pp. 4–5.
3. See for example M. Olson, 'A Theory of the Incentives Facing Political Organisations: Neocorporatism and the Hegemonist State', *International Political Science Review*, **7**, 1986, pp. 165–89.
4. J. Madison, *The Federalist*, 1787, New York, Modern Library, 1941, p. 54.
5. J. Downs, *An Economic Theory of Democracy*, New York, Harper Rowe, 1957, p. 25.
6. Downs, *An Economic Theory of Democracy*, p. 28.
7. M. Maor, *Political Parties and Party Systems*, London, Routledge, 1997, p. 6.
8. Ware, *Political Parties and Party Systems*, p. 5.
9. Alan R. Ball, *British Political Parties*, London, Macmillan, 1981, p. 3.
10. Edmund Burke, *Thoughts on the Causes of the Present Discontents*, first published in 1770.
11. L.D. Epstein, *Political Parties in Western Democracies*, London, Pall Mall, 1967, p. 5.
12. For example, T.B. Macaulay's *History of England*, New York, Harper and Brothers, 1861, esp. vol. IV.
13. See S.B. Chrimes, 'Before 1600', in S.D. Bailey (ed.), *The British Party System*, London, Hansard Society, 1952.
14. Quoted in H.R. Williamson, 'The Seventeenth Century', in Bailey, *The British Party System*.
15. Williamson, 'The Seventeenth Century', p. 18.
16. David Hume, *History of Great Britain*, vol. II, London, 1824, p. 532.
17. T.F.T. Plucknett, *Taswell Langmead's Constitutional History*, 10th edn, London, Sweet and Maxwell, 1946, p. 692.
18. See Brian Harrison, *The Transformation of British Politics 1860–1995*, Oxford University Press, 1996, pp. 33–5.
19. K. Feiling, *The Second Tory Party*, London, Macmillan, 1938, p. v.
20. See G.K. Roberts, *Political Parties and Pressure Groups in Britain*, London, Weidenfeld & Nicolson, 1970, p. 18.
21. This view is certainly accepted by modern historians, for example J.Cannon, *The Fox/North Coalition*, London, Cambridge University Press, 1969. Also F O'Gorman, The Emergence of the British Two-Party System 1760–1832, London, Edward Arnold, 1982.
22. M. Ostrogorski, *Democracy and the Organization of Political Parties*, London, Macmillan, 1902, p. 6.
23. Ostrogorski, *Democracy and Organisation*, p. 22.
24. G.K. Chesterton, *Return of Don Quixote*, London, Chatto & Windus, 1917, p. 262.
25. Ernest Barker, *Reflections on Government*, London, Oxford University Press, 1967, p. 86.
26. Ian Gilmour, *The Body Politic*, London, Hutchinson, 1969, p. 24.
27. R.S. Katz and P. Mair, *How Parties Organise: Change and Adaptation in Party Organisations in Western Democracies*, London, Sage, 1994, p. 12.

28. Ostrogorski, *Democracy and Organisation*, p. 57.
29. Quoted in S.H. Beer, *Modern British Politics*, London, Faber, 1965 p. 36.
30. Quoted in Ivor Bulmer Thomas, *The Party System in Great Britain*, London, Phoenix House, 1953, p. 14.
31. See Philip Tether, 'Conservative Clubs: A neglected aspect in Conservative Organisation', *Hull Papers in Politics*, no. 42, University of Hull Politics Department, 1988.
32. Ostrogorski, *Democracy and Organisation*, p. 142.
33. See, for example, Philip Tether, *Conservative Clubs*, unpublished PhD thesis, University of Hull, 1990.
34. See M. Pugh, *The Making of Modern British Politics 1879–1939*, Blackwell, Oxford, 1982, pp 15–17.
35. Justin Fisher, *British Political Parties*, London, Prentice Hall/Harvester Wheatsheaf, 1996, p. 7.
36. Feuchtwanger E.J., 'J.E. Gorst and the Central Organisation of the Conservative Party (1870–82)', *Bulletin of the Institute of Historical Research*, **33**, 1959, p. 199.
37. Pugh, *The Making of Modern British Politics*, p. 50.
38. H.J. Hanham, *Elections and Party Management*, Longmans Green, London, 1959, p. 126.
39. M. Pinto Duschinsky, *British Political Finance 1830–1980*, London, American Enterprise Institute, 1981, p. 49.
40. Quoted in Rodney Barker, *Studies in Opposition*, London, Macmillan, 1971, p. 132.
41. Quoted in Barker, *Studies in Opposition*, p. 145.
42. For example, George Dangerfield, *The Strange Death of Liberal England*, London, McGibbon and Key, 1966.
43. For an account of how this was accomplished see R.A. Butler, *The Art of the Possible*, Harmondsworth, Penguin, 1973, Ch.7.
44. For a discussion of this see Stephen Ingle, 'The Emergence of Multi-Party Politics', Hayward J. and Norton P. (eds), *The Political Science of British Politics*, Brighton, Wheatsheaf, 1986, pp 105–19.
45. G. Sartori, *Parties and Party Systems: A Framework for Analysis*, Cambridge, Cambridge University Press, 1976.
46. See 'Was Guy Fawkes right?' in Isaac Kramnick (ed.), *Is Britain Dying?* London, Cornell University Press, 1979.
47. See Anthony Seldon (ed.), *How Tory Governments Fall*, London, Fontana Press, 1996.
48. See H. Drucker, *Multi-Party Britain*, London, Macmillan, 1979.
49. A. Lijphart, *Democracies, Patterns of Majoritarian and Consensus Government in Twenty-One Countries*, New Haven, Yale University Press, 1984.
50. R. McKenzie, *British Political Parties*, London, Heinemann, 1955.
51. Quoted in Gilmour, *The Body Politic*, p. 33.

CHAPTER TWO

What is Conservatism?

'Conservative belief,' wrote Anthony Quinton, 'becomes explicit only in reaction to a positive, innovative attack on the traditional scheme of things. What exists speaks for itself simply by existing.'[1] Conservatism is to be understood, then, as the defence of the established order. This apparently straightforward statement, however, can hardly go unchallenged. What are we to understand by 'speaks for itself'? Presumably the phrase implies that what exists justifies itself; but can anything justify itself merely by existing? And anyway, does not the fact of existence contain within it not merely a sense of stability and permanence but a propensity, indeed a certainty, of both change and decay? It will come as no surprise, consequently, that few Conservative thinkers would seek to justify an established political order just because it was there. It seems to follow that such an order would need to embody certain qualities to be sure of Conservative support and, if we are fully to understand the nature of Conservatism, then we must elucidate and identify the principles which would ensure such support. We may hope to be able to tackle this problem later in the chapter but we must begin by investigating what we know about Conservatism in theory and in practice.

The fundamental principles of Conservatism

Quinton adduces three chief principles of conservatism which will provide as good a beginning as any. He speaks first of traditionalism, a strong emotional attachment to existing procedures and institutions.

Traditionalism

A traditional system which evolves over a long period of time will surely come to represent, in some measure, the accumulated wisdom of the community, or at least of that part of the community habituated to making decisions. A fixed and settled constitution should be seen as representing the aggregated outcome of innumerable compromises, struggles and adjustments over the years; it may be regarded as a kind of residuum of practical political experience, capable of adaptation but not of sudden and major change.

Now reverence for tradition can be seen as a perfectly natural disposition but is far from universal; equally natural is the radical disposition to assume that institutions require constant change if they are to remain efficient. Conservatism tends to take consolation from the longevity of institutions and can rationalise this disposition by arguing that, after all, it is only when we know institutions thoroughly that we can make the fullest use of them, bend them to our purposes, learn how to avoid their pitfalls. Such is the complexity of society that it would be impossible to design institutions to fulfil social purposes; much better and safer to adapt those that have proved their value over time.

Organicism

Quinton's second major principle is what he calls 'organicism', which holds that society is analogous to a natural living body and not a machine or other man-made structure. There are two characteristics of most organisms: they are extraordinarily complex and thoroughly interconnected. Thus in the organic society citizens are seen as social beings connected to each other in a complex pattern of mutually beneficial relationships. It is precisely because of the complexity and mutuality of these relationships and, crucially, because they arise naturally, that they are not amenable to wholesale change. Machines, on the other hand, are designed for a specific purpose and may be adapted to fulfil that purpose optimally. Whole sections can be dismantled and replaced, and however complex the machine it is less complex than the mind that made it and gave it a purpose. But an organism has developed to fulfil a certain function, or array of functions, and bits cannot be chopped off and replaced without grave repercussions for the whole organism. Moreover, the complexity and interconnectedness of organisms is not limited by the brain-power of a human designer, and indeed modern theories such as catastrophe theory show graphically how minor events in one part of an ecological system can have completely unforeseen and even sinister repercussions elsewhere. Likewise, even minor changes to a social system must be considered with the greatest care because of their possible effect upon other parts of the living body of the state. Major changes are always likely to be calamitous.

Some Conservative thinkers have understood the existing social order to represent a reflection of divine intention, a view which they shared with medieval thinkers such as Saint Augustine. In the well-known nineteenth-century hymn *All Things Bright and Beautiful*, we are reminded of God's design:

> The rich man in his castle,
> The poor man at his gate.
> He made them high and lowly,
> He numbered their estate.

Although this line of argument is difficult to pursue very far, it makes little practical difference whether society is hierarchical – a place for everybody and everybody in his place – at the behest of God or as a consequence of natural design. What follows is that things should not or cannot (or both) be other than they are. Conservatives, as O'Sullivan tells us, see the existing social order as representing the culmination of an historical process, a 'more complete and more profoundly rational expression of the human spirit than any deliberately contrived social order could ever be'.[2] O'Sullivan locates the origins of this version of Conservatism in the German romantic movement, whose exponents were greatly influenced by Hegel's dialectical view of history. Its influence on British Conservatism was mediated by nineteenth-century writers such as Samuel Taylor Coleridge and Thomas Carlyle.[3]

Whatever its philosophical origin, the organic view of society has had a profound influence upon Conservatism, tending to stress the mutuality of duties and obligations. That the rich man in his castle has obligations to the poor man at his gate is central to the organic view and gives to Conservatism a paternalistic dimension found, for example, in Coleridge's idea of a national church, the clerisy, founded and organised by the wealthy, society's 'natural' leaders, but dedicated primarily to the welfare of the poor; or in Disraeli's 'one nation' philosophy; or more recently in the compassionate Conservatism of so-called Tory 'wets' such as Sir Ian Gilmour.[4] For all its compassion, however, organicism implies the retention of hierarchy; the poor will always be with us. Indeed as Dr Johnson told his friend Boswell: 'You are to consider that it is your duty to maintain the subordination of civilised society; and where there is gross or shameful deviation from rank, it should be punished so as to deter others from the same perversion.'[5] This was precisely the fate of Thomas Hardy's Jude the Obscure, a man who tried to 'rise above his situation' and suffered accordingly. He came to regard himself as a 'frightful example of what not to do'. Poor men should stay at the gate; the rich will come down from the castle to care for them.

Scepticism

Quinton's third major principle is that of scepticism, which holds that life is not very amenable to 'improvement' by the application of social and political theories. H.G. Wells once remarked that socialism was based upon the same principle as all scientific work: the assumption that 'things may be calculated upon, may be foreseen'.[6] The Conservative, on the other hand, believes pretty well the opposite: that in the end things may not always be calculated upon, not always foreseen. As far as the Conservative is concerned it is certainly better to put one's faith in established institutions and customary procedures than in untried political theories such as Wells' socialism.

Underpinning Quinton's principle of scepticism (and traditionalism for that matter) is the overpowering certainty of human fallibility. As Quintin Hogg[7] argues, this belief has traditionally been associated with the Christian concept of original sin which holds that since the fall of Adam we have all of us been tainted with sin, or to put it more prosaically, none of us is capable of moral perfection. Such a belief is not restricted to traditional Christianity, however. There are important modern secular theories which stress man's moral limitations. At the beginning of the twentieth century Freud's hugely influential psychological theories exposed man as severely limited by the effects of early childhood experiences; towards the end of the century some geneticists pictured man as the prisoner of his genetic structure. Conservatives, then, can feel that they have strong support for their scepticism. The consequence of their belief in man's limitations is clearly to make Conservatives suspicious of any Utopian scheme and strongly supportive of institutions that, though far from perfect, have stood the test of time.

Moreover, it is not merely man's moral imperfection which disposes the Conservative against grand designs but also man's intellectual limitations. Believing, in Kant's words, that nothing straight could be built from the crooked timbers of humanity, Conservatives have tended to disregard abstract theories of progress and settle for the piecemeal redress of proven grievances. Given man's moral and intellectual limitations, Conservatives believe that civil life only becomes tolerable to the extent that man is constrained by customs and institutions with which he is familiar and which are broadly acceptable to him. O'Sullivan adds another consideration: politics is after all about choices. Now to the extent that they advance the interests of one person or group, choices are almost certain to injure the interests of others. Moreover, in securing a benefit for himself a man will often forfeit some other presumably lesser good, from which he had previously benefited. No advantages in this world, said David Hume, are pure and unmixed. From this it follows that governments ought always to move in a spirit of compromise and moderation which emphasises individual liberty, the rule of law and constitutional government.

Defence of property rights

'The possession of property by the individual is the essential condition of liberty,' wrote Quintin Hogg,[8] and indeed the party has been unequivocal in its defence of property. Existing property rights, though by their very nature enshrining inequalities, are the essential characteristic of 'the established order' which Conservatism seeks to defend. Property owner-ship is a talisman of a free society for it guarantees the dis-aggregation of economic power, guarantees to individuals some small castle of which they can be kings (or queens). Property, moreover, gives the individual a stake in society, thereby offering an inducement towards social stability. This is why post–1945 Conservative governments sought to encourage and extend the ownership of property, to promote what Anthony Eden called a 'property-owning democracy'.[9] But the right to own property has two important concomitants: the right to transfer property, usually to one's children, and the right to own a means of production. It should also be borne in mind that Conservative belief in the organic nature of society means that ownership of property brings with it social obligations as well as rights, and a Conservative state could legitimately exercise a custodial function in securing the fulfilment of such obligations.

These are the main principles of Conservatism: they may be summarised, to paraphrase O'Sullivan, as the defence of a limited style of politics based upon the idea of imperfection.[10]

Operational principles

The principles we have discussed so far could be described as basic or fundamental principles, and taken cumulatively as providing an ideology of Conservatism. I should like to move now to what I shall call the operational principles of Conservatism, of which there are four. The first is pragmatism.

Pragmatism

Pragmatism is defined by the *Concise Oxford Dictionary* as being a belief that assertions or doctrines should be estimated principally by their impact or bearing upon human interests. Conservative pragmatism is certainly linked to the amount of time that the party has spent in office, for as Blake reminds us, 'political parties seldom philosophise when they are in office'.[11] Richard Rose thought that the Conservative party was consumed by electoral greed and holding office[12] and that all other considerations, including ideology, were secondary. Ian MacLeod's dictum was: 'The Socialists can scheme their schemes and the Liberals can dream their dreams but we, at least, have work to do.' Julian Critchley agreed: 'the object of political activity is power, and ... sustained and obvious disunity [the by-products of ideology] would oblige us to relinquish it'. Gilmour, too, recognised that the Conservative party gives a lower priority than do its opponents to ideological considerations and that it 'believes that politics grows out of the needs, fears, hopes and wishes of the people and out of the demands of the time'.[13] Enoch Powell argued that principles did not define what Conservatives might be expected to do in office, but rather that they were abstracted from 'the way the Conservative Party … acts in politics'.[14] Indeed, largely because the party leaders were motivated by pragmatic considerations – chief among which was the obtaining or retention of power – they were traditionally able to count upon the loyalty of the parliamentary party to an extent that their rivals envied. Disraeli's famous advice to Bulwer-Lytton during the debate on Corn Law reform sums this attitude up succinctly: 'Damn your principles! Stick to your party.'

In historical terms this pragmatism has stood the party in good stead. In the nineteenth century the principal threat to 'the traditional scheme of things' was posed by the individualistic doctrines of Liberalism. These doctrines threatened the existence of even a limited form of government for, in stressing above all the rights of the individual, Liberalism called into question the very notion of government by consent. In the twentieth century, however, the threat to the established order came not from individualistic Liberalism but from collectivist Socialism which, in order to achieve its objectives, invariably sought to aggregate substantial state power at the expense of individual liberty. So in the modern era Conservatism has had to react to challenges from 'individualistic' Liberalism and 'statist' Socialism, with Conservatives defending the state against the individual and then the individual against the state.

Limited government

The second operational principle I wish to discuss is that of limited government, and it follows naturally from the fundamental principles of Conservatism. Those who are convinced of human frailties, of the benefits of tradition and order, of property-owning rights, and of the difficulty of making large-scale social and political change, are hardly likely to favour placing great power in the hands of governments. Governments are always a potential threat to individual liberty and the more powerful the government, the greater the threat. Governments, then, should be constrained by a series of constitutional, political and indeed social checks and balances: a plural society, as Philip Norton points out,[15] is a *sine qua non* of limited government.

The rule of law

Closely associated with the idea of limited government is that of the rule of law. The law is the chief expression of the accumulated wisdom and experience of a society and as such is a far safer guide to proper political action than the programme of the party which happens to be in government at any time. The rule of law constrains governed and governors; it is the rock on which a stable society may be constructed. Its concomitant, equality before the law, provides a framework for social transactions and, in the process, enshrines that basic Conservative principle, the right to private property. The constraints of the law, which derive from social experience and not the arbitrary will of the governors, will provide a protection for the rights of the individual. 'The rule of law,' as Norton and Aughey conclude, 'provides that essential breathing space of predictability and security of redress which is at the heart of liberty'.[16]

The national interest

Norton draws our attention to the word 'nation' in Disraeli's 'one-nation' Conservatism. It was Disraeli who first associated Conservatism with one specific embodiment of the national interest – empire – and he managed this so successfully that they seem to form a natural association. It is not generally remembered that the main thrust of Conservative thought in the nineteenth century had been anti-imperialist; Disraeli himself once referred to the colonies as 'millstones around our necks'. The idea of an imperial 'mission' cut very little ice with Conservative politicians until well into the second half of the century, but Disraeli was one of the first to recognise its electoral value. By 1872 he was publicly extolling the virtues of empire, for example in his famous Crystal Palace speech. As S.H. Beer wrote, 'in imperialism the party had found a cause with a mighty appeal to the voter … only from the election of 1886 … did the party win those majorities of the popular vote which eluded even Disraeli.'[17]

But imperialism was not the only aspect of the national interest which the Conservative party championed. The Conservatives were also the party of the Union. They stood opposed to Irish Home Rule and this was a position which won them a great deal of working-class support in Lancashire and the West of Scotland; indeed in Scotland Conservatives were often referred to as 'the Unionists'.

In emphatically championing the assertion of national interest the Conservatives 'most successfully exploited the patriotic theme, reinforcing claims to stand above narrow class interests and for the nation as a whole'.[18] Particularly appropriate for the last quarter of the nineteenth and the first half of the twentieth centuries, the politics of national interest continued to feature among Conservative operational principles, though as the bitter battles over European unity and the party's complete disappearance as an electoral force in Scotland and Wales in 1997 were to show, the consequences nowadays are hardly as beneficial.

Tensions within Conservative ideology

This completes our analysis of the main threads of what might collectively be called Conservative ideology. There are within this body of thought some central tensions and apparent incongruities, however, which need to be considered if we are fully to understand the nature of Conservatism.

Tory and Conservative

Although the modern Conservative party can trace its origins back to the Tories of the late seventeenth and eighteenth centuries, and although nowadays the words 'Tory' and 'Conservative' are used even by party members indiscriminately, to speak correctly they are by no means synonymous. Toryism has always been essentially hierarchical and paternalistic and the Tories were traditionally the 'country party'. Although its parliamentary opponent was Whiggism, and although the modern Liberal Democrats can trace an unbroken history back to those Whigs, Whiggism also became part of the Conservative tradition. In fact the philosopher whom most British Conservatives would consider as their most significant thinker, Edmund Burke, was an Irishman and a Whig. As a Whig, Burke was not only a champion of the Glorious Revolution of 1688 but also of the Americans colonists in their war of independence against the Crown. What made Burke a champion of Conservatism, however, was his stinging attack on the revolutionary forces in France. He distinguished between the earlier revolutions and the French one, arguing: 'all the reformations we have hitherto made have proceeded upon the principle of reference to antiquity, taking full account of precedent, authority and example. The French revolution, by contrast, sought only to overturn tradition. The very idea', he continued, 'of the *fabrication* of a new government is enough to fill us with disgust and horror'.[19] This is Conservative scepticism par excellence: individuals should not trust to their reason but 'avail themselves of the general bank and capital of nations and ages'.[20] We should not ignore the fact, however, that this founder of modern Conservatism was actually a Whig who would defend some revolutions and oppose others on grounds which were perhaps not always as clear-cut as he would have us believe.

Conservatism: attitude and ideology

In his classic work *Conservatism*, Lord Hugh Cecil[21] speaks of a 'natural conservatism' which is to be found in most people. It amounts to little more than a 'distrust of the unknown and a love of the familiar'. It makes little sense to the majority of men, says Cecil, to depart from the known. Taking any risks is clearly dangerous and requires considerable forethought. 'Why not let it alone?', he advises, 'why be weary instead of at rest?' The implicit problem here must now be made explicit. If we assume that even in a sophisticated democracy parties other than the Conservatives will come to power (although this has not happened very often in Britain), and if when in power they implement certain liberal or socialist policies (and this has happened even less often), then the problem for an incoming Conservative government is: is it radically to undo what the past government has done or is it to conserve what has become *ipso facto* 'the traditional scheme of things'? Clearly the radical course of action will invite uncertainty and perhaps danger: why not follow Cecil's advice and 'let it alone'? Why not heed the advice of Michael Oakshott and eschew innovation because 'a known good is not lightly to be surrendered for an unknown better'?[22] If Conservatism is an ideology and not simply an attitude of mind, however, it will not do for Conservatives to hide behind their belief in limited government; their political opponents are not likely to be so modest. During the 1960s the Liberal party leader Jo Grimond said of the Conservative government that it was conserving Socialism whereas previously it had conserved Liberalism. This paradox represents a major tension within Conservatism.

Stability and change

Now we come to an even more significant tension for Conservatism, and in discussing it we may return to the question posed at the beginning of this chapter. Under what circumstances should Conservatives support the 'traditional scheme of things'? The Conservative writer T.E. Uttley believed that in the modern world a Conservative government must embody the social disciplines of capitalism, maintaining the unequal distribution of property necessary to that discipline, and backing it up with an emphasis on law and order.[23] A limited government perhaps, but a strong one. But Uttley ducks the real issue: is the social order based upon capital accumulation to have any regard for social harmony as well as social order? Peter Walker, a long-serving Minister in Mrs Thatcher's governments, posed and answered the same question. The test of capitalist inequalities, he declared, is the contribution they make to the general welfare of society. If they make no contribution, there would have to follow 'drastic and radical reforms to secure a socially responsible capitalism in which inequalities do contribute to public welfare'.[24] Walker's tests seem to be largely economic and not to take account of the argument of writers like George Santayana whose concern was chiefly cultural: hierarchy must be defended because it has provided 'the source from which all culture has hitherto followed'.[25] It is hard not to see a conflict, anyway, between the view that hierarchy is natural or God-given, or the fruit of some inexorable historical development, and the view that hierarchy must be assessed by some almost Benthamite-like measure of utility, with radical reform threatened if it falls short.

Norton and Aughey, aware of this tension, declare: 'This is the essence of the Conservative Party's role – to formulate policy that conserves a hierarchy of wealth and power and to make this intelligible and reasonable to a democracy.'[26] Yet when the authors go on to discuss the kinds of policies which are likely in a democracy to make inequalities seem reasonable to the less favoured, they come exactly upon Walker's problem – the perennial tension within Conservatism – when should Conservatives support the 'settled order of things' and when should they not?

Historians of the Conservative party have addressed these tensions. Maude referred to the inconsistencies as 'archaeological strata, specimens from all its historic stages'[27] but, added Gilmour, with 'common characteristics imposed by the geography and topography of the site'.[28] Inconsistencies and tensions, then, tend to be regarded by some Conservatives as simply a rich diversity within a common theme. For practical purposes, though, these tensions may be rendered down to one single choice: to change or to preserve. The guiding principles for changing and preserving will vary – organicism versus limited government for example – but in the real world of politics the actual decision will be '… which interests to defend and which expectations to disappoint.'[29] But change, especially when delayed, may involve Conservatives in precisely the kind of radical transformative actions to which they are temperamentally opposed.

Conservatism in action

What I propose now is to consider some of the chief events in the history of the Conservative party in order to understand the extent to which its ideology, and more especially the tensions within it, help to explain that history. The history of the modern party opens with a resounding defeat for the Tories: the Great Reform Act of 1832. The unreformed constitution embodied each of the four dominant conservative values – traditionalism, organicism, scepticism and the defence of property rights – and the operational principles of limited government and the rule of law. Tory leaders fought strongly to prevent reform but were eventually forced to give ground, and the reform which Russell's Whigs pushed through parliament marked a decisive move away from the aristocratic dominance exemplified by and institutionalised in the House of Lords. It soon became obvious that the Tories would have to live with the change since to reverse it was impossible.

Sir Robert Peel

The party leader whose task was to accommodate the party to the new world was Sir Robert Peel, and in many senses he was well-suited to that task. He had been instrumental in bringing the party to accept basic changes to which it had long been opposed, the best example being the extension of civil liberties to Roman Catholic citizens referred to in shorthand as Catholic Emancipation. In securing the acceptance of Catholic Emancipation and parliamentary reform, Peel is usually credited with founding the modern Conservative party. For Peel the tension between change and stability was intensified by the emergence of a new wealthy class whose interests were in many respects opposed to those of the landed aristocracy. The focal point of this opposition was the Corn Law question. The Corn Laws had been enacted to protect British agriculture from the importation of cheap foreign wheat, and many Tories had come to see them as somehow representative of the traditional, organic, hierarchical society which needed to be protected against further blows from destructive radical forces. For the new wealthy class of mill and factory owners, moral arguments about cheap bread apart, clearly the availability of cheaper food would be a disincentive for their work-force to press for higher wages. But there were other important factors in the equation. The 1840s witnessed a series of failures of the Irish potato harvest with mass starvation as a direct consequence. It was argued that the availability of cheap bread in England might release other foodstuffs such as potatoes for Ireland. It is not clear how logistically convincing these arguments were, though it was important not to leave undone anything which might ease the suffering across the Irish Sea: paternalistic organicism demanded no less.

Here was the classical problem for a Conservative leader:[30] how to 'sell' necessary change to the landed interest so as not to arouse what Norton and Aughey call a 'blind emotional reaction' which would surely have damaged their cause even further. History shows that Peel was unable to carry his party with him: the Corn Laws were indeed reformed but in the process the newly created Conservative party was shattered. Though he failed his party the judgement of historians has been kinder to him than was the judgement of many of his contemporaries, especially Lord George Bentinck and the waspish Mr Disraeli.

Peel's failure to persuade his party to accept change a third time is not difficult to understand: after all, the Corn Laws were central to the maintenance of the domination of the landed aristocracy, or so members of that class believed. Norton and Aughey describe Peel as a statesman; perhaps the situation needed a strategist and not a statesman. Peel failed to resolve the tension between change and stability and as a consequence the party set its face against change and was broken.

Benjamin Disraeli

That the Conservative party managed to reassert itself so successfully after its period in the wilderness was thanks in no small measure to the leadership of the second of its great men, Benjamin Disraeli. It would be difficult to overestimate the importance of Disraeli in the history of the Conservative party – the only party leader to whom the Conservative young of successive generations have turned for inspiration. Disraeli was one of the few Conservative leaders able to 'bring warmth to conservatism and to add to its basic common sense a degree of romance, generosity and excitement'.[31] This was certainly not the judgement of his contemporaries, however, many of whom viewed him with deep distrust.[32] Disraeli's great achievement was to secure an electoral base for future Conservative governments, and the most important single step by which he managed this was the Second Reform Act of 1867. Much has been made of Disraeli's opportunism in seizing upon a Liberal Bill, making it more radical, and thereby earning the lasting gratitude of the workers. The truth seems to be that Disraeli was reluctant to become enmeshed in electoral reform; Ward argues that Derby had to press the case for reform upon Disraeli.[33] It is true that the radical nature of the 1867 bill had not been a question of design but of concession; Disraeli needed the support of the radicals to get the measure passed at all. Norton and Aughey conclude that 'as an act of long-term political strategy the passage of the Reform Bill proved that the Conservatives were no longer bent upon reaction but could accommodate the demands of the day and do so competently.'[34] In fact this was not so much a strategy as a stratagem, a piece of political opportunism, though Disraeli clearly believed it could only be beneficial to the Conservative interest in the long run. If there was a direct pay-off to the Act it came not in the next election in 1868 but in the following one in 1874. Disraeli's achievement was impressive: the party which had opposed parliamentary reform so vehemently thirty-five years before had itself introduced a measure of further reform more radical than that proposed by its reformist opponent. Disraeli had persuaded his party to take a 'leap in the dark'; not so much a reluctant acceptance of change but an enthusiastic and opportunistic welcoming of change, and as such quite out of character with Conservative ideology.

Disraeli's six-year ministry from 1874 to 1880 was another substantial development of Conservatism in terms of its organicist 'social harmony' programme of domestic reforms which equalled anything attempted by the Liberals. Disraeli incorporated the traditional support for property and hierarchy (extended to include the new owners of industrial wealth) with a paternalistic concern for the well-being of the industrial poor. The thrust of Disraelian Conservatism set out imaginatively in his novel Sybil,[35] sought to establish a new sense of organicism: 'One Nation', a true community, based upon hierarchy, but with the wealthy classes taking a compassionate concern over the conditions of the poorer classes. The interests of this national community could only be secured by the governance of the truly national party, the Conservatives. Moreover, the Conservatives would also protect the interests of the national organic community overseas by building up the empire and calling into being an imperial community of kith and kin.

Conservatism, Unionism and Empire

The next two decades were years of Conservative dominance, the result more of Liberal disunity than of Conservative strength. One important consequence of this disunity, primarily the result of Gladstone's growing preoccupation with Ireland and of the strength of radicalism within the Liberal party, was the inexorable transfer of middle-class support from the Liberals to the Conservatives, as James Cornford has demonstrated.[36] But not just middle-class opinion. The Whigs, too, had seen their party drifting towards the dangerous rocks of radicalism. Warnings to alter course had not been heeded by the bridge; as the century drew to its close the Whigs decided to abandon ship, thereby making the Conservatives for the first time unmistakably the party of wealth. More surprising was the defection of another part of the crew who saw only danger in the swirling currents of Gladstone's Irish policy. The defection of the Whigs and Chamberlain's radical Unionists, and their eventual merging with the Conservatives, was a major event in British party history, adding another dimension to the Conservatives' claim to champion the national interest.

In the early years of the twentieth century, a policy issue was to emerge as injurious in its consequences for the party as Irish home rule proved to be for the Liberals: that issue was later to be known as imperial preference.[37] Imperial preference implied the creation of an empire-wide tariff barrier, important in its own right for British industry, but which was seen as a first step on a long road which was to lead on, through a common defence strategy, to nothing less than imperial federation. As such, although the policy was pursued principally by Chamberlain the Unionist, it can be seen as fitting in with the Disraelian concept of an empire-wide organic community of kith and kin. The subsequent history of the twentieth century might suggest that Chamberlain's ambitious plan, had it been achieved, would have been quickly doomed. But at the time it was seen by many to hold enormous possibilities and indeed many (including Lenin) thought it inevitable. All the same, imperial federation was not achieved and the only palpable consequence of this fiercely contested battle between change and stability inaugurated by Chamberlain's campaign was to 'cast the Conservative Party into confusion and internecine strife and help to achieve [in 1906] what had seemed inconceivable in 1900 – a Liberal government'.[38]

In the years before the First World War the Conservative opposition championed a cause that, once again, brought it face to face with change, that of Irish home rule. With the advent to the leadership of Bonar Law, of Ulster Presbyterian stock, the party's natural reluctance to see the Union weakened intensified to the extent that it offered support to Ulstermen prepared to take up arms. 'Ulster will fight and Ulster will be right' was an unequivocal message whose implication was support for the gun against the ballot box and the dispatch box. True, the passage of the Bill through the House of Commons had been possible only because the Irish held the balance of power; true the House of Lords' constitutional powers of restraint had recently been severely clipped by the Liberal government – with Irish support. But most Conservative thinkers are quite clear about the primacy of the constitution and the rule of law; to pick and choose which laws a man will and will not obey is simply not compatible with Conservatism. Winston Churchill, a minister in the Liberal government, remarked that Bonar Law's motion of censure on his government's Irish policy constituted support for an attack by the criminal classes upon the police. Where all of this might have led is a matter for conjecture because events on the continent of Europe in 1914 were to take precedence over Irish affairs.

Socialism, one-nation Conservatism and the decline of empire

In the inter-war period Conservatives had to come to terms with a new political order the chief features of which were the apparently terminal decline of the Liberals and the inexorable rise of Labour. That the party proceeded, either alone or in coalition, to run the nation for almost the entire period is a testimony not so much to its ability to accommodate itself to running a modern economy but rather to the division between its opponents. When, following World War Two, Labour was strong enough to provide a coherent challenge, the Conservatives were swept from power in a comprehensive electoral defeat almost as great as that caused in 1906 by the Chamberlain split. Not only was the election lost but lost to a Socialist party with a massive majority. So stunning was this defeat that it provoked a major reappraisal of Conservative ideology and policy. Once again the balance between stability and change had shifted, wrong-footing a party out to recreate the conditions of a pre-war world which most citizens rejected.

The party was fortunate to possess men like R.A. Butler, Harold Macmillan and others who were committed to transforming the party so that it might convince the electorate, in Butler's words, that '... we had an alternative policy to socialism which was viable, efficient and humane, which could release and reward enterprise and initiative but without abandoning social justice or reverting to mass unemployment'.[39] The research department and industrial policy committee, under Butler's guidance, promulgated a new Industrial Charter, committing the party to a policy of full employment and Keynesian demand-led economic management. The Charter and the others which followed provided the party with modern, more inclusive policies while at the same time restoring confidence among the shell-shocked party faithful that Socialism could be defeated.

The public proved ready to respond to a modern non-socialist party: the austerities of the late 1940s were beginning to sap morale. Between 1945 and 1950 the Labour government had built the foundations of post-war Britain; perhaps no other party could have done this. But after all, it was no fun living on a building site, and soon enough the new occupants hankered after better amenities, landscaping and the like. So it was that in 1951, after Labour had found it impossible to sustain itself in government following a very narrow electoral victory of 1950, the Conservatives came into power for thirteen years. These were to be the years of de-registration, of the burning of ration books, of growing affluence among the working class, of the spread of material benefits among all classes in a way never seen before. The benefits were not equally spread but on the other hand nearly everybody became better off. For ten years and three successive elections there was no serious challenge to Conservative domestic and economic policies. The British people were convinced, in a phrase attributed (erroneously) to Prime Minister Harold Macmillan, that they had 'never had it so good'. The party had responded to large-scale political and social change during this period with great success.

The foreign policies of the Conservatives were not so successful, however. The party of empire found it almost impossible to face up to the reality of declining British military and economic power in the post-war world and sought to sustain a British military presence on a world-wide scale. Yet within ten years or so British colonies would be achieving independence with almost indecent haste and the dominions of the 'white Commonwealth' would soon become very much their own men. But this did not happen without an ill-advised struggle when, in 1956, British and French troops invaded Egypt in order to regain control of the Suez Canal which the Egyptians had nationalised. Although in military terms the operation was successful, it was a failure in all other terms and had to be abandoned. Suez proved a very painful lesson to the Conservatives: the world had changed, and that change had to be accommodated.[40]

The Prime Minister of the day, Sir Anthony Eden, chose to resign. His successor, Harold Macmillan, had to educate the nation and, more pertinently, his party to the inevitability of the loss of empire. Macmillan was far-sighted enough to realise that Britain's future lay in sloughing off the vestiges of empire as quickly as possible and pressing its case for membership of the European Economic Community (EEC) with equal speed. These two processes were so radical that they seemed certain to break the stability/change balance. The dismantling of empire was obviously against Disraeli Conservative tradition and to associate the nation's future directly with that of continental Europe had never been part of Britain's diplomacy. In fact the strongest opposition to entry into the EEC came not from the ranks of Tory die-hards but from the Labour party whose leader Gaitskell spoke of Britain 'turning its back on a thousand years of history'. In the event Macmillan was more successful in wrapping up the empire than in joining the EEC, but to win his party over to the attempt was an enormous achievement.

Macmillan's leadership probably represented the fullest expression of Conservative organicism since Disraeli. The policies of his government sustained the privileges of the wealthy and yet improved the lot of ordinary people. Moreover, Macmillan saw the necessity of those most fundamental changes in British foreign policy and managed to make many of them, though his failure to gain British membership of the EEC as a result of a French veto proved humiliating.

Managerialism and the eclipse of the Tory tradition

The issue of membership of the EEC returned to the Conservative agenda in 1970 with the election of a new leader and a new brand of Conservatism. Edward Heath had his own ideas on the proper balance between stability and change. In many respects Heath represented a departure for the Conservatives; although he was not the first non-patrician to lead the party (even Macmillan had been a patrician only by marriage!), he was the first lower-middle-class leader, the first 'man of the people'. In *The Making of Conservative Party Policy*, Ramsden quotes a letter from a middle-aged industrial manager and lifelong Conservative which sums up the expectations which Heath aroused in certain kinds of Conservative. The manager writes: 'We were sick of seeing old men dressed in flat caps and bedraggled tweeds strolling about with 12 bores ... The nearest approach to our man is Heath ... He is our age, he is capable, he looks like a director [of the country].'[41] That phrase 'he looks like a director' sums up the new managerial balance in Conservatism which Heath sought to build. If he had a picture of an ideal Britain when he came to office it was of a meritocratic society built upon the success of the technological revolution. Not only this, but his whole approach to politics, the ethos of his cabinet, was optimistic, 'managerial' and almost utilitarian rather than sceptical, organicist and traditional.

Heath was nothing if not a pro-European and he it was who piloted Britain through the dangerous waters towards membership of the EEC. Not for him the nostalgia for empire nor Powell's belief in national sovereignty, both more plausible traditional conservative policies.[42] Heath's overriding concern was for the efficiency and competitiveness of British industry, a laudable if not specifically Conservative goal. His approach, nicknamed the politics of 'Selsdon Man' (after a conference at Selsdon Park in 1970 from which this general approach emerged), was to oppose macro-economic planning, to oppose statutory incomes policies and to favour the statutory limitation of trade union powers, which Labour had backed away from. What Britain needed was resolute business management to bring it out of economic stagnation.

By mid-term, however, Edward Heath's policies had not provided the expected up-turn in the economy. More particularly the centrepiece of Heathite policy, the Industrial Relations Act of 1972 which sought to constrain the power of the unions, was acknowledged to have failed. Thus the Industry Act of 1972 constituted a complete rejection of the politics of Selsdon Man; it gave governments unprecedented powers to aid and indeed to regulate private companies. Heath may be accused of reneging, Peel-like, on party commitments; alternatively he may be applauded for having learned from his mistakes. He certainly may not be congratulated on having convinced his party of the necessity of change: indeed he hardly attempted to do this. Within the space of a year Heath was transmogrified from Selsdon Man to Neo-Corporatist Man, a change as complete as that from Jekyll to Hyde (or vice versa). If these brands of politics had one thing in common it was that both were difficult to accommodate within the framework of traditional Conservatism. In any event the phase-two Heath government proved no more successful than had phase one and the party was defeated in 1974,[43] not to return to office until 1979 under the leadership of Margaret Thatcher.

Thatcherite Conservatism

Margaret Thatcher described herself as a 'conviction politician', which makes her a rarity amongst Conservative leaders. The nub of her conviction was that the social democratic state of the post-war consensus had failed. 'The Thatcher leadership', said Andrew Gamble in one of the best accounts of her governments' objectives and policies,[44] 'united the Conservative party around the claims that the country had become overtaxed, over-governed and undisciplined.' Under Thatcher, on the other hand, a Conservative government would be strong and would 'impose, nurture and stimulate the business values, attitudes and practices necessary to relaunch Britain as a successful capitalist economy'.[45]

Gamble attempted to unravel the interwoven strands of Thatcherite Conservatism, though he warned 'her right wing views always appeared to be much more of a matter of instinct than rational argument'.[46] He associated Thatcherism with the politics of the new right and discerned two quite different tendencies here. First is the neo-liberal; the neo-liberal new-right thinkers were concerned with freeing the economy. Markets, they believed, were inherently superior to any other form of organisation, and so a policy of 'sound money' (absence of inflation), reduction in taxation and public expenditure, deregulation and privatisation was recommended by writers such as Milton Friedman[47]. Monetarists saw the reduction of inflation as the highest priority regardless of its short-term social consequences, and supply-side economists sought the restoration of incentives and the stimulation of enterprise.

Neo-liberals also wished to see the state's role in welfare diminished. They argued that welfare programmes destroyed choice and encouraged dependency, and they wished to see self-help, independence and financial prudence encouraged. Neo-liberals took consolation from the fact that critics on the left as well as on the right were pointing out that the welfare state had failed anyway and that a new approach was needed. Gamble concludes that, generally speaking, 'the intellectual case for markets appeared overwhelming, much as the intellectual case for planning had appeared overwhelming to an earlier generation of intellectuals'.[48]

Although we can plainly recognise elements of neo-liberal thinking in the economic and social policies of Thatcher administrations,[49] it is important to remember that Thatcher made no claim to be a neo-liberal. 'Never let it be said that I am laissez-faire,' she insisted. 'We are a very strong government. We are strong enough to do these things that government must do and only governments can do. We are strong enough to say "over to the people" because we believe in their fundamental dignity and freedom.'[50] She declared with some passion: 'We are not just interested in power, but in power to release people from power' – a crucial distinction about which more will need to be said.

New-right Conservatives wanted to build a strong state. They believed that the will of social democratic governments to resist 'challenges' had been seriously weakened. Both Heath in 1974 and Callaghan in 1978–9 were believed to have been defeated by militant trade unionism. The government's whole position had been undermined by what was at the time a growing army of public sector professionals whose influence had spread into nearly every corner of public service. Moreover, in the 'corporatist' world of the 1960s and (especially) the 1970s an ability to come to some arrangement with the unions seemed indispensable, and clearly this was an easier task for Labour governments. For both practical and ideological reasons, then, Thatcher made no secret of her ambition to break with corporatism,[51] though while in opposition she masked any intention of seeking confrontation with the unions. All the same, two internal reports were commissioned to consider options for a future Conservative government in case of just such a major confrontation. In terms of defence, law and order and industrial relations, Thatcher sought a strong government willing and able to intervene in these areas which traditionally and properly belonged to the state. More than this, Thatcher's government sought to use the state to intervene in education, health and social services, broadcasting, and within the civil service and local government in order to maximise conditions favourable to the values of the market economy. Her government, as Gamble put it, was prepared to force people to be free. If only the grip of collectivism and social democracy could be loosened people would instinctively exhibit those values of enterprise, initiative, robust independence and patriotism which were seen to be the foundations of a successful market system.

Thatcher's goals seem to have been marked out not by Disraeli nor indeed any traditional Conservative figure but by Samuel Smiles, the prophet of self-help. Given Thatcher's small-town petit bourgeois background this is not surprising. Nevertheless we can see in Thatcherism the resolution of a paradox presented by Gamble in which the state is simultaneously to be rolled back and to be rolled forward. Thatcher appropriated the neo-liberal ideas of market forces and coupled them to a Conservative notion of the strong state representing the interests of the whole nation (perceived as a free economy). It is not true, however, that she pursued these policies relentlessly. The 'hands-off' monetarism of earlier years gave way, under Chancellor Lawson, to more pragmatic fiscal and monetary policies internally and to more co-ordinated actions externally.

To what extent may Thatcherism be accommodated within the Conservative tradition? Clearly a leader who directed her party's fortunes for fifteen years and through three successive electoral triumphs has some reason to regard this question as redundant. Nevertheless it has some intrinsic interest to our investigation and is therefore worth pursuing. As for defending property rights, Thatcher's governments did more than any to extend property ownership through the sale of council houses to people who could not normally have even aspired to own their own homes. As for traditionalism, Thatcher had nothing but scorn for those institutions which helped to run the despised social democratic consensus. The Church of England, the BBC, the House of Lords, the Civil Service, the army, the navy, the universities, the National Health Service (NHS), even the Football League all came under threat from 'the handbag'. When Quinton spoke of fixed constitutions embodying innumerable compromises and adjustments he was certainly not speaking the language of Thatcherism. Organicism, too, was anathema to Thatcher, who declared that there was no such thing as 'society'. She felt no attachment to the idea of a traditional ruling class, nor was she enamoured of paternalism which did not gel with her notions of independence and self-help. Gilmour indicated the anxieties that One Nation Tories felt about 'the prospective creation of a nineteenth-century liberal paradise ... there is nothing Tory about a powerful government presiding over a country of atomised individuals, with its intermediate institutions emasculated or abolished, and with the state progressively abandoning its activities and services – except of course for a strong police force to keep the under-class and everybody else in order.'[52] Gilmour's criticism was echoed by David Levy who claimed that the autonomous individual, free of the 'encrustation of cultural formation', is not only a Liberal rather than a Conservative aspiration, but is also self-destructive.[53]

Quinton's other Conservative principle was scepticism. Thatcher's whole philosophy rested upon the assumption of the demonstrable superiority of the market and she was prepared to legislate to create the right domestic framework for the market, though ironically, since its proper functioning owes everything to global economic factors, her own government had no control over global market forces – the disadvantages of what has been called 'Thatcherism in one country'. Nevertheless Thatcher was not sceptical about the operations of the market: she was a true believer.

As for limited government, David Marquand pointed out that the 1988 Education Reform Act, one example among many, was *dirigiste* in method and centralist in intent.[54] Thatcher used the state to reshape society – precisely the kind of enterprise Conservatives have traditionally considered both inappropriate and obnoxious. And we should be under no illusions as to the extent of this *dirigisme*. The 1988 Education Reform Act conferred no fewer than 240 new powers upon the Secretary of State, more than 60 of which were the direct result of government amendments. Moreover, in July of 1988 over 500 House of Lords amendments to the Education Bill (and over 400 to the Local Government Bill) were driven through the House of Commons in three days.[55] So much for the rule of law, limited government and rolling back the state.

Any claim that Thatcher was a pragmatist (sustainable in her first few years) must be weighed against her government's policy regarding the replacement of domestic rates. That the rating system had all but broken down, especially in Scotland, is generally accepted; that the community charge (the soon to be notorious Poll Tax) was a suitable replacement can be argued. What cannot be accepted or argued is that a pragmatist would have persevered with the Poll Tax when it received such intense universal opprobrium. It was her failure to respond to unease over the Poll Tax which led directly to the party's series of disastrous by-election performances and thus to her own vulnerability as leader. But in truth the Poll Tax was only symptomatic of an inflexibility which exasperated senior colleagues. The lady *was* not for turning, even by colleagues offering sound advice. Eventually those colleagues withdrew their support and Britain's most powerful Prime Minister since Lloyd George was obliged, by her own party, to resign in 1990.

Conservatism after Thatcher

John Major, Thatcher's successor, was to prove that pragmatism might be a necessary attribute of a Conservative leader but it was by no means a sufficient one. Although he attempted to lead by consensus it was Major's apparent complete lack of ideological ballast that received critical comment. Major managed to win the 1992 general election against all expectations (including his own) but a majority of twenty-one – small by Conservative standards, – an economic embarrassment when Britain was forced out of the European Exchange Rate Mechanism within six months of his victory; growing opposition to his European policies, together placed severe constraints on Major's position. Major had been chosen by the party because he was seen as a disciple of the previous leader and many who voted for him looked forward to 'Thatcherism without Thatcher'. In the event Major continued with Thatcher's policies of privatisation and civil service reform but sought to couple this with a far less abrasive style and an inclusivity exemplified by the introduction of Citizens' Charters which were intended to give the public guaranteed rights in respect of both public and privatised service provision. Major's room for manoeuvre was limited by the Conservatives' small and diminishing majority but even more by the accelerated programme of European integration to which the government had to respond. In ideological terms Major's government became impaled upon the issue of sovereignty, especially in respect of the move towards European Monetary Union (EMU) and Britain's response. Conservatism after Thatcher became, above all else, a battle fought ferociously between the anti- and pro-Europeans, a battle certain to cause the party's defeat at the polls.

Major's resignation immediately after that defeat catapulted the party into a leadership election at a time of maximum confusion when one of the foremost contenders, Michael Portillo, had just lost his seat. In the event the parliamentary party, reduced to 165, elected William Hague, a 35-year-old Yorkshireman and ex-Secretary of State for Wales, as its leader. Hague immediately set about establishing his party's unequivocally Eurosceptic credentials, having presumably decided that Major's attempted balancing act could only prove self-defeating. He won the party over to a policy of remaining out of EMU for at least ten years and in doing so earned the enmity of senior pro-Europeans such as Clarke and Heseltine. At successive party conferences Hague declared a belief in community, in a Conservatism that had 'compassion at its core'. He reached out to younger women, to ethnic minorities and to homosexuals.[56] Hague launched a campaign in 1998 to 'reconnect' the party with the people of Britain – the 'Listening to Britain' campaign, launched not at party headquarters but significantly at the ultra-modern Imagination Gallery in Bloomsbury. The party would be guided by key principles such as championing the family and marriage, the commitment to a stable and democratic constitution, low taxes and the importance of enterprise, and of course an unswerving belief in the nation state, but within those parameters Hague's would be a 'listening party'.[57]

In a lecture to his party in January 1999 William Hague outlined his vision of Conservatism in the twenty-first century. The fate of his party, he said, was to define and champion British values, a rebuke to those within his party who would 'abandon Scotland outright and exploit an emerging sense of English nationalism' which he described as a 'sinister, uncontrollable force'.[58] Hague emphasised the need for the party to accept Britain as it was rather than to 'wallow knee-deep in nostalgia', to accept change and inclusiveness. In anchoring his philosophy to 'Britishness', Hague was sending a coded message of Euroscepticism – no further transfer of power and sovereignty. He did not indicate, however, what would be the distinctive features of his inclusive, British society. But William Hague commands a parliamentary party of only 165. He will need great political acumen and a lot of luck if he is not to become only the second Conservative leader in the entire twentieth century never to have been Prime Minister. Indeed even the *Yorkshire Post* felt obliged to point out that a year after taking office more than ten million voters did no know who William Hague was.[59] The story of Conservatism after Thatcher has not been a happy one.

Conclusions

Having established the chief characteristics of Conservatism, a brief history seems to suggest that the actual policies pursued by Conservative leaders frequently shows little more than a symbolic relationship to that ideology and tradition. Conservatives were opposed to parliamentary reform and then its champion; opposed to Corn Law Reform and then its agent; opposed to the development of the empire, then an enthusiastic supporter, and finally the dismantler of empire; in favour of state intervention to the extent of setting up the frame of a pseudo-corporatist state and then an unrelenting critic of such a state. If Conservatism (defined as what Conservative governments 'do', not what Conservative thinkers say) has any consistency, then, it must surely reside in some other general principle which we have not uncovered so far.

There is another such principle which is worth considering. Suppose we take Conservatism to represent – substantially though by no means entirely – a rationalisation of the interests of the advantaged, political actions consciously taken by the socially privileged classes. Conservatism defined in these terms would develop as the interests of that class developed.[60] The ideological principles we have considered, moreover, are certainly not harmful to those interests. Traditionalism, for example, favours the retention of institutions and customs which, by definition, have allowed the advantaged to dominate the polity. Organicism, too, favours the advantaged. After all, it is far easier to believe that the hierarchical society is natural, God-given or the product of history when one is nearer the top than the bottom. Again, we should be more inclined to be dismissive of large-scale plans for human betterment – more inclined, that is, to be sceptical – if our own interests were already well catered for. Finally, it is safer to argue that man's moral and intellectual imperfections commend strict limits to government when, because of good fortune or wealthy forebears, we are quite capable of maximising our own interests in society as it exists. For the 'poor man at the gate', any injury to his individual liberty produced by government intervention would seem secondary when his family is hungry; indeed he might consider the 'liberty' to go hungry to be a blessing that he would be willing to manage without.

Let us put this putative principle to a more controlled test. How did Thatcherism, for example, safeguard the interests of the wealthy? After all, high interest rates, a feature of her governments' policies in the early years, were harmful to industry. Gamble argues that the disadvantages of Thatcherism were short-term and limited, and were more than balanced by long-term general advantages; short-term bankruptcies were more than balanced by the longer-term improvements in the environment for expansion. 'The essential requirement for this', says Gamble, 'was a government prepared to confront and permanently weaken the organised power of labour.'[61] The weapons used were mass unemployment, trade union reform, privatisation and the dismantling of the corporate framework.

All the same, Thatcherism was more than a front for the interests of capital. In fact some of Thatcher's policies struck such an obvious chord with popular sentiment that Stuart Hall called Thatcherism 'authoritarian populism'.[62] Indeed the policies of Conservative governments in the past have always embodied more than class interests. On the other hand, it is hard to believe that the principles which make up Conservative ideology, only symbolically related to the policies of Conservative governments, could have survived had they not also suited the interests of the advantaged. The interests of capital offered a reference to party leaders during times of change which, as Peel's experience shows, they ignored at their peril.

The constant tension between conserving and changing could be described as attempting to optimise social and economic privilege when the pressures completely to resist change become too great. A Marxist would argue that in sustaining the interests of the capitalist class as a whole the Conservative party found it expedient from time to time to sacrifice a fraction of capital. Well, Conservatives were seldom as clear-sighted as Marx implied but the evidence suggests a relationship between the interests of capital and Conservative ideology. Social cohesion linked to a degree of political change is important to the well-being of modern capitalism, and the ability to provide that link through the balance of its fundamental and operational principles has traditionally guaranteed the Conservative party the alliance of wealthy capitalists and the support of the middle class (and sections of the working class).

As John Gray notes however,[63] in its scorn for the identity and continuity of long-established institutions such as the civil service, local government and the NHS, the Tories under Thatcher wrought havoc among many of their natural supporters. Her governments' policies weakened, even destroyed, the natural trust of the British for their institutions. Job insecurity and shrinking equity, Gray continues, have pauperised sections of the middle class – the reversal of 'bourgeoisification'. Thatcherism was partly concerned to modernise Britain's *ancien régime*; its success was predominantly at the expense of its own supporters, especially in Scotland and Wales.

More importantly, to the extent that Thatcherism overturned the neo-Keynesian shibboleths of the post-war consensus and replaced them with a new consensus – that markets work – it made itself redundant. At the beginning of this chapter we saw that Conservatism became explicit in response to attack from radicals. Only in terms of constitutional reform has the late 1990s Blair government acted radically, and those battles are largely over. In its opposition to EMU the Conservative party may well be setting itself against the interests of capital: as Peter Riddell pointed out,[64] in 1998 it was to the Labour and not the Conservative conference that the 'businessmen and lobbyists flocked'. Because of its failures but also because of its successes, Thatcherism has detached Conservatism from its traditions and its allies – from its anchorage – and it is adrift. The one issue which could be said to define the party – Euroscepticism – is also that which most bitterly divides it. William Hague will need all his undoubted acumen and Yorkshire grit if the party is not to drift in a direction some would say Thatcher had already charted, towards the rocks of a narrow-minded English nationalism.[65]

Notes

1. Anthony Quinton, *The Politics of Imperfection*, London, Faber & Faber, 1978, p. 24.
2. N.K. O'Sullivan, *Conservatism*, London, Dent, 1976, p. 24.
3. See F.J.C. Hearnshaw (ed.), *Social and Political Ideas in the Age of Reaction*, London, Harrap, 1932.
4. See Ian Gilmour, *Inside Right*, London, Hutchinson, 1977.
5. Frank Brady (ed.), *Boswell's Life of Johnson*, London, Signet Classics, 1968, p. 297.
6. Quoted in W.Wagar (ed.), *H.G. Wells: Journalism and Prophecy*, London, Bodley Head, 1965, p. 277.
7. Quintin Hogg, *The Conservative Case*, Harmondsworth, Penguin, 1959.

8. *Ibid.*, p. 99.
9. Robert Leach, *British Political Ideologies*, London, Prentice-Hall, 1996, p. 117.
10. O'Sullivan, *Conservatism*, p. 12.
11. Robert Blake, *The Conservative Party from Peel to Churchill*, London, Eyre and Spottiswoode, 1972, p. 1.
12. Richard Rose, *Politics in England*, London, Faber, 1965, p. 143.
13. Gilmour, *Inside Right*, p. 12.
14. Enoch Powell, 'Conservatism and Social Problems', *Swinton Journal*, Autumn 1968, p. 8.
15. Philip Norton, 'The principles of Conservatism', in Philip Norton, *The Conservative Party*, 1996.
16. Norton, P. and Aughey, A., *Conservatives and Conservatism*, London, Temple Snith, 1981, p. 27.
17. Samuel Beer, *Modern British Politics*, London, Faber, 1965, p. 272.
18. Leach, *British Political Ideologies*, p. 124.
19. Edmund Burke, *Thoughts on the Causes of the Present Discontents*, first published in 1770.
20. *Ibid.*
21. Lord Hugh Cecil, *Conservatism*, London, Home University Library, 1912.
22. Michael Oakshott, *Rationalism in Politics*, London, Methuen,1962, p. 168 ff.
23. T.E. Uttley, 'The significance of Mrs Thatcher', in M. Cowling (ed.), *Conservative Essays*, London, Cassell, 1978, p. 51.
24. Peter Walker, *Ascent of Britain*, London, Sidgwick & Jackson, 1977, p. 20.
25. Quoted in Norton and Aughey, *Conservatives and Conservatism*, p. 37.
26. *Ibid.*, p. 47.
27. Angus Maude, 'Party paleontology', *Spectator*, 15 March 1963.
28. Gilmour, *Inside Right*, p. 144.
29. Norton and Aughey, *Conservatives and Conservatism*, p. 92.
30. Peel had been persuaded to support Catholic emancipation, for example, twenty years before. It is interesting to recall that in his political novels Disraeli spoke of Peel's 'Conservatism' as a betrayal of what he termed 'true toryism'.
31. Gilmour, *Inside Right*, p. 86.
32. R.J. Feuchtwanger, *Disraeli, Democracy and the Conservative Party*, Oxford, Oxford University Press, 1968, p. 10.
33. See J.T. Ward, 'Derby and Disraeli', in D. Southgate (ed.), Conservative Leadership 1832–1932, London, Macmillan, 1974.
34. Norton and Aughey, *Conservatives and Conservatism*, p. 107.
35. Benjamin Disraeli, *Sybil*, Harmondsworth, Penguin, 1980, Book ii, ch. 5, p. 96 (first published 1845).
36. See James Cornford, 'The Transformation of Conservatism in the late nineteenth century', in *Victorian Studies*, **VII**, (1) September 1963, pp. 35–66.
37. See R.R. James, *The British Revolution 1886–1939*, London, Methuen, 1978 for a full account of this issue and its consequences.
38. Norton and Aughey, *Conservatives and Conservatism*, p. 117.
39. Quoted in *Ibid.*, p. 128. For a full account of the work of this group see R.A. Butler, *The Art of the Possible*, Harmondsworth, Penguin, 1973, ch. 7.
40. See Anthony Nutting, *No End of a Lesson*, London, Constable, 1967.

41. J. Ramsden, *The Making of Conservative Party Policy*, London, Longman, 1980, p. 226.
42. See D. E. Schoen, *Enoch Powell and the Powellites*, London, Macmillan, 1977.
43. Heath held an election in order to strengthen his hand to deal with a miners' strike. His platform was 'Who runs Britain?'
44. Andrew Gamble, *The Free Economy and the Strong State*, London, Macmillan, 1988, p. 231.
45. *Ibid.*, p. 232.
46. *Ibid.*, p. 85.
47. Milton Friedman, *Capitalism and Freedom*, Chicago, Chicago University Press, 1962.
48. Gamble, *The Free Economy and the Strong State*, p. 50.
49. See Peter Clarke, 'The Keynesian Consensus and its enemies', in David Marquand and Anthony Seldon (eds.), *The Ideas that Shaped Post-War Britain*, London, Fontana Press, 1996, pp 67–88.
50. *Independent*, 14 September, 1987.
51. See Shirley Robin Letwin, *The Anatomy of Thatcherism*, London, Fontana Books, 1992, chs 1, 2.
52. *Independent*, 21 July 1987.
53. See 'The Politics of Self', in Roger Scruton, (ed.), *Conservative Thinkers*, London, Claridge Press, 1988; see also Scruton, *The Meaning of Conservatism*, Harmondsworth, Penguin, 1980.
54. *Sunday Telegraph*, 6 March 1988.
55. *Independent*, 19 July 1988.
56. *Daily Telegraph*, 10 October 1997.
57. *Daily Telegraph*, 15 July 1998.
58. *The Times*, 20 January 1999.
59. *Yorkshire Post*, 5 October 1998.
60. See H.G. Schumann, 'The problem of Conservatism', in *Journal of Contemporary History*, **13**(4), October 1978, p. 807.
61. Gamble, *The Free Economy and the Strong State*, p. 192.
62. 'Popular democratic versus authoritarian populism', in A. Hunt (ed.), *Marxism and Democracy*, London, Lawrence & Wishart, 1980.
63. *Guardian*, 15 May 1995.
64. *The Times*, 5 October 1998.
65. *The Times*, 6 October 1998.

CHAPTER THREE

Who runs the Conservative Party?

This chapter considers the key features of party leadership and organisation, both within and outwith parliament, and seeks to locate power within the party. We shall begin this investigation with the office of leader.

Leadership in the Conservative party

Many who write about the relationship between Conservative leaders and their party seek to provide an analogy to clarify the relationship, presumably because it is not formal and so may not be stated in strictly constitutional terms. The most common is probably the monarchical analogy, with the leader seen as a monarch surrounded by a court from among whom advisers will be chosen. A second analogy is that of the baronial system, with more emphasis on bargaining and coalition-building.[1] A third analogy may be described as Hobbesian,[2] with the leader seen as Leviathan, to whom absolute power is surrendered so long as the interests of the supporters are protected (by electoral victory). If the covenant is broken (by electoral defeat) then the obligation to obey is no longer binding. In Winston Churchill's words: 'The loyalties which centre upon number one are enormous. If he trips he must be sustained. If he makes mistakes they must be covered. If he sleeps he must not be wantonly disturbed. If he is no good, he must be pole-axed.'[3] Norton and Aughey prefer a more homely analogy: that of the traditional family. 'As in most families', they tell us, 'there may be occasional discord, but the members remain bonded to one another by ties of loyalty, respect and kinship.'[4] Heads of household, though, are not elected nor are they bound by obligations beyond what the law imposes (which are minimal) and which they themselves choose to adopt. Moreover, families differ: indeed some are nowadays described as dysfunctional. The family head model is cosy but misleading, though its emphasis on mutuality is important.

There is another model – a modern one – which appears to offer some possibilities: that of the manager of a soccer club. Here what is being emphasised is the freedom of manoeuvre that the manager has; his ability to make, shape and break the careers of his players. He needs the committed support of the fans and the team and the success of his tactics will be the chief determinant of the extent to which he gets it. But his control over match outcomes is incomplete and there are a range of external factors over which he has little control. And if his tactics fail his security of tenure is weak. Conservative leaders, like soccer managers, are only as good as last month's result as portrayed in the nation's media! True their tenure in office is nothing like as easily terminated but bad results may well find them in power but powerless.

No Conservative leader was elected by his party until 1965; prior to that date Conservative leaders were judged to have 'emerged'. This system provided continuity and no open struggle for the succession; however, history shows that as often as not there was no natural successor, and informal soundings had to be taken so that a compromise candidate could be agreed. At the resignation of Harold Macmillan in 1963, for example, no natural successor emerged. Contenders for the leadership used the party conference to launch public 'selection campaigns', making the proceedings not unlike an American party convention. The traditional procedures simply could not cope with this kind of pressure, and in the event the decision was taken to select a compromise candidate, Lord Home. Home's ministry was so generally unpopular that it proved to be the *coup de grâce* for the traditional method. What finally emerged from the party's subsequent review was election by the parliamentary party, with an overall majority plus 15 per cent of those voting required for victory on the first ballot. Additional candidates could join the second ballot but if no overall majority was obtained the three top candidates would proceed to a third ballot using the alternative vote method.

This system remained unaltered for a decade and then an important limitation was placed upon the leader's powers: re-election. Again this development was the consequence of a practical problem: that of removing Edward Heath, the first elected leader. Not only had he lost an election but he had become generally unpopular with the parliamentary party. Provision was consequently made for elections at the beginning of every new session, and the 15 per cent above an overall majority required for victory in the first ballot now became 15 per cent above an overall majority of all eligible voters. Much to his surprise Edward Heath lost the leadership of the party to Mrs Thatcher in the first such challenge, thus becoming both the first elected and de-elected leader of the party.

It is arguable, though, that re-election has strengthened the hand of the party leader, because a leader under threat may well risk re-election, banking on the instinct to loyalty of the average Conservative backbencher. In the event of a challenge being beaten off the leader's position clearly becomes stronger. This is what persuaded John Major to resign as leader in 1995. Fed up with backbench and indeed frontbench sniping at both his style of leadership and his policies, he sought to strengthen his hand by a decisive victory in the subsequent leadership election. His attempt to draw his opponents out into open battle was successful. One of his leading right-wing critics, John Redwood, stood against him. His subsequent victory rid him of Redwood's criticism within the Cabinet and strengthened his position in the party at least temporarily, but it was not a convincing win and its fruits were not enjoyed for long. Major's eventual resignation, following defeat in 1997, was precipitate and a sure indication of his disillusionment with party colleagues. Anthony Bevins described his action as desertion, a 'gross abdication of responsibility, a dereliction of duty.'[5]

In 1997 William Hague instituted a major reform of the party which included the system for leadership elections. The thrust of Hague's reforms was to 'give power to the members' and in terms of leadership elections this meant the establishment of a two-stage process. Henceforth an election would be triggered either by the resignation of the leader or by the leader losing a vote of no-confidence in the parliamentary party (to be triggered by 15 per cent of MPs writing to the chairman of the committee comprising all Conservative backbenchers, the 1922 committee). If the leader won then no further vote could be initiated for a period of at least a year. However if the leader failed to win a simple majority he or she would be obliged to resign and would be deemed ineligible to stand in the election which followed. The chairman of the 1922 would call for nominations for the position of leader, and first-past-the-post elections would then be held to reduce the number of contenders to two. At that stage the full membership of the party would vote for the new leader. This new system, currently untried, seems to balance the demands of party democracy with the practical need for 'guidance' from party managers. Conservatives claim that it makes them a more democratic party than Labour, with its electoral college system.

We can best conclude this initial analysis of the Conservative leader by returning briefly to those analogies with which we began. From their different perspectives they sought to show both the extent and the limitations of the powers of a Conservative leader. As Norton points out,[6] of the thirteen party leaders this century (before William Hague) – twelve of whom has been Prime Minister – seven held office for at least nine years, Major for seven years. Of the remainder, two retired through ill health and thus only three could be said to have felt obliged to resign through political failure – the two Chamberlains and Douglas Home. Nevertheless if we shift the focus to other indices of stability – principally the extent to which leaders enjoyed the confidence of the party when in office – then a radically different picture begins to emerge. Each was subject to various pressures from an early stage in his or her period of leadership; most, though not all, were able to withstand the pressures. Like the soccer manager, however, the best insurance against pressure is success. When the party feels that its manager is likely to lose the Big Match even the most secure of them, as the case of Margaret Thatcher in 1990 illustrates, becomes a candidate for the pole-axe.

Recent leaders in action

The Conservative party has spent the greater part of this century in power, its leader acting as Prime Minister. It is accepted wisdom that Conservative Prime Ministers are required to achieve a balance when constructing their Cabinets in which the principal ideological strains and sectional interests are represented. In the case of Edward Heath it is argued that his original appointments were unduly weighted towards colleagues known to be personally loyal to him. Norton and Aughey clearly believe this to have been a major source of weakness rather than strength because he 'deprived himself of any means of communication between the pro- and anti-marketeers. The latter feel dispossessed. They are on the other side of the tracks'.[7] Norton and Aughey contrast Heath's attitude with Mrs Thatcher's, who, they claim, rated parliamentary ability higher than personal loyalty. Her inability to persuade Cabinet to accept a second round of public expenditure cuts in 1981, however, convinced Mrs Thatcher that balanced cabinets were not always a good thing. A Cabinet reshuffle produced a swing to the right and Shirley Williams commented that Mrs Thatcher had replaced her Cabinet with an echo chamber.[8] After the electoral victory of 1987, the traditional Tory wing of the party was largely unrepresented in Mrs Thatcher's last cabinet.

The most severe test of Mrs Thatcher's leadership and judgement occurred in 1985-6 when her Minister of Defence, Michael Heseltine, resigned because he claimed that the Prime Minister had prevented full discussion in Cabinet of the future of the Westland helicopter company. These events illuminated the animosities within Mrs Thatcher's second Cabinet and they were equally plain during her third ministry. In the bitterest Cabinet dispute since Westland, the Prime Minister sought to prevent Chancellor Lawson from intervening to support sterling's exchange rate. Lawson, with public support from Sir Geoffrey Howe, refused to give way. Eventually it was the Prime Minister herself who was obliged to withdraw. But worse – much worse – was to follow.

In 1988 in Scotland and the following year in England and Wales the government introduced a replacement for the domestic rating system – the predominant source of funding for local government – the Community

Charge. The 'poll tax' as it quickly became known was almost universally hated and in the autumn of 1989 a backbencher, Sir Anthony Meyer, stood as a 'stalking horse' candidate in a leadership challenge. Although Meyer entertained no hope of success, some 60 Conservatives failed to support their leader. A further number – probably around 60 – let her campaign managers know that their support for the leader was conditional upon a more conciliatory approach to the poll tax and to European issues. The government was shaken by serious and widespread poll-tax riots and disastrous by-election results. In November 1990 Sir Geoffrey Howe, Leader of the House and Deputy Prime Minister, resigned. His resignation speech to a packed House could hardly have been more damaging to the Prime Minister or more critical of her style of leadership. The following day Heseltine triggered a leadership election with the announcement of his candidacy. Although Mrs Thatcher headed the first ballot she was four votes short of the margin necessary for victory. After initially declaring, with her usual vigour, her intention of pressing on to a second ballot, she was persuaded by Cabinet colleagues to stand down. John Major won the ensuing election; although he had won two votes short of the necessary majority in the first round, his opponents withdrew from the field.

In a sense Thatcher's Prime Minister's story is paradigmatic: it shows how by skilful management and good fortune a Conservative leader can strengthen her hand and eventually mould the Cabinet to her purpose, and yet in doing so immunise herself against the kind of criticism from Cabinet colleagues that would normally be productive of sensible compromise. Finally, like Shakespeare's Richard III, having alienated many of her more powerful supporters, she took the field defiantly against all challengers only to suffer even graver defections on the day of battle. Her eventual defeat was no less decisive.

John Major, her successor, held office for seven years. His leadership style was more naturally collegiate than his predecessor's but it was also more circumscribed by external factors. During his first ministry Thatcher's sometimes baleful presence hovered over the new Cabinet. Following the unexpected Conservative electoral victory of 1992, considered by many to be a personal triumph for the new leader, Major's parliamentary majority was only twenty-one and began soon to diminish further as a result of by-election defeats. He attempted to run a balanced Cabinet and to seek accommodation where Thatcher had sought confrontation. Major was supportive of 'failed' Cabinet colleagues when a more ruthless leader would have dismissed them or required their resignation, and this approach was to earn him the caustic comment from the former Chancellor of the Exchequer, Norman Lamont, in his resignation speech in 1993 that the government was in office but not in power and that it lacked a sense of direction and purpose. Major was opposed in Cabinet and in the parliamentary party over his European policies (ambivalent if more conciliatory than his predecessor's). He was caught in a trap. Overt divisions in the party over Europe led to disastrous by-election performances and opinion-poll standing; these in turn led to increasing criticism among his parliamentary colleagues of his leadership.

Moreover, the leader's adoption of a 'back to basics' campaign at the 1993 conference – widely seen as signalling a return to traditional family values – rebounded, as a seemingly endless sequence of financial and sexual scandals – the 'sleaze factor' – hit the headlines, leading to the establishment in 1996 of the Nolan Commission on standards in public life. There occurred a veritable cascade of falling Ministers and discredited backbenchers whose misdemeanours stretched from three-in-a-bed sex scandals[9] to accepting money for asking parliamentary questions and for more direct forms of lobbying.[10] Less than two months before the 1997 election no fewer than three MPs decided to stand down as a result of personal indiscretions.[11] To adapt a judgement on one of Gladstone's ministries, 'born down by a torrent of division and sleaze' would be a suitable epithet for the 1992–97 government. The administrations of both Prime Ministers, then, had their failings, but whereas Major's leadership seemed to indicate that Conservative Prime Ministers need to lead, Thatcher's and Heath's show that they should listen before leading.

Leaders and the party bureaucracy

One key indicator of the power of Conservative leaders is the relationship with the party bureaucracy. Formally that relationship is unequivocal: party chairmen are appointed by the Prime Minister, and indeed their main responsibility – Central Office – has been referred to as the leader's personal machine, a subject to which we shall be returning. Although the leader must make symbolic gestures towards the effective two-way transmission of views, chairmen who saw it as their main task to act as tribunes for the broader movement seem not to have been favoured by past leaders. Accordingly when party chairmen are chosen they will ideally be well-known party figures, preferably on the front bench, with proven administrative skills and a good ability to mix with and inspire the party faithful, and above all a loyal supporter of the party leader. Pinto-Duschinsky has pointed out that it is by no means always easy to find people with the requisite skills or to persuade them to take on the job.[12]

The party in the country wants a chairman it can look up to, a major figure in the party hierarchy. Thatcher's appointment of Cecil Parkinson in 1983 and Norman Tebbit in 1985 indicated the importance which the party leader attaches to the post.[13] But such men (never, so far, a woman) are often reluctant to forsake a ministerial post. Leaders have therefore sometimes been obliged to make appointments they would probably have preferred not to make. Between 1979 and 1993 eight chairmen were appointed, none of whom lasted two years and only one of whom, Cecil Parkinson – later to be re-appointed by William Hague – could be considered to have enhanced his reputation in the post.[14] The leader will also influence other appointments, for example the director of the research department, or the deputy chairmen. However, the leader traditionally had no direct authority over the voluntary wing of the party; the National Union had to be persuaded and not cajoled,[15] though its instinct was invariably for loyalty to the leader.

Leaders and party policy

We shall shortly be considering the machinery of policy-making within the party, but the establishment of the main thrust of policy – 'agenda-setting' – is something different. It is a function of the Conservative leader to provide a policy context within which priorities may be established, and this context will affect policy-making at two levels. First, at the level of policy options: under Thatcher, for example, it would have been unthinkable for policies favourable to reflating the economy to have emerged from the machine at least before 1986; under Major no gesture towards devolution was possible, whatever the consequences for the party in Scotland and Wales. Second, at the level of selecting policy priorities when the party is in office: here the powers of Conservative leaders are quite formidable and they are able, indeed expected, to imprint their personality upon government policy in a manner to which past Labour leaders have seldom even aspired. Yet it is essential for Conservative leaders to sustain contacts with the party at all levels, so that a process of consultation is perceived to operate. 'To impose a policy, however good it may be,' say Norton and Aughey, 'without adhering to the accept "form" can constitute an affront to [party] sensibilities'.[16] This may be too sanguine: a leader whose policies are generally considered successful will have greater scope regarding party sensibilities; but there is very little sympathy if the policies begin to fail.

The clearest exposition of party policy is the election manifesto. The leader's influence on this document has always been substantial, but the very comprehensiveness and detail of the modern manifesto requires a formal process of preparation. In 1949 a broadly representative advisory committee serviced by the research department of Central Office was established which, in its monthly meetings, would consider reports from study groups and discussion groups. The committee was discontinued under Thatcher, and the groups began to report directly to the leader. The research department, too, lost its influence. Thatcher tended generally to look outside the party structure for policy advice. Nevertheless a small group, with the chairman of the research department and the head of the No.10 policy unit, would produce a paper based upon the groups' reports. Senior ministers would be called in for advice on the paper and then a manifesto committee of trusted advisers would report directly to the leader, and the shape and detail of the manifesto would be finalised. Major's approach differed little in 1992 but by 1997 senior ministers and their advisers exercised more influence, though still the final word rested with the party leader. As part of his reform measures, William Hague has promised members a direct influence (via a referendum) on the chief aspects of the party election manifesto. Indeed, his referendum on whether the party should rule out membership of a single European currency for the life-time of the next parliament was held in 1998. Central Office sent out 344,157 ballots of which 202,674 (59 per cent) were returned. Of these 84 per cent supported the leadership and 16 per cent were opposed. It was widely argued that Hague had held the ballot simply to wrong-foot Heseltine and Clarke.[17] There *were* strategic advantages to such a course, but it was also in line with the new leader's pledge to involve the membership.

In day-to-day policy matters the party leader, as Prime Minister, simply cannot control all the policies of Ministers. But they can interfere and attempt to control some of them. Norton offers two examples from 1995 when Major exerted influence on the Secretary of State for Education, on policies relating to competitive sport in schools and the nursery education voucher system.[18] Some ten years earlier Thatcher had personally prevented the reform of the English 'A' level system of examinations despite widespread departmental support for change and the report of a government-sponsored committee, the Higginson Report, which also recommended change. These are small beer, though, in comparison to Heath's personal influence on his government's *volte-face* on economic policy or Thatcher's unremitting support for the poll tax, unpopular even with her own party and massively so with the voters.

Conservative party organisation

Traditionally the Conservative party comprised three separate entities: the parliamentary party, the National Union of Conservative and Unionist Associations together with the constituency organisations, and finally Central Office. There is no doubt in Conservative history and mythology which body dominated: the parliamentary party is 'the party'. It is the task of the other parts, 'the movement' (the National Union) and 'the bureaucracy' (Central Office) to support and sustain the party and its leader. So let us begin with the parliamentary party.

The parliamentary party

Traditionally such party structure as existed at Westminster allowed the leader to communicate with the backbenchers, transmitting instructions downwards. Yet in the same way as the ideology of Conservatism developed in response to changing circumstances and events, so did the party in parliament. By far the most significant development occurred as a reaction against Lloyd George's continued dominance of the post-1918 coalition government: it was the founding of 'The 1922'. This committee took its name from the meeting of Conservative backbenchers at the Carlton Club in that year when opposition to the coalition was so strong as to oblige the compliant Conservative leader, Sir Austen Chamberlain, to resign. Backbenchers in the next government formed a permanent committee to 'enable new members to take a more active interest and part in parliamentary life'.[19] The new committee elected officers and an executive committee. Official recognition followed and a whip began regularly to attend meetings to give details of business for the following week. Within a few years membership of the 1922 was extended to any Conservative private member and as it grew so its activities became more institutionalised. A structure of permanent and ad hoc committees, with their own officers, began to emerge, eventually with frontbench spokesmen as chairmen. Party whips began to attend the meetings of these committees and so a comprehensive structure had developed by the 1950s allowing for the transmission to the leadership of advice and opinion, with the chairman of the 1922 having ready access to the party leader. There has been no major change to this structure since.

The oil which keeps the party machine running smoothly is provided by the whips of whom there are fourteen in all. The chief whip has a deputy, seven whips and five assistant whips. Their tasks are often thought of as being to 'organise' the backbenchers so as to maximise support for the leader. This is not surprising, for the word finds its origin in the world of fox-hunting where the 'whippers-in' keep the hounds in good order. In the pre-reform House of Commons the role of the whip was not so much to enforce discipline as to inform backbenchers of government business, since most of them devoted much of their time to other activities. After the 1832 Reform Act the number of whips rose from two to five[20] but their function was still basically one of providing information, though this became a two-way process. Conservative MPs were grateful for the support, especially when the whips began to underline the weekly document of government business circulated to backbenchers (also referred to as the whip) to indicate the more important issues and votes. Nowadays the whip system has as much to do with informing the leadership of the feelings of the backbenchers. Nevertheless, it is an important task of the whips to attempt to persuade disgruntled backbenchers to support the leadership, for example by arranging for them to meet the relevant minister, or spokesman, to whose policy they are objecting, but they have few formal sanctions at their disposal should this fail. On major issues very considerable pressures are put on reluctant government supporters,[21] though some 'rebels' are beyond threat. In the 1970–74 parliament Enoch Powell voted against his government on 113 occasions. In the first eighteen months of Mrs Thatcher's second term of office (1983–7), Mr Heath supported his government on only six occasions out of a possible 129. For mere mortals, however, the pressures which whips can apply are very substantial. It has been rumoured (and not denied!) that the whips' office has a black book listing the indiscretions of their backbenchers. Enough said.

Nevertheless it has been clearly demonstrated, especially by writers like Norton,[22] that since 1970 Conservative MPs voted against their government more often, in greater numbers and with greater effect. Heath's government was defeated three times on a three-line whip; even the Thatcher administration was defeated on a three-line whip in 1986 on the bill to allow Sunday trading. The Major government, with its small and ever-diminishing majority, was much more prone to being derailed. In November 1994 eight backbenchers voted against the government on a motion of confidence following the government's defeat on the European Finance Bill, the ultimate – and previously unthinkable – act of disloyalty. The leadership responded by withdrawing the whip, effectively temporarily expelling them from the parliamentary party. No Conservative MP had had the whip withdrawn for over fifty years. But worse was to follow when the eight, joined by a ninth who voluntarily relinquished the whip, acted as a party within a party – and a party which to all intents and purposes held the balance of parliamentary power – '… the tail which wagged the Tory dog'.[23] The whip was restored five months later with the rebels giving no undertakings as to their future conduct. Conservative backbenchers were on occasion openly hostile to their party leader during Prime Minister's Questions over the issue of European Monetary Union (EMU), one declaring that he would support the government 'only if it looks after our freedoms'.[24]

Although less exciting than 'rebellions', the meetings of the 1922 provide a useful forum for the discussion of general issues, though more detailed policies are the prerogative of the twenty-four subject committees or perhaps the seven geographical area committees which also usually meet on a weekly (or fortnightly) basis. The 1922 is a force to be reckoned with especially during elections to its own executive (a good barometer of the strength of ideological groups) and to the party leadership – which it organises. Meetings of the 1922 are frequently addressed by Ministers, and their reception may have a considerable effect on that Minister's subsequent career. In 1982, for example, the Foreign Secretary Lord Carrington's rough ride in the face of the government's lack of preparedness for the Argentine invasion of the Falkland Isles confirmed his intention to resign from office; likewise the Trade and Industry Secretary, Leon Brittan, met a hostile reception in 1986 and resigned the next day. Junior

Ministers, too, have been persuaded to resign by direct and indirect pressure from the 1922, for example David Mellor in 1992 and Michael Mates in 1993. In popular mythology the leaders of the 1922 – the famous 'men in grey suits' – have the power even to remove a party leader. This despite the fact that they have never actually done so.[25]

It is not in the interest of even a powerful Minister completely to ignore messages from the troops. For example, in 1984, the Secretary of State for Education Sir Keith Joseph sought to increase parental contributions to the cost of university education. Some 180 backbenchers signed a motion of protest, reacting, said one, to months of irritation and frustration. At question time Sir Keith faced one of the most concerted onslaughts ever experienced by a Tory Cabinet Minister from his own side. A few hours later he met the 1922 and more hostility; of thirty speakers only three supported the Minister. In what was described as 'one of the swiftest and most effective assertions of backbench power over the executive' in many years, Sir Keith felt obliged to give his tormentors most of what they wanted.[26]

On his accession to the leadership, William Hague sought to tackle the lack of unity in the parliamentary party by organising a 'bonding' weekend at a hotel in Eastbourne. His proposal was not universally welcomed. Former deputy leader Michael Heseltine, for example, commented: 'I'm sure I must have a prior engagement'; Nicholas Soames refused to go 'on principle'.[27] At Eastbourne a late-night sing-song led by soon-to-be-party chairman Michael Ancram on acoustic guitar encapsulated one at least of the party's principal problems: although they managed the 1960s songs 'Mr Tambourine Man' and 'Blowing in the Wind' with some aplomb, they collapsed completely when attempting an Oasis number; nobody knew the words.[28] Although such exercises, described caustically by one MP as 'American psycho-twaddle',[29] can do little harm they are unlikely to heal the deep divisions within the party, especially over Europe.

Conservative organisation in the Lords is a pale reflection of that in the Commons.[30] The whipping system comprises a chief and deputy whip and five whips, but contact with backbenchers is fairly perfunctory except on major issues, such as the debates in 1985 on the bill to abolish the Greater London Council and those in 1988 over the 'poll tax' and the introduction of a fee for dental and optical check-ups. There is an association of independent Unionist peers which meets weekly with a role similar to that of the 1922, but it possesses no permanent committee structure. Those who wish will attend relevant meetings of the Commons committees, though surprisingly little formal contact exists between the party in the Lords and the Commons. Although Conservative peers have no vote in the election of the party leader they continue to sustain greater Cabinet representation than their Labour colleagues, with such senior posts as Foreign Secretary and the Ministers for Employment and Trade and Industry being held by

Conservative peers in recent years. They have an additional importance. Although among working peers Conservatives can be outvoted by an alliance of their opponents and crossbenchers, they are still the most important party in the second Chamber. Should the need arise the party can still muster an overall majority by appealing to the so-called 'backwoodsmen' in the shires. The changes to the composition and functions of the Lords outlined by the Blair government in 1999 will put an end to this essentially undemocratic state of affairs.

In the first direct elections to the European parliament held in Britain, shortly after the general election of 1979, no fewer than sixty of the eighty-one seats fell to the Conservatives. In the second such election in 1984 the Conservatives dropped to forty-five seats. Their numbers declined further in 1989 when they won thirty-two seats and again in 1994 when party representation was reduced to a mere eighteen seats. Originally this group, together with one Ulster Unionist and three Danish MEPs, formed the European Democrats, with a chief and two deputy whips. This became a fairly cohesive group though its contacts with the party in Westminster were few. In 1993, however, the group joined the much larger European Peoples' party which currently comprises 173 members among whom the forty-seven members of the German Christian Democrats are the dominant force. Until the British electorate takes a greater interest in European affairs, MEPs are unlikely to play an important part in the activities of their party, especially given the Conservative party's general coolness to the development of European institutions.

The movement

The National Union was set up in 1867 to orchestrate the activities of existing local associations and to help create new ones. One of its chief activities was the dissemination of information, but from the beginning its role was entirely supportive of the party at Westminster; it was never considered to be a means by which to assure accountability of the party to its supporters. Robert McKenzie quotes the chairman at the inaugural meeting as declaring that members had not met to discuss Conservative principles because they were all in agreement as to what these were; their task was 'to consider by what particular organisation we may make these Conservative principles effective among the masses'.[31] From its inception the National Union jealously guarded its integrity against the encroaches of the party bureaucracy, Central Office. In recent years two enquiries have been held into the nature of the relationship. The first, headed by chairman Sir Norman Fowler, created a Board of Management which brought together the voluntary, the elected and the professional wings of the party. Tether referred to this process as the 'colonisation' of the National Union,[32] but the structure of the National Union defied complete domination. Until 1997 that is, when William Hague established a committee under party chairman Lord Parkinson. The declared aim of the committee was to create a 'mass volunteer party equipped to spread the Conservative message to all parts of the nation'. The ensuing reform package was to represent 'the biggest reorganisation of the party since Disraeli's time'.[33]

The Hague reforms sought the endorsement of the entire membership, and to that end some 400,000 ballot papers were distributed by Central Office, though in the absence of a centralised membership list this was probably wishful thinking. In the event 176,391 were returned of which 142,229 (81 per cent) voted in favour and 34,092 (19 per cent) against: Hague's reforms, then, linked to support for his leadership, were heavily endorsed, though what percentage of the 'real' membership had voted is impossible to say. What is known is that only 418 constituencies in England, Wales and Northern Ireland out of 580 responded, and this after the leadership had mounted twenty-six road shows to tour the country.

The effect of these reforms was to unite the two wings of the movement into a National Conservative Convention (NCC). At the apex of the movement now is the Board, meeting monthly, consisting of the party chairman, two deputy chairmen (one elected by the NCC, one appointed by the leader), four members elected by the NCC, the leader in the Lords, the chairman of the 1922, a representative of the Scottish Conservative and Unionist party, the chairman for Wales, the chairman of the Conservative Councillors Association, the party treasurer, a senior member of the professional staff (nominated by the chairman) and one potential further member nominated by the party leader. The Board can establish any committees it wishes, though it is required to have three standing sub-committees on candidate recruitment, conference (preparation and management) and membership. The Board's functions are the development of policy, campaigning, membership and fund raising, and the party organisation. It approves and monitors the Central Office budget, appoints senior staff, manages the membership and candidate lists, oversees constituency association matters, ensures that women and young people are properly involved and represented, resolves internal disputes, implements decisions of the ethics and integrity committee, and oversees leadership elections.

Under the Board comes the NCC itself, meeting twice yearly, and comprising the chairmen of the constituency associations of England, Scotland, Northern Ireland and Wales, the members of area management executives and their Scottish counterparts, regional co-ordinating chairmen and their deputies, representatives of Conservative Future, the Conservative Women's National Committee and other recognised organisations, the three immediate past presidents, two immediate past chairmen of NCC and the immediate past Area and Regional co-ordinating chairmen. NCC provides a focus for the views of party members and links membership and leaders. The party leader, officers and Board members are invited to attend.

Reference has been made to the ethics and integrity committee, another Hague reform. The behaviour of some of its representatives in the 1990s caused the party grave concern. As a response the Board was empowered to establish this new committee to be chaired by a Queen's Counsel, with the chairman of the 1922 and the national convention. (The Scottish Conservatives established their own discipline committee but all cases involving Scottish constituency MPs or MEPs would be the business of the ethics and integrity committee.) The task of the committee is to investigate instances of misconduct referred to it by the leader or by the Board – though the expression of disagreement with party policy will not of itself constitute misconduct. A right of appeal exists.

The movement in England

At the grass roots of the party are the constituency associations with four main responsibilities. The first is to 'sustain and promote the object and values of the Conservative party' (thus putting it on much the same footing as the other parties' constituency associations). The others are to provide an effective campaigning organisation, to secure the return of Conservative candidates and to contribute to party funds. The constitution sets out a core management structure, with a chairman who runs the association with two deputies, one responsible for membership and fund-raising and the other for campaigning and coordinating political activity (including the discussion of policy under the umbrella of the Policy Forum). Every association is required to produce annual objectives and a plan of activity for the following year and to specify the attainment of certain minimum criteria for association. Each association is represented on the area committees and indeed at the annual party conference.

The party's new area structure comprises forty-two areas, based on county and metropolitan boundaries. Each has a council made up of constituency chairmen and representatives and a management executive (mirroring the constituency set-up) whose task is to coordinate between the constituency associations and the Board. The area executive has wide responsibilities in managing the associations and coordinating general, local and European elections. Above the area are nine regions in England (based upon the European electoral regions) and one in Wales. The regions, with a coordinating chairman and two deputies, will have limited roles, overseeing their areas and providing back-up at the request of the Board.

A word now on recognised organisations: bodies such as the Conservative Trade Unionists, The Conservative Medical Society and the Countryside Forum will be encouraged to contribute appropriately to the party but the Board will additionally recognise other bodies which promote Conservatism among professional or specialist groups. Particular attention, however, has been given by reformers to the resuscitation of the party's youth wing. The Young Conservatives had witnessed a dramatic decline in their membership and Norman Tebbitt as chairman had felt obliged to disaffiliate the Confederation of Conservative Students which had come under the influence of right-wing libertarian groups – many of whom thereafter infiltrated the Young Conservatives and generally became a mild irritant.[34] The reformers' response was to establish an umbrella youth organisation, Conservative Future, for members under thirty. Conservative Future will be represented at the party conference and in the National Conservative Convention. Overall responsibility for the effective running of the organisation is the responsibility of the Board but a democratically elected executive will be in day-to-day charge. The organisation will operate in universities and colleges under the title Conservative Students but in the constituencies (or areas) as Conservative Future. The executive will represent students but will be dominated by non-students, with a special provision for the representation of those under twenty-two.

The Conservative Women's national committee, which heads constituency-based women's committees, will consider its own structure in the light of the new reforms. Already, however, there has been established the Network for Conservative Women, one of whose functions will be to provide advice, seminars and training for those who wish to play a representative role or who wish to develop party policy. The intention is explicit: to encourage more women to seek election at local and national level and to provide appropriate support.

This machine is oiled by the work of the party agents, now substantially fewer in number and having responsibilities for groups of constituencies. Agents will henceforth be responsible not to the constituencies but to the Board, which will assume responsibility for training and career development. Regional directors (or equivalent) will have a key strategic role to play in the deployment of party agents. Their tasks will become far less secretarial in nature and more concerned with new communications technology, handling the media and fund-raising.

One of the principal tasks of the party organisation is to select parliamentary candidates. A permanent sub-committee of the Board has responsibility for maintaining an approved candidates' list. Not only will this broadly representative sub-committee exclude 'unsuitable' candidates but as well it will 'seek out' suitable ones. All candidates on the list will be required to abide by the rulings of the ethics and integrity committee. There exists a more specialist list of candidates thought to be particularly suitable for by-elections, and constituency associations are generally required to select candidates from this list. Some activists claim that the second list of allegedly more able candidates constitutes an attempt to ensure that more women are selected for winnable seats but also that 'extremists' (presumably those opposed to the leadership's line on key issues) will be disadvantaged.[35] A standardised candidates' curriculum vitae has been developed, and all candidates on the approved list are now trained in campaigning and in handling the media. The candidates' association, to which all belong, also provides public-speaking opportunities and mentoring by sitting MPs. Constituency associations, in reality, retain a considerable influence in MP and MEP candidate selection and have complete control over selecting candidates for local elections. For example, age criteria were established by the party for MP and MEP selection (thirty-five to fifty-five for the former and forty to sixty for the latter). A list of approved candidates for the regional lists for the European elections was sent to regional screening committees. There was no interview involved and no appeal against non-selection.[36]

Celtic Conservatism

Conservatives north of the border traditionally reacted to poor electoral performances by organisational reform.[37] In 1997 they recorded their lowest support (17.5 per cent) since 1865 and won not a single seat. If that were not reason enough for wholesale change, they soon knew that they would have to contend for seats in and devise policies for Scotland's new parliament. Accordingly the Scottish Conservative and Unionist Association, always distinct and autonomous, set up a review under Lord Strathclyde most of whose recommendations were accepted at a special conference in 1998. Basically Strathclyde recommended that the Scottish leadership, formerly the gift of the party leader, should become an office elected by a college comprising party members (30 per cent) and the members of the Scottish parliament (MSPs – 70 per cent); that the party should rename itself the Scottish Conservative party; that candidate selection for Edinburgh, Brussels and Westminster should not be open to residents in England; that policy for the Edinburgh parliament would (as for the English party) be a joint product of the Scottish Policy Forum, the Scottish executive (to be elected by party members) and the conference of the Scottish party; that the two wings of the party in Scotland would amalgamate like their English counterparts under the executive; that there should be a Scottish policy commission and centralised membership lists.

Wales too followed suit. Henceforth to be known as the Welsh Conservative party, the party will be unified under a management board to include the Conservative leader from the Assembly and the chairmen of the four area management executives in Wales. Northern Ireland, for its part – the Conservatives are the only major party to operate in Northern Ireland – will become an area of the party with its own management executive.

It was suggested earlier that Hague's reforms had at their heart the notion of involving the membership, and this entailed not simply the creation of a more coherent organisational structure but the greater involvement of party members in the formulation and development of policy. There had existed, since the party had responded to its last major defeat in 1945, the Conservative political centre whose task was to encourage members in the constituency associations to comment on policy, though most critics thought that it was only a limited success.[38]

Hague was aware that many Conservative constituency associations had traditionally attached little importance to ideology and a lot to fund-raising. Constituency associations tended to see themselves principally as electoral machines; certainly this was how they were seen by many in the party at Westminster. The model rules set up to guide constituency associations listed eleven functions of which only one was not expressly and directly related to optimal electoral efficiency, and that was to spread the knowledge of Conservative principles and policy. Ideological debate within the party, as we have seen, was the responsibility of the Conservative Political Centre (CPC) which operated what it called a contact programme, in which issues were regularly selected (at national level) for local debate; it also prepared a contact brief outlining various questions for discussion. Reports on these local discussions were then forwarded to the CPC at party headquarters where a collating exercise took place, with summaries sent on to the party leadership. Norton and Aughey considered the process a success chiefly because it provided 'a reinforcement to a sense of belonging',[39] but they do not suggest that this process had any effect whatever on party policy. In 1989 considerable effort was put into revitalising the contact programme and the objective was quite clear: the better selling to the faithful of government policies.

It may well be that nothing more 'bottom-loaded' existed because there was no wide demand for it. The 1972 Chelmer report on party organisation recommended an increase of discussion of policy within the party but the institutional changes required for this were simply never implemented. Yet there were always 'revolutionaries' within the party who sought genuine participation: the Charter movement, with its own newsletter, regularly campaigned for greater democracy within the party. ' "Traditional party democracy" is not democracy. It is a substitute for the real thing, intended to divert the unwary into believing that no further scrutiny is necessary. Nothing could be further from the truth.'[40] Yet Charter remained small and and most members appeared to be largely unconcerned about their lack of involvement in policy-making, a point made much earlier by McKenzie[41] and reiterated almost thirty years later by Gamble who spoke of a 'largely sleeping membership'[42] as far as policy-making was concerned.

Following the Hague reforms, organising conference has become the business of the Board, through a committee comprising the president of the NCC (who will chair the conference) and the director of the policy forum. The committee will set the agenda based upon motions submitted by the various organs within the new structure. Although there is no formal process through which conference decisions become binding on the party, an innovation – the new Spring assembly in which the policy forum will play a leading role – will ensure that issues of policy are aired not only through full debate but also through workshop sessions.

Among the 1997/8 reforms was included the establishment of the Conservative Policy Forum (CPF) whose task was to encourage a genuine 'two-way movement' of ideas between leaders and members. The new Forum will seek to coordinate the work of constituency deputy chairmen with responsibility for political activity. These chairmen will have the responsibility for setting up constituency discussion groups. The chairman of CPF (appointed by the Board) will seek to establish a consultative structure through the area deputy chairmen, who will be brought together twice a year. One of their tasks will be to elect representatives to a CPF council, thus representing the areas and Scotland, together with the director of the research department and five co-opted members, such as academics and business people. The council will be chaired by a Cabinet or Shadow Cabinet Minister appointed by the leader. Additionally, regional policy congresses will be established to discuss proposals formulated by policy groups. The party has declared its intention to initiate regular surveys of members and indeed, as we have seen, membership approval was sought by ballot for these changes and also for the leader's policy of ruling out membership of European Monetary Union for the period of the next parliament. Moreover CPF will have a major influence on future party policy agendas. Motions will be submitted to the director who will publish them all. CPF will also have the task of ensuring adequate opportunity for the discussion of policy at the new annual Spring Assembly.

The annual conference

The chief function of the National Union, and now of the Convention, has been to organise the annual conference. The essence of the Conservative party conference has traditionally been consolidation, rallying the troops and inspiring them to greater efforts; in the words of one Conservative backbencher, 'to repay party workers for the tedious business of selling endless raffle tickets'. It is an opportunity for the faithful to see and perhaps actually to meet their leaders, and for the leaders, if they are wise, to listen to the grumbles of their troops. The constitutional status of the annual conference as a 'primarily deliberative and advisory' body was formally acknowledged by the 1948 Maxwell Fyfe committee on the party organisation. Indeed given its size – at around 9000 – it is one of the largest political gatherings in Western democracies.[43] In terms of policy-formulation, Balfour's much-quoted comment that he would as soon take advice on policy matters from his valet as from conference was probably realistic if not diplomatic. On the other hand, as an exercise in public relations, both within the party and with the outside world, the conference fulfilled a function of considerable importance. And while there was little open criticism of the party leadership at conference, the leadership would leave the conference with a good idea of the mood of the party, and this mood may well have influenced the general direction of policy, for example over issues such as immigration and law and order in the late 1970s and early 1980s.

The importance to the leadership of this public-relations exercise is indicated by the fact that the party leader who, before Heath, did not actually attend any of the debates but simply addressed conference before it broke up, became a regular attender. Frontbenchers or ministers would sit on the platform in full view of the faithful and were keen to make a good impression. Their own contributions to conference debates could and can still be crucial to their standing in the party, and a number of very able ministers have progressed less far and less fast than they might otherwise have done because of lacklustre conference performances. Indeed, such a performance is said to have been decisive in Maudling's failure to achieve the leadership in 1965; only two years earlier Quintin Hogg had similarly destroyed his chances of the leadership by his general demeanour at the 1963 conference. Virginia Bottomley, Minister of Health, chose to sing to conference in 1995; her political career never recovered – neither did a stage career beckon. Other ministers, though, have greatly enhanced their standing in the party, none more so than the ex-Ministers of Defence, Michael Heseltine, a 'darling' of the conference, and more recently Michael Portillo. In 1998 Ann Widdecombe captivated delegates at an otherwise largely lacklustre conference with her barnstorming assault on the Labour government.

In the days of televised conferences it is arguable that the traditionally bland and packaged Conservative conference is more appropriate than its traditionally rumbustious Labour counterpart. It is, after all, one thing to practice internal party democracy but quite another to parade party divisions remorselessly before potential voters. The objectives of Conservative conferences, though they were not always achieved, were more limited than those of their opponents: in Gilmour's now dated words, 'the conference now has to cheer the faithful and to impress the infidel ... and much of the proceedings are more of an exercise in revivalist enthusiasm than a serious discussion of issues and policies'.[44] A recent example of the attempt to cheer and impress was the official video of 1994 which showed an enthusiastic conference warmly cheering the loyal words of party chairman Mawhinney and a more restrained conference politely receiving the right-wing, anti-European onslaught of Defence Secretary Portillo. The party had later to admit that owing to unfortunate 'editing errors' the two speeches had become attached to wrong audience response.

Notwithstanding what has been said, the annual conference has, from time to time, taken on the leadership: Balfour over protectionism, for example, Baldwin over India.[45] Indeed Whiteley *et al.* have suggested that it would be quite wrong to believe that party members had traditionally felt unable to influence the leadership.[46] On the other hand, Kelly, while generally supporting this view, quotes one of thirty-three critical resolutions to the 1986 conference calling upon organisers 'not to manipulate proceedings or to stage-manage debates'. None of these resolutions was selected for debate.[47] In the 1990s, however, the government's disastrous electoral performances, its pit-closure programme, Post Office and rail privatisation programmes, the imposition of VAT on domestic fuel, but above all its perceived pro-European policies following Britain's removal from the Exchange Rate Mechanism, produced a series of party conferences (1992–97) which were simply bilious: many members had become incensed at their inability to hold their leaders accountable on a regular, formal base. The membership had been rocked in the 1990s by two earthquakes: the dismissal (against the wishes of most party members) of Mrs Thatcher and the inability of the government subsequently to maintain unity, effectiveness or integrity. What tended to happen as a consequence – and it has happened to the other major parties also – is that leadership controls over full-conference debate have led to the development of flourishing fringe meetings. They now occupy, at least for the Conservative and Labour parties, as significant a position as does the Fringe at the Edinburgh Festival.

The party bureaucracy

We now turn our attention to what we have called the party bureaucracy. One of the chief features distinguishing the Conservative and Labour parties has been the hold that the Conservative party leader has over the bureaucracy. 'Constitutionally the Conservative party, my party, is no better than the old Soviet Communist party and it stinks.' So said the Tory 'dissident' Eric Chalker.[48] He went on to complain that absolute control of party headquarters – Central Office – and of party funds was passed from the old leader to the new as if they comprised some personal property.

Central Office

True the transfer formally required a properly framed resolution, properly voted upon, but this had never happened. The leader's power to appoint the Chairman and other senior officers seemed to be doubly undemocratic. Though strongly defended, this had been a minority view until the 1990s. Its wider prevalence was one of the impulses behind the Hague reforms.

Pre-reform party headquarters had traditionally comprised three separate bodies, the Central Office, the research department and the advisory committee on policy. Each, though separate, was none the less responsible to the party leader. Established under Disraeli in 1870, the Central Office was soon fully committed to all the professional supportive work required by the party both nationally and locally and, despite some lean periods, its position has become stronger over the years. Initially the Central Office was run by the chief whip but by the turn of the century it was felt necessary for the party leader to appoint a chairman. After the 1987 and 1992 elections party headquarters was substantially restructured and by 1997 Central Office had been required to shed 25 per cent of staff. Central Office now comprises three departments, each under its own director: research, political operations (the field of press and communications) and field operations (previously known as campaigning). The research section, established in 1929 and reorganised in 1948, has traditionally been headed by a senior politician, the most celebrated being R.A. Butler, who was head from 1945 to 1964. On appointment of one head, Angus Maude, to Cabinet in 1979 the post was abolished, and the department is now run by a full-time director. In the past the research department earned a reputation as the party's 'think-tank', offering a home for young men of intellect and promise who were later to make a name for themselves in the House; for example Maudling, Macleod, Powell and, more recently, Chris Patten. It also earned a reputation for being somewhat to the left of centre and its influence in policy-formulation consequently declined after 1979, its role being increasingly taken on by the Centre for Policy Studies, an independent body established by, among others, Sir Keith Joseph and Margaret Thatcher.

Gamble has described the whole headquarters edifice as 'antique and ramshackle',[49] Norton and Aughey coyly declare its antiquities to be 'understandable' to a Conservative. Its basic role has traditionally been to give advice on how to achieve power when the party is in opposition and to provide loyal though largely uncritical support for the leadership when in office. Whatever its shortcomings Central Office was usually considered as superior to its Labour and Liberal counterparts. Popular wisdom suggested that Central Office efficiency was worth twelve seats in any general election. The last three general elections, however, exposed serious deficiencies in presentation and in services to candidates and local parties. In 1997 for example, Central Office canvass returns were massively inaccurate because the party had insufficient canvassers and because Central Office did not even have a membership list. Although it might still be worth twelve seats in a general election, these days Central Office provides that advantage to the party's opponents. John Major's off-the-record description of his bureaucracy was terse: 'hopeless'.[50]

In 1998 Archie Norman, the new chief executive at Central Office, and future party chairman Michael Ancram were given the task of modernising Central Office and of saving money. Norman argued that Central Office had proved incapable of the kind of teamwork necessary for success.[51] 'People in different departments don't speak to each other', claimed one party worker, 'they scribble away in dark corners ... we are out of date and out of touch'.[52] Norman planned to trim the workforce at the party headquarters by a further forty from one hundred and thirty. Faced with an annual budget of £3 million and a dependable income of some £600,000, hard decisions were obviously required. Graham Mather MEP recommended privatising Central Office, though in the event this was resisted. However, the chief agent and director of campaign was forced out after twenty-seven years because he had resisted £3 million spending cuts.[53] Norman, who was credited with turning round the ailing ASDA chain, made an immediate impact on management practices, but Central Office has a long way to go to recapture its former prestige, and is very likely to move out of Smith Square which is seen as being expensive and unsuitable for a modern party.

Party funding

The funding of the Conservative party has, as we have just seen, become an issue of major controversy. Pinto-Duschinsky[54] identified three phases in the development of party fund-raising: the aristocratic era when voters were habitually bribed and parliamentary seats bought; the plutocratic era when honours were sold in return for party donations; and the modern era of mass membership subscriptions and major corporate donations. Fisher suggests a post-modern era in which personal donations dominate.[55] He shows that donations as a percentage of party income have risen to 83.2 per cent whereas constituency-quota income now comprises 5.7 per cent. Running a national party, he reminds us, is an expensive business, with routine expenditure comprising 80 per cent of the total (thus permanently expensive and not just in election years). The cost of fighting elections, nevertheless, is not far short of £20 million these days and, unlike constituency election expenditure, is not limited by law. The Conservative party is kept afloat financially through undeclared donations by individuals on behalf of major, usually multinational companies. But only just. After the 1992 election the Conservatives were in deficit to £19,200,000 and were obliged to appoint a Director of Finance to oversee expenditure. The Central Office apparatus was overhauled, and the number of staff employed fell from 224 to 159. The numbers of regional staff were pruned and full-time constituency agents declined to 207, the lowest number since 1945. It is simply not known how the party could sustain its activities with such a deficit. Its bankers, the Royal Bank of Scotland, would certainly have required some form of security to allow its client to continue its activities (especially bearing in mind the cost of fighting elections), but what form that security took is unknown.

The capacity of the party to raise substantial funding for its electoral activities, however, should not be in doubt. The party paid the advertising agency Saatchi £13 million for the 1997 election campaign, bringing total expenditure for the two years prior to the election, according to Lord Parkinson, to £28 million.[56] Party accounts show that the party had raised £38 million in the year ending 31 March 1997, though this still left them with a post-election deficit of £4 million. In 1998 it was revealed that the party had accepted a donation of £13 million from a Hong Kong businessman.[57]

As part of his reform measures William Hague sought to address the question of party funding, requiring that all donations of over £5,000 be declared and that no donations from overseas be accepted. He did not, however, recommend the publication of full party accounts. These reforms are likely to be overtaken, however, when the Blair government implements the recommendations of the Neill Committee on Standards in Public Life. Neill recommends the banning of all foreign donations, full disclosure of donations (with names of donors) above £5,000 centrally and £1,000 locally, a ban on all anonymous donations above £50 and a cap of £20 million on general election campaign expenditure. An electoral commission would be established to oversee the implementation of these proposals.

Whatever the outcome of Neill it is clear that the financial stability which characterised the party bureaucracy has been shattered; the party is currently caught between the rock of insolvency and the hard place of undisclosed and potentially dubious overseas financing. Perhaps the disciplines which Neill's recommendations would require are the best way forward for the party.

Conclusions

A brief conclusion to this analysis of who runs the Conservative party must inevitably lead to a reassessment of the thrust of McKenzie's treatise on power within the Conservative party, written forty years ago, which highlights the very substantial power of the leader. We can be more assertive than he about the informal constraints upon the powers of the Conservative leader, which are real and considerable; more clear about the relationship between ideology and leadership: much of the leaders' traditional power could be ascribed to the fact that, pragmatists themselves, they were not much constrained by ideological opponents within the party. We could demonstrate with certainty that organisational efficiency and financial strength can no longer be taken for granted.

So while we have to acknowledge the fundamental strength and considerable personal prestige still enjoyed by the Conservative leader throughout the party, we would want to add that much of this was a reflection of the popular perception that the Conservatives were a party not so much of ideology as of government. Margaret Thatcher, a towering figure, used the personal powers of a Conservative leader to the maximum. Her power and prestige were unexampled. Yet after three consecutive electoral victories the party brought her down. Perhaps her demise signalled the end of the Conservative leadership tradition. The changes inaugurated by William Hague suggest that no future leader is likely to enjoy the eminence that hitherto he or she could have taken for granted.

Notes

1. See Richard Rose, *The Problem of Party Government*, London, Pelican, 1976, pp. 154-5.
2. R.T. McKenzie, *British Political Parties*, London, Heinemann, 1953, ch. 5.
3. Quoted in Sir Nigel Fisher, *The Tory Leaders*, London, Weidenfeld & Nicolson, 1977, p. 3.
4. Philip Norton and Arthur Aughey, *Conservatives and Conservatism*, London, Temple Smith, 1981, pp. 242-3. Norton was happy enough with this model to retain it in his more recent *The Conservative Party*, Prentice Hall/Harvester Wheatsheaf, 1996, ch. 9.
5. *Independent*, 14 May 1997.
6. Norton, 'The Party Leader', in *The Conservative Party*, p. 147.
7. Norton and Aughey, *Conservatives and Conservatism*, pp. 250-2.
8. *Observer*, 16 December 1984.
9. Richard Spring MP, the unfortunate subject of this story, was the seventeenth Conservative to attract newspaper headlines of this general nature during Major's second administration. (See *Guardian*, 11 April 1995).
10. Graham Riddick and David Treddinick were found by the House's Privilege Committee to have brought Parliament into disrepute. (See *Guardian*, 5 April 1995.)
11. *Independent on Sunday*, 30 March 1997.
12. M. Pinto-Duschinky, 'Central Office and "power" in The Conservative Party', *Political Studies*, **20**(1), March 1972.
13. Hugo Young, *Guardian*, 7 March 1986.
14. *Sunday Telegraph*, 12 September 1993.
15. Norton, *The Conservative Party*, p. 154.
16. Norton and Aughey, *Conservatives and Conservatism*, p. 258.
17. *The Times*, 9 October 1998.
18. Norton, *The Conservative Party*, p. 152.
19. Philip Goodhart, *The 1922*, London, Macmillan, 1973, p. 15.
20. See A. Aspinall, 'English Party Organisation in the Early Nineteenth Century', *English Historical Review*, **41**, 1926, pp. 389-411.
21. Michael Brown, 'Confessions of a Tory Rebel', *Guardian*, 2 August 1985.
22. Philip Norton, *Does Parliament Matter?*, London, Harvester Wheatsheaf, 1993, ch. 5.
23. *Guardian*, 25 May 1995.
24. *Independent*, 12 November 1996.
25. Norton, *The Conservative Party*, p. 131.

26. *Guardian*, 21 May 1985. It is worth pointing out that the experienced chief whip, John (later Lord) Wakeham, was in hospital at this time. His might otherwise have been a crucial restraining influence.
27. *Sunday Telegraph*, 19 October 1997.
28. *The Times*, 23 October 1997.
29. *Independent*, 25 July 1997.
30. See D. Shell and D. Beamish, *The House of Lords at Work*, Oxford, Oxford University Press, 1993.
31. McKenzie, *British Political Parties*, p. 151.
32. See Philip Tether, 'The Party in the country: development and influence', in Norton, *The Conservative Party*, pp. 109–11.
33. *The Times*, 2 February 1998.
34. *Guardian*, 5 April 1986.
35. *Daily Telegraph*, 14 December 1996.
36. *The Times*, 4 June 1998.
37. See Peter Lynch, 'Preparing for devolution: the Scottish Conservatives after the 1997 electoral wipeout', *Regional Studies*, forthcoming, pp. 1–14.
38. See Philip Tether, 'Members and Organisation', in Norton, *The Conservative Party*, p. 122.
39. Norton and Aughey, *Conservatives and Conservatism*, p. 218.
40. *Charter News*, Spring 1985.
41. McKenzie, *British Political Parties*, p. 24.
42. Andrew Gamble, 'The Conservative Party', in H.M. Drucker (ed.), Multi-Party Britain, London, Macmillan, 1979, p. 40.
43. J. Kelly, *Conservative Party Conferences*, Manchester, Manchester University Press, 1989.
44. Sir Ian Gilmour, *The Body Politic*, (rev. edn) London, Hutchison, 1971, p. 80.
45. Tether, 'The Party in the country: development and influence', p. 104.
46. P. Whiteley, P. Seyd and J. Richardson, *True Blues: The Politics of Conservative Party Membership*, Oxford, Oxford University Press, 1994, pp. 38–9.
47. Kelly, *Conservative Party Conferences*, p. 140.
48. *Independent*, 25 June 1997.
49. Andrew Gamble, 'The Conservative Party', p. 39.
50. *Independent*, 11 December 1996.
51. *The Times*, 24 June 1998.
52. *Ibid.*, 9 June 1998.
53. *Daily Telegraph*, 15 August 1998.
54. M. Pinto-Duschinsky, *British Political Finance 1830–1980*, Washington DC, American Enterprise Institute, 1981.
55. Justin Fisher, 'Party Finance', in Norton, *The Conservative Party*, pp. 157–69.
56. *Daily Telegraph*, 14 February 1998.
57. *The Times*, 13 February 1998. This article reveals that the donor's father, who had left Hong Kong in 1978 following police enquiries, had been hoping to return.

CHAPTER FOUR

Who are the Conservatives?

One of the most striking features of the Conservative party, according to Burch and Moran, has been its ability, over many years, 'to combine electoral success with social elitism' in a democratic age.[1] They draw our attention to the paradox that a party which makes no secret of its belief in privilege is able to convince sufficient of the less privileged to support it, to the extent that it has been far more successful over the last one hundred or so years in its quest for power than its more overtly egalitarian rivals. In this chapter we shall examine three areas of party activity, namely Conservative parliamentarians (especially MPs), party activists and finally party supporters – those who regularly vote Conservative – in order to discover who the Conservatives are and what really motivates them. So let us begin with Conservative MPs.

The parliamentary party

The most noticeable feature of the current parliamentary party is its size – or lack of it: at 165 it is smaller than at any time since 1906. It is unlikely that such a transformation in size would not imply changes in character and structure. In fact, as we shall see, it has been claimed that the tenure in office of Margaret Thatcher had already transformed the character of the parliamentary party. We need to assess the validity of this claim, and so we need a basis for comparison: we need to know what the 'traditional' Conservative party looked like.

The backbenches: social background

The first authoritative modern work on the background of members of the House of Commons, Colin Mellors's *The British MP*,[2] considered each new wave of MPs from 1945 to 1974. The Conservative party was shown to be traditionally resistant to social change. In 1945 the typical Conservative MP came from a privileged background, over 80 per cent having been to public school. More than 25 per cent had been to Eton and almost 50 per cent had gone on to Oxbridge from their public school. Mellors said that the Conservatives, in choosing their parliamentary candidates, 'concern themselves more with rank and achievement than party political experience. Breeding and educational attainment are customarily seen as the two most important qualifications ... for recruitment to the political elite.'[3] He went on to say that the 'old school tie' was the single most important qualification for would-be Conservative MPs. 'As a guarantee of success it ranked with sponsorship from the mineworkers' union in the Labour party.' It would be difficult to overstate the preponderance of public school-boys in the Conservative party up to 1979. They represented an unusually narrow channel of recruitment implying a tight network of old school friends. Moreover, Mellors indicated that this preponderance of public school backgrounds found an echo at the university level. It was not simply that Oxbridge dominated the Conservative party but that the products of four specific Oxford colleges (Christ Church, Balliol, New and Magdalen) and four Cambridge Colleges (Trinity, Trinity Hall, King's and Gonville and Caius) dominated. As far as educational background went, the Conservative parliamentary party was homogeneous to an unparalleled degree.

Education has always tended to be an indicator of social class, and it may be stated quite simply that the post-war Conservative parliamentary party was (and remains) overwhelmingly upper-middle-class. It has, as we shall see, some aristocratic connections (not as strong as they were), but since the war has produced only a handful of MPs who could be classified as working-class. So the party was traditionally characterised by a remarkable educational and social homogeneity. Moreover, the careers from which Conservative candidates tended to come reinforced this homogeneity to a high degree. It may be true, as Robert Louis Stevenson once wrote, that politics is the only profession for which no preparation is thought necessary, but it is clear that Conservative candidate selection committees believed that some professional backgrounds were eminently more suitable for aspiring politicians than others. Mellors characterised the parliamentary Conservative party as representing 'law, land and business' but acknowledged that it was in fact business and not the law which provided the preponderance of MPs – the cornerstone of the parliamentary party. Again, we can be more precise and say that a certain category of businessmen traditionally provided the overwhelming majority of these MPs: company directors.[4] In the thirty years after the second world war 273 company directors were elected to parliament of whom no fewer than 245 were Conservatives. As Mellor concludes, 'it is by far the largest single occupation group represented at Westminster'.[5] It seems abundantly clear, then, that for a substantial majority of Conservative MPs, 'training' traditionally consisted of having succeeded in a previous career, usually business, a finding supported by the fact that 75 per cent of MPs of both parties during this period did not enter the House until they were in their thirties or forties. What also characterised the parliamentary party in these years was a concomitant of their professional backgrounds: wealth – professional, commercial, industrial and, even more traditionally, landed wealth (in the last parliament before World War Two well over one-third of Conservative MPs were aristocrats by birth or by marriage).[6]

There is ample evidence, none the less, that the Conservatives had actively sought to broaden the social base of the parliamentary party. When Lord Woolton became party chairman after the war he initiated a review of party organisation under Maxwell-Fyfe which turned its attention to the general problem of the party's unrepresentativeness. It recommended, among other things, that the entire election expenses of candidates should be the responsibility of the constituency association and that candidates should be permitted to make no contribution to their campaign.[7] The aim of the recommendations, which were accepted by the annual conference and by the central council of the National Union, was to remove the financial considerations which might deter ordinary people from standing as Conservative candidates or, more probably, might dispose constituencies to prefer more wealthy candidates. The pre-war selection procedures were described as being exercises in plutocracy, with three categories of potential candidate: those willing to meet all their election expenses and contribute handsomely to local association funds, those willing to pay half their election expenses and able to contribute modestly to funds, and those unable to do either. Needless to say, those in the first category stood the best chance of being selected as candidates.[8] For all that, Butler and Pinto-Duschinsky point out that these developments had very little effect upon the social composition of the party, either within or outwith the House of Commons.[9] The Conservative party remained as élitist and as hierarchical as ever, though the influence of the aristocracy and of rich businessmen was replaced to a considerable extent by that of professionals and managers.

The Thatcher 'revolution'

It was only in 1979 that changes in the party started to make themselves felt. For the first time the proportion of those following what Burch and Moran[10] had called the meritocratic route – that is, state education followed by university – outnumbered those who followed the traditional public school followed by Oxbridge route. What is more, Etonians counted for only about 6 per cent of these new intakes. In 1979 there were more new members educated in the provincial and London universities than there were from Oxbridge.

When they sought to account for this change Burch and Moran argued that the wider opportunities of the Butler Education Act of 1944 were making themselves felt but also that the appeal to the privileged of a parliamentary career was diminishing. Such a career could no longer easily be coupled with a long-term career in the law or in industry. While it can be argued that the House of Commons has been and will continue to be the poorer for having deprived itself of this experience, the move towards full-time politics has only gathered pace since and, with specialist committee work taking up more of the backbenchers' time and energy, the process is likely to continue.

Not only were the 1979 newcomers distinctive socially but they were also recognisably different in so far as many of them were already, in effect, full-time politicians. By 1983 over half of new Conservative MPs had local government experience, in Burch and Moran's words 'the most striking index of the change'. They continued: 'They would have been amongst the ablest councillors. As chairmen of committees, they would influence budgets worth millions of pounds. Articulate, experienced and opinionated councillors do not make good lobby fodder in Westminster.'[11] The difficulties that Conservative whips experienced 'spring in part from the party's success in broadening its social base in parliament'. For a variety of reasons this is not so plausible an argument as it sounds. First, the Conservative whips, as we have seen, started to experience disciplinary problems in the early 1970s; second, we should remember that those whom the new group have tended to replace were themselves successful and influential career people, no doubt also being involved in transactions worth millions of pounds or in important legal cases. On the face of it they would have been even less amenable to party discipline. At least the ex-local councillors would have been familiar with and would have recognised the importance of 'party'. However, between 1983 and 1992 the size of the government majority simply lessened the need not merely for Conservative backbenchers to be tightly disciplined but even for them to be physically present at the House for much of the time. For these reasons the new wave of backbenchers became, as the 1980s wore on, altogether less amenable to the old-style party discipline than their predecessors.

Selection procedures also changed in 1980, however, and these had some effect upon the kind of candidates being chosen.[12] From that year residential selection boards operated a system rather like that of the civil service. Prospective candidates were assessed in groups in a number of different situations over a period of forty-eight hours by a team including an MP, an industrialist and a member of the National Union. About 25 per cent failed at this hurdle; the remainder were scrutinised by the party vice-chairman in charge of candidates and about 40 per cent failed here.

Competition for places on the resulting approved list increased substantially and this helped to improve the quality of candidates, though to what extent is an open question. These new vetting procedures were denounced by one respected agent as a 'hopelessly haphazard process', especially the vetting by the vice chairman who 'lets everyone go unless they're a raving monster'.[13] However no gains are made without losses. Like the Maxwell-Fyfe reforms, these procedures tended to replace men with considerable varieties of background, interest and ideological persuasion who had chiefly one thing in common, their wealth, by candidates who corresponded most closely to an amalgam of all desirable Conservative qualities. Selection committees began to use candidate 'profiles' in their task: the day of the party clone had arrived.

There were countervailing pressures. It is in the nature of a large majority that many of the new MPs elected in the 1980s represented previous Labour seats, with a more working-class electorate than Conservative MPs will usually represent. The logic of this situation, argued David Thomas,[14] was that in being more attentive to constituency needs they tended to reflect a distinctive, 'uncloned' brand of Conservatism. Moreover, as Baker and Fountain point out,[15] under the influence of Norman Tebbit, the party began actively to portray itself as representing the upwardly mobile – the party, in Julian Critchley's exuberant if rather inaccurate phrase, of the estate agent not the estate owner.[16] These changes produced not simply a more independent party but arguably also a more able one. 'The standard of professionalism and intellect among Conservative MPs', said Sir David Price (himself an MP for over thirty years) in the mid-1980s, 'is infinitely higher than when I first came here'.[17] Those hoping for revolutionary changes in the parliamentary party may have welcomed the election in 1983 of the great-grandson of the famous socialist agitator Tom Mann.

The question of 'new' versus 'old' Conservative parties was raised first in 1983 when Francis Pym established a parliamentary ginger group called Centre Forward. Critics attacked Pym's self-confessed group of moderates as 'squirearchs and landed gentry from another era' though the journalist Anthony Howard defended them. 'Backbench knightage and baronetage with its roots in the soil', he claimed, 'provided the Tory party with its ballast – and some of them at least … were markedly enlightened and modern-minded in their outlook … their successors have tended to be young, thrusting professional politicians, for whom party, if not faction, means all'.[18] Pym's group sought a more compassionate and less radical approach to government, hence his claim to represent a Conservative tradition which Thatcher despised. Julian Critchley went on the attack, describing the 1975 leadership campaign which brought Thatcher to power as 'the Peasants' Revolt'. Thatcher changed the Conservative party into a Liberal party, he claimed. Traditionally it had never been a party of conviction and crusade but rather a 'non-political political party', eschewing ideology, tempering belief with scepticism, and flying 'by the seat of [its] pants'.[19]

Pym and his colleagues were concerned by the fact that the new intake of MPs tended to be on the Thatcherite wing of the party, 'more aggressively business minded ... the sort for whom capitalism doesn't have an unacceptable face.'[20] Butler and Pinto-Duschinsky wrote: 'The relatively dumb knight of the shire is said to be a dying breed, replaced by the thrusting city banker or the advertising man.'[21] With Thatcher's policy of mass ennoblement of Conservative backbenchers, it might be simpler to say that the knights of the shires were being replaced by the knights of the suburbs! One senior backbencher MP declared in interview that these changes had made the party less 'gentlemanly'. He said of new members: 'their behaviour is boorish and they don't have any real sympathy for the place [parliament].' Another experienced member took a similar position adding: 'they're mostly hard-nosed businessmen who are here for their own reasons, and that includes quick promotion come what may. But they've no time for party loyalty unless it happens to suit.' A third backbencher felt: 'they're a pretty disaffected lot, by and large, with the whole set-up, actually. Their attendance at the House is pretty dismal ... one of the disadvantages of such a big majority I suppose.' One final comment from a backbencher of long standing: 'they may be a clever lot – everybody says they are – but they're not my idea of gentlemen. I think they behave as badly as the other side personally.'

As we have seen, these 'new' Conservatives claimed to be articulating the interests of the majority of ordinary people, and in some senses they clearly were. Crewe and Sarlvik[22] argued that on issues such as law and order, education and morality (populist-authoritarian issues they called them, reflecting Stuart Hall's description of Thatcherism) they took a pugnacious stand substantially to the right, which was to prove electorally popular throughout the 1980s. They concluded: 'in a large number of policy areas – foreign affairs, defence, crime, minority rights, sexual morality – the majority view aligns with Conservative rather than Labour instincts'. It was no electoral disadvantage for the Conservatives to become more like the rest of the nation, for 'the Conservatives [had been] damaged by being seen as a class party.'[23]

On the other hand the picture of a 'new' parliamentary party inexorably becoming more lower-middle-class is not sustained by figures from 1987, 1992 and 1997 (though perhaps on grounds of size the latter should be discounted). Baker and Fountain[24] and Whiteley, Seyd and Richardson[25] indicate that, if anything, the decline in what they call social exclusivity of the early 1980s was later reversed. 'The Conservative party is led in parliament', say the former, 'largely by men and women whose education, particularly in the more exclusive institutions such as private schools, Oxford and Cambridge, indicates a continuation of social exclusivity.' They continue:

'the media image of Major as the leader and creator of a more 'classless' Conservative party ... appears largely groundless ...' Moreover, the new intake of forty-one in 1997 contained more than its share of 'clones', including four former Central Office staff. Dame Angela Rumbold had been given the task of trying to place more women on the candidates' list but in the event she was able to place approximately 100 of whom only thirteen were elected (five new MPs). Three sitting MPs, meanwhile, had been deselected and a further two retired rather than face re-selection committees, one for perceived incompetence, one for perceived disloyalty to the party leader and three for reasons which had to do with their private lives. Ten other sitting MPs were the subject of tabloid comment on their private lives and of these only three retained their seats. In other words Conservative party selection in 1997 appeared to be motivated not by any desire to substantiate some supposed social revolution but to eliminate 'sleaze' wherever possible. The banner of a new post-Tebbit party was carried among the new intake by one, Julie Kirkbride (Bromsgrove), a journalist: Cambridge-educated, right-wing, the daughter of a lorry driver from Halifax.

Altogether the 1997 parliament contained only thirty members who had been elected before 1979, so if the party had undergone a Thatcher or Tebbit 'revolution' it would have been obvious in 1997.[26] In educational terms, 65 per cent of the 1997 parliament went to public school and 53 per cent to Oxbridge. Of newly elected MPs 61 per cent went to public school and 49 per cent to Oxbridge. Although the number of MPs from public school has not changed significantly, the number of old Etonians in the parliamentary party dropped from fifty-five in 1945 to fifteen in 1997. In both of these elections the party had been heavily defeated and so it was the backbone, so to speak, that was represented. Even in its best seats, then, the party seems to have turned away from this prime source of candidates to a much greater extent than it has from Oxbridge. In terms of occupation 52 per cent of the 1997 parliament have a background in business, the majority as company directors. A further 22 per cent have a professional background of whom by far the largest category is barristers. There are, in addition, three teachers and one manual worker. The new intake comprises 17 per cent professionals, with barristers again by far the largest component, 54 per cent businesspeople (company directors slightly less dominant), one teacher and no manual workers. If we make a comparison with the 1992 parliamentary party we find a slightly smaller percentage of professionals in 1997 and a considerably larger proportion of business-people. Interestingly, the number recruited from local government actually fell from one in three to one in four. So we can say that, with the exception of recruitment from the very top public schools (there were none at all from Harrow), in its social background at least, the post-Thatcher/Tebbit Conservative party remains to a large extent what it has been since the war: the representative of business and the older professions.

Social background in itself is not as important as the narrow perspective that it frequently instils. There may have always been a wealth of knowledge among members on matters of finance, commerce, agriculture and the law, but this has been balanced by an absolute dearth of first-hand experience of poverty, unemployment, the sharp end of the welfare state, the problems of living in the inner cities, and so on. Voters' perceptions of the parliamentary party may be reflected by the following extract from a tabloid newspaper. Entitled 'School Report',[27] it tells of the decision of Bob Dunn MP to send his son to a local fee-paying school. Nothing very unusual in that, except that Dunn happened to be a junior minister in the Department of Education and Science. 'Perhaps', wrote the journalist, 'if it were his child whose future depended upon how he came through the state system, his child who came home semiliterate, rude and uninterested, he might get off his backside and do something to improve it.' Norman Tebbit told the story of one Tory grandee who, as preparation for a Cabinet discussion on the subject, had to ask his senior civil servants what mortgages were and how they worked.[28]

In brief, then, Thatcher's and Major's Conservative party was less homogeneous, more factious, more abrasive, and less deferential. These leaders assisted in something of a change in the parliamentary party; if they led a revolution in the social background and character of the party, it turned out to be more apparent than real and it did not last.

The backbenches: ideological background

No social revolution, apparently, but what of ideology on the backbenches? Norton has commented on the Conservatives under Major that they were in office but not in power.[29] He elucidates four reasons for this state of affairs: incompetence (especially economic), disunity, weak leadership, and the lack of what he calls 'the public service ethic' which is similar to the paternalism that Gilmour associates with traditional Tory values. We are not interested here with incompetence or weak leadership, but the divisions on Europe (a leitmotif of Conservatism in the 1990s) and the decline of the public-service ethic do tell us something about the modern parliamentary party that we should consider carefully.

The issue of Britain's relationship to the European Union as its member states became more closely aligned, always a sore, achieved major medical salience during the passage of the Maastricht Bill in 1992. Although originally the deal that Major had struck at the Maastricht conference of 1991 had been hailed as a triumph, two events changed the nature of the debate. First was Denmark's original refusal (by referendum in June 1992) to endorse the treaty – which derailed the legislative process in the House of Commons – and second was the United Kingdom's withdrawal from the Exchange Rate Mechanism (in September). An early day motion signed by sixty-nine Conservatives urged the government to make a 'fresh start' to future progress.[30] They sought not greater integration but an enlarged Europe which would be 'a fully competitive common market'. Henceforth Major's diminishing majority would need the support of Liberal Democrats and Ulster Unionists to secure the tortuous progress of the Maastricht legislation.[31] The continuing crisis within the party led to an attempt by the Eurosceptics to scale the heights of intra-party influence: Sir Nicholas Bonsor contested the chairmanship of the 1922 with the incumbent loyalist Sir Marcus Fox. In the event Fox held on, winning by 129 to 116 – anything but a comfortable victory.

The most remarkable confrontation, however, followed the decision of the government to make the vote on the annual contribution to the EU budget in 1994 an issue of confidence. A 'constitutional outrage' declared the Eurosceptics, eight of whom actually failed to support the government. The whip was withdrawn from them immediately and a ninth resigned the whip in protest. Of these eight MPs only one had entered the House before the first Thatcher government and each represented a 'southern British' constituency. They posed as almost a quasi-independent party and were we to invent a name for them, it might be the Little Englanders.[32] They provided a focus for Euroscepticism though they certainly were not its only expression. In 1996 two bills introduced under the ten-minute rule sought drastic limits on EU influence; both received the support of more than one Conservative in four. Later that year the paymaster-general resigned from the government because of its allegedly pro-European stance; further, at the party conference the former party Treasurer Lord McAlpine defected to the Referendum party, and three leading party figures addressed large fringe meetings of anti-Europeans.[33]

Norton provided a tabulated summary of the structure of the parliamentary party around the axis of European policy which suggested that what he classified as the Eurosceptic right amounted to 32 per cent. Major could count on the loyalty of some 49 per cent but almost half of these were 'Eurosceptic leaning'. Norton described the remaining nineteen per cent as 'pro-European integration left'.[34] In terms of specific group loyalties the Eurosceptic Fresh Start, the Bruges and European Research groups could claim a combined membership of at least 120; the closely allied Conservative Way Forward (Thatcherite) group had between eighty and one hundred members. Much of the membership between these right-wing and Eurosceptic groups overlapped but all in all they amounted to over half of the parliamentary party. Norton's analysis shows that for more than half the party Europe was an issue so important that it transcended party loyalty, and two-thirds of these were Eurosceptic and right-wing. Such was their animosity to the leader that John Major decided to resign after meeting the Fresh Start group in June 1995. Martin Holmes has argued that Major saw the Eurosceptics as his principal enemies. 'They were "bastards" who were "spreading poison".'[35] Perhaps the right, who had by and large voted for him in the 1990 leadership election – as representing Thatcherism without Thatcher as Chris Patten put it – saw Major as a traitor.[36] Gilmour compared the party to 'some crazed American cult ... intent on mass suicide' whose leader, though not intent on encouraging his followers to commit suicide, 'was merely unable to talk them out of it'.[37]

Such is the importance of the European fissure that it has rendered the old categories of partisanship in the parliamentary party more or less irrelevant. It used to be argued that a rough balance existed within the ranks between the left-of-centre groups, such as the Bow group, the Reform group, the One Nation Group and the Lollards (who used to meet in the tower of that name in Lambeth Palace), and right-of-centre groups such as the 92 (called after the Cheyne Walk address of its founder, the late Sir Patrick Wall, MP for Beverley), the Selsdon group and the No-Turning Back group – with the Monday Club further to the right. Now the issue that counts is Europe. The association of Euroscepticism with the right and pro-Europeanism with the left may be approximate but it is not inaccurate. In the parliamentary party after 1997 there was no balance. The preponderance of Eurosceptics which Norton noted in the 1992–97 parliament was enhanced in the new parliament. True, Portillo and Forsyth lost their seats, but of the new intake only one or arguably at the most three were pro-Europe. Of the 165 Conservative MPs in the house after 1997 only approximately thirty-five were pro-European.[38] For their self-protection Michael Heseltine organised them into a Europhile group called Mainstream by its supporters, Slipstream or even Backwater by its more numerous opponents.[39]

Norton referred also to the decline in the public-service ethos and we have already considered the allegations of 'sleaze' as it affects the party. It would be invidious to suggest that the average Conservative MP in the 1990s was less honest or indeed less public-spirited when entering parliament. But we have already noted the increased professionalisation of politics among the parliamentary party, and it would be strange if a government whose leader had declared that there was no such thing as society, and who had 'professionalised' the civil service in such a way as to make civil servants feel that the public-service ethos was of no value, did not have some impact on the thinking of backbenchers. When that factor is coupled with the self-confidence (critics would say arrogance) of such a long period in office we begin to understand that in this respect there was something new about the parliamentary party in the 1990s. Thus the gamut of sex scandals, of MPs accepting cash payment for asking parliamentary questions, of a Minister with responsibilities for arms sales allegedly being treated to a stay in a luxury Paris hotel, with tales of over-close relationships between MPs and lobby groups, and with an independent enquiry announcing that a Minister had deliberately misled the House,[40] all seemed to add up to a party which somehow had lost contact with its 'public-service' or paternalist roots. The description of the 1919 administration as comprising a large number of 'hard-headed Unionists on the make' might easily be transposed by critics to the 1997 government. David Willetts accepts this line of argument, concluding: 'It is because people believe, wrongly, that Conservatism just stands for every man for himself and the devil take the hindmost that they also came to dislike the Conservatives.'[41] There is confusion here: it is the public perception of Conservative parliamentarians that has caused a reaction against Conservatism and not the other way about. Willetts asserts that this perception is nothing more than a caricature. He would have to acknowledge, however, that in what he refers to as a major division in political philosophy between the adherents of Gemeinschaft (community-based politics) and those of Gesellschaft (contract-based politics), Thatcherite Conservatism was unmistakably in the latter camp. So when Willetts calls this picture a caricature he is more accurate than perhaps he realises. The chairman of the National Union executive who had criticised the parliamentary party thirty years earlier because 'nowadays too many MPs become [company] directors instead of too many directors becoming MPs'[42] would no doubt have been stunned by the number of Ministers who retire and almost immediately take up key positions in major companies.

And so by the general election of 1997 it is plausible to argue that some kind of a revolution had indeed taken place within the ranks of the Conservative parliamentary party. The struggle between new and old, left and right, wet and dry had been perpetual but containable. The new struggle, crystallising by 1997 as the battle over Britain's future in Europe, had become more corrosive than this and does not seem to be containable. As the retiring backbencher Julian Critchley observed, 'what is so remarkable about the Conservative party is the extent to which we hate each other'.[43]

Party leadership

The most striking social feature of the modern Conservative leadership is the fact that the four most recent Conservative leaders have been meritocrats of modest social origins. Mrs Thatcher defended grammar schools, for example, by declaring: 'people from my sort of background need good schools to compete with children from privileged homes like [Labour Cabinet Ministers of the day] Shirley Williams and Anthony Wedgwood Benn.'[44] Heath before her was of lower-middle-class origins as was her successor John Major and his successor William Hague (who, even more unusually, is from the North of England – industrial Yorkshire). Despite this clean break with tradition at the top, Conservative Cabinets were not affected by the same social change as the backbenchers. The proportion of Cabinet Ministers born to working-class families or with only an elementary or secondary education actually fell during the period 1955–85 compared with earlier periods.[45]

While on the one hand it is true that the proportion of ministers with an aristocratic background had also declined, their places had not been taken up to any noticeable extent by meritocrats from the state schools or by self-made businessmen. Burch and Moran examined new entrants to Conservative Cabinets after 1970 (thirty-four in all) and discovered no great break with the past: over 80 per cent were from public schools and 75 per cent were Oxbridge educated. There was, however, one noteworthy change: whereas between 1916 and 1955 Eton and Harrow supplied about half the membership of Conservative Cabinets, they have since supplied only 15 per cent and the trend confirmed in 1997 is downward.

In general, since 1885 the percentage of Conservative Cabinet Ministers from an aristocratic background had varied from 44 per cent in that year down to 22 per cent in Heath's 1970 cabinet, with the principal fall-off occurring during Churchill's last government in 1955. Over these years aristocrats provided an average of 37 per cent of Conservative Cabinets.[46] Burch and Moran went further and examined the backgrounds of non-Cabinet Ministers who were under forty-five years of age on appointment in 1983. This group, it could reasonably be expected, would comprise those from whom future Conservative senior figures would emerge. Of these (twenty-nine in number), ten were from an aristocratic background, twenty-four were public school educated and seven were old Etonians. Baker and Fountain brought the ministerial statistics up to date in 1994,[47] and their figures showed that in fact the numbers of Cabinet Ministers who had been privately educated fell from Heath's government to Thatcher's and from Thatcher's to Major's: but only from 86 per cent to 73 per cent. The number of old Etonians at Cabinet level also fell, more dramatically, from 27 per cent down to 9 per cent. Oxbridge-educated Cabinet Ministers also declined from 73 per cent to 55 per cent. Baker and Fountain concluded their study: 'The Conservative party is led in parliament largely by men and women whose education, particularly in the more elite institutions such as private schools, Oxford and Cambridge, indicates a continuation of social exclusivity. Major and Tebbit remain unrepresentative examples of the 'upwardly mobile' in the top ranks of the parliamentary party … If "meritocracy" or "classlessness" is growing in the Conservative party, there are few clear signs yet visible in its parliamentary elite.'[48]

Yet as John Major frequently reminded all who would listen, the fissure over Europe which transformed the backbenches divided Cabinet too. So while Baker and Fountain's picture shows no Thatcher-inspired social revolution among the leadership, if the camera is pointed at ideology a different image emerges. The seeds of deep division had already been sown. Thatcher had been the opponent of consensus and never regarded the idea of her own party as a coalition ('broad church') with any favour: coalitions do not get difficult things done. Such an observation would not have concerned many traditional Conservatives whose scepticism led them to favour what Edward Pearce of the *Guardian* called 'chug-chug government'. Thatcher's clarity of purpose led to three electoral victories but in fact, as Ramsden shows,[49] her party never achieved the levels of support that those of traditionalists such as Disraeli, Salisbury, Baldwin and Macmillan had done. Her victories owed much to the weakness of the Labour party. Her departure, engineered by her opponents in Cabinet, connived at by her supporters, left a bitterness which solidified into a despising of Major's leadership especially over Europe. Europe dominated the Cabinet as it did the party and it became the touchstone of ideological loyalties. And it became so corrosive an issue that a British Prime Minister would allow his opinion to be reported: that a number of his Cabinet colleagues were 'bastards' and that he was 'out to get them'.

As far as the party leadership is concerned, then, Thatcher's legacy has been transformative. The party is now divided in a way that it has not been since 1906 and there is no simple answer to the question: who are the Conservative leaders? Socially they may be much like the last generation of leaders: ideologically they are divided. Just as with the parliamentary party at large, the ideological divisions within the leadership have contracted to one issue – Europe. When Philip Cowley analysed the 1997 leadership contest he considered ideological support as an indicator of voting. His division was into three: Eurosceptic, Europhile and Centre.[50] His conclusion was that Hague got into a winning position because he was not disliked by either group and could command general support from the centre. Yet when one considers the greater experience and public standing of his Europhile opponents one can only reiterate what was said in Chapter 2, the Eurosceptics were winning.

Party members

We turn now to that body of citizens which, unpaid, works for the return of Conservative governments, the (former) National Union. We must try to discover who belongs to the party and why, and in doing so have the signal advantage of Whiteley, Seyd and Richardson's study of party membership, *True Blues*, whose findings will help us to answer a number of fundamental questions.

Before turning to this study, however, we might consider a detailed study of the motivations and aspirations of the members of one local party. Philip Tether examined in detail the structure of the local party in the city of Kingston upon Hull.[51] He argued that local parties provide a framework for aspirations that are only tangentially connected to politics. Tether distinguished two levels of membership, the total and the visible. The first comprised all who pay a subscription; the second was restricted to activists and comprised, in the constituencies he looked at, between twenty and fifty members (though in more successful constituencies the figure would be substantially greater). He continued: 'The party is seen by much of this visible membership as a social organisation. It serves the function of a social club for a limited type of clientele – middle-aged to elderly, predominantly female but not exclusively so and completely middle-class in origin.' This visible membership sets the tone of the association. 'They tend to regard the party proprietorially since they are all long-established members. Membership of the group is by co-option through evolution …' The social goals which this group set up are straightforward: the maintenance of an agreeable and congenial coterie of companions and the control of social events. The status goals of the 'visibles' are provided by their office, a confirmation of local social prestige.

Tether emphasised that local associations differ one from another, but his cameo of the personalisation, what he calls 'privatisation', of constituency party politics was applicable to all but the best-organised and most active of constituencies. One final point: Tether highlighted the importance of married women in the local structure, but constituency parties being run – though seldom led – by women are becoming rarer as more married women return to full-time employment; the work of some local associations has clearly suffered as a consequence.

On now to the broader picture, and we can begin with an interesting reflection: nobody currently knows how many members the party has. Estimates varied in the recent past from 1.5 million to 750,000, though the figure was certainly far lower than that by the time of the 1997 general election, and fell badly thereafter. Not only are commentators guessing (however intelligently) but so, for the time being, is Central Office, and indeed so are the constituency associations themselves. Whiteley et al.[52] discovered that in their sample the differences between claimed and actual membership varied from an over-estimation of 69 per cent to an under-estimation of 194 per cent. Perhaps the best indication is that Central Office distributed 400,000 ballot papers for the referendum on Hague's reforms. Only 176,391 were returned. Bearing in mind that 28 per cent of constituency associations in England and Wales chose not to participate and that Scotland was excluded, we can calculate a current membership of somewhere between 250,000 and 300,000.

If there is some doubt as to the size of membership there is much less regarding socio-economic characteristics. The party in the 1990s, according to Whiteley et al., comprised men and women in almost equal number; only 16 per cent of members were under forty-five, whereas no fewer than 43 per cent were over sixty-five. In terms of educational background 23 per cent worked for a private company or firm but 32 per cent were employed in the public sector. No fewer than 91 per cent owned their own homes although only 13 per cent enjoyed a household income of more than £40,000. In occupational terms 55 per cent were salaried and only 8 per cent were working-class. Not only is the Conservative party nationwide an overwhelmingly middle-class party but only a minority of its members (29 per cent) were in full-time work, most having retired. We are told that the Church of England is traditionally seen as the Conservative party at prayer: 70 per cent of party members nowadays are members of the Churches of England or Scotland – only 7 per cent are Roman Catholic and 7 per cent Non-conformist.

It will come as no surprise to discover that the political views of these Conservatives are informed by the Tory press: only 8 per cent took a paper other than the *Daily Express, Mail, Telegraph* or *The Times* – and these included readers of the previously loyal *Sun*. All in all then, the party membership represents a remarkably homogeneous group. But what motivates them to join and to become active?

Tether's cameo of local party membership emphasises the psychological motivation of key members; Whiteley *et al.* provide a broader picture of ideological motivation. They quote an arresting statistic for a party which prides itself on its 'statecraft': when asked if the party should stick to its principles even if it meant losing an election 81 per cent replied in the affirmative. Members were shown to see themselves as patriots, proud of Britain's achievements and institutions and approving of authority and discipline. Although in many senses progressive – 81 per cent felt that governments should spend more money to eliminate poverty, 80 per cent wanted more money spent on the NHS and 64 per cent wanted to give workers more say in the workplace – attitudes towards immigrants presented a different picture: 70 per cent thought a future Conservative government should encourage their repatriation. On the thorny issues relating to Europe the image was not clear-cut: although 68 per cent thought that Britain's sovereignty was being lost in Europe, 67 per cent supported Britain's position in the Exchange Rate Mechanism (ERM). Disapproval of a British membership of a single European currency was limited to 57 per cent, though the issue lacked its present (1999) growing salience when this study was undertaken.

On the question of whether Margaret Thatcher transformed the ideological disposition of the rank-and-file members, the authors found some ambivalence. We have already seen the strong support for acting to abolish poverty and improving the NHS. Furthermore, 57 per cent favoured protection against the effects of the free market. These findings suggest that Thatcher failed completely to convince her supporters that there were no such things as society and its concomitant, social obligations. It is true that 61 per cent believed that the welfare state undermined self-reliance and enterprise and 60 per cent wanted to reduce government spending generally, but it is hard to believe that these figures had been much inflated by the influence of Margaret Thatcher. The study of party members concludes that 'in many respects the grass-roots Conservative party is rather anti-Thatcherite': 41 per cent of members described themselves as left-of-centre, and only 20 per cent as being on the right.[53] 'Many grass-roots Conservatives', the authors conclude, 'are ... more progressive than conventional wisdom suggests'.[54]

Whiteley *et al.* also explore levels of activism within the membership and make some interesting discoveries: only a relatively small proportion (20 per cent) of members 'frequently' undertook even the minimum activity for the party – delivering election leaflets. Even fewer (15 per cent) frequently attended meetings. For the majority of members, then, membership seems to constitute some way of making a statement – after all, however inactive they generally are politically 83 per cent described themselves as fairly or very strong Conservatives, and 55 per cent claim to have been motivated to join the party to support Conservative principles (or oppose Labour ones). The authors conclude their study into activism by observing that the better-educated members with relatively high incomes are likely to be the most active, and their reasons are a mixture of the psychological, social and ideological.

As for the great European divide, it is evident that the majority of party activists are opposed to further European integration, as the 80 per cent support for Hague's policy on European Monetary Union shows. Whether members feel as strongly as some parliamentarians about this issue is not known. All evidence suggests that party loyalty and unity are more significant issues for the activists than those concerned with the pooling of sovereignty.

Conservative voters

The third and final category of Conservative that we need to consider is the voter. The traditional relationship between class and voting has been clear enough at least since 1945 with the middle and upper-middle class tending to vote Conservative and the working class and the very poor tending to vote Labour. Further, support for the Conservatives has traditionally been strongest in the upper-middle class (about 75 per cent) and the further down the middle class the less substantial was Conservative support, though these voters were more important because there were many more of them, and many tended to be located in the more marginal constituencies.[55]

Even with this substantial middle-class vote, the Conservatives, to secure election, always needed the support of a sizeable number of working-class voters. That they have managed this so frequently since universal male suffrage was granted has been described as 'one grand historical paradox'.[56] Why should it be considered paradoxical for working-class voters to support the Conservatives? The answer is, because of the accepted relationship between class and voting. But that relationship cannot be assumed to be causal and is a long way from being exact: we cannot be certain that class determines voting at all. The generalisation 'class determines voting' (more accurately: 'class and voting are related') has never been much more than 70 per cent accurate, and no predictive theory which is wrong on about every third time can be taken too seriously. To call the working-class Conservative vote a paradox makes little sense, especially when we remember Stuart Hall's description of Thatcherite Conservatism as authoritarian populism: indeed it may be considered somewhat patronising. Paradoxical or patronised, however, the working-class Conservative has always been of interest to the political sociologists who have sought to explain such 'deviant behaviour'. Three theories have been developed in this attempt, those of deference, embourgeoisement and generation cohort.

The theory of deference argues that a number of working-class voters see the Conservatives as the 'natural rulers of Britain – sensitive to her traditions and peculiarities and uniquely qualified to govern by birth, experience and outlook'.[57] Deference theory also speaks of a second category of working-class Conservatives who vote more instrumentally; they believe quite simply that the Conservatives' record shows them better able than their opponents to run the country. The first category of voters has been called 'deferential' and the second 'secular'; moreover, although the loyalty of the first category could be relied upon, the second had to be persuaded. According to McKenzie and Silver, writing in the late 1960s, the second category was younger, larger and growing.

The second theory, generated by the Conservative victories of the 1950s, held that as workers' disposable incomes rose, so they acquired more middle-class attitudes, among which was support for the Conservatives. According to this, the theory of embourgeoisement, the better sections of the working class were simply becoming middle-class, or bourgeois. This thesis,[58] which was not without influence on the Labour leadership at the time – and indeed since – was generally held to have been invalidated by Labour's victories in the 1960s, though, not surprisingly, it resurfaced in the 1980s. Yet even the elections of the 1950s, when analysed in detail, showed the theory to be less than wholly convincing, for the working-class Conservative voters were by no means exclusively the better-off.

The third traditional explanation of working-class Conservatism was that of the generation cohort. 'Given the extent to which party loyalties are transmitted in the childhood home', said Butler and Stokes, 'time was needed for historic attachments to the "bourgeois parties" to weaken and for "secondary" processes to complete the realignment by class.'[59] This theory had an obvious potential for self-destruction if the working-class Conservative vote did not decrease as the years went by. Analysis of the elections of the 1960s and 1970s seems to corroborate the theory, but wholesale working-class defections to the Conservatives in the period 1979–1992 blew it out of the water. There has been no sign whatever of the permanent collapse of the working-class Conservative vote; quite the reverse in fact.

Perhaps we should not regard the working-class Conservative vote as a paradox at all, but as at least in part a rational appraisal of self-interest. The lives of a considerable number of people have been changed by totally different patterns of consumption, by social mobility, greater educational opportunities, and so on. This may have led not necessarily to voting Conservative but to voting instrumentally. When he led the Labour party Harold Wilson targeted these instrumental voters by presenting his party and its polices as theirs, and with considerable success, though Labour lost their allegiance with the Winter of Discontent. Research published in 1988 indicated that the working class as a whole was more disposed towards Conservative moral values (not related to welfare provision) than they were to Labour's, with working-class Conservatives more in favour of these values even than their middle-class counterparts.[60] In their election campaign of 1992 Labour moved perceptibly towards this agenda, especially on issues such as law and order. By 1997, as we shall see, New Labour had committed itself very largely to the values of what had become known as the 'aspiring' working class.[61]

Instrumental voting is by no means confined to the working class, neither is it the only characteristic of that group. It is, in fact, another dimension of the process which Crewe, Barrington and Alt referred to as partisan dealignment: that is, the erosion of the whole class–party correlation.[62] This is a general development, well documented by the authors, in which voters are seen to be less and less tied by traditional party loyalties. The Conservatives were the chief beneficiaries of this process in 1979 but in 1983 and 1987 had to share them with the Alliance parties. Yet as 1997 so clearly demonstrated, these votes are not the Conservative party's as of right; the party must prove its ability to 'deliver the goods'. Of course there have always been instrumental voters among the so-called floating voters; what is new is the growth of the dealigned instrumental vote. Partisan dealignment means, quite simply, that instrumental voters have grown in influence so as to be decisive in modern general elections.

Moving finally from the general to the specific, let us look at the Conservative vote in the 1980s and 1990s. It comprises around 60 per cent of the managerial and professional groups (though only 55 per cent in 1983), that is, social classes A, B, and C1; about 40 per cent of the skilled working class, social class C2; and between 30 and 35 per cent of the unskilled working class and the poor, that is, social classes D and E. These social differences may also be expressed geographically. In 1979 the Conservatives won 146 of the 193 seats in the south of England (compared with 127 out of 189 in 1970) while losing support in the north. In 1983 this apparent re-emergence of 'two nations' was reinforced; the Conservatives won no fewer than 183 of the 186 seats south of a line from the Wash to the Severn (excluding London) whereas there were swings to Labour in the northern cities. The net result of this trend was a voting pattern (when adjusted to a 50:50 ratio) of 61.4 per cent Conservative support and 38.6 per cent Labour support in 'the South' – what Butler and Kavanagh[63] referred to as Tory Britain – and exactly the reverse of this in 'the North', what they refer to as Labour Britain (Inner London, the West Midlands, the North of England, Wales and Scotland). This division, replicated almost exactly in 1987, was considered by some commentators to have become permanent. It should not be thought of as a new phenomenon however; the Conservative party has traditionally been the party of 'the South' since before the advent of universal male suffrage, with sometimes as many as 80 per cent of its MPs representing southern constituencies. But the extent of the polarisation in the 1980s was new.

In 1992 the pendulum began to swing back, although the Conservatives won 192 seats to Labour's 23 in Tory Britain. In Labour Britain, by contrast, the Conservatives won 87 seats to Labour's 223. In 1997 the pendulum swung through the whole arc; Labour won 85 seats to the Conservatives' 104 in 'the South' and in 'the North' they took 277 seats to the Conservatives' 23. Labour, massively victorious in its own territories, also managed to do well in the Tory South. Indeed, the swing to Labour, though more or less uniform, was in fact proportionately strongest in parts of the South (though no doubt because it was building on a smaller base). In 1997 the two-nations explanation of voting behaviour, which appeared to indicate that 'the South' would be in a permanent majority and that swings were likely to be differential, was in need of considerable refinement.

If the Conservative party, in parliament and the constituencies, can be said to be the party of the 'haves', Conservative voters cannot be classified so easily. Not only have the Conservatives traditionally secured the majority of their votes from the working class but in 1979–92 they actually secured more than half of the working-class vote. Norton and Aughey feel sufficiently confident to conclude that Conservatism 'can be seen as the articulation of the interests not only of those who benefit from the present institutional structure and who wish to preserve the privileges they derive from the status quo, but also those who prefer, despite not having these privileges, what is known and predictable in the present system, and who believe that this is how things should be'.[64]

There is much in what Norton and Aughey say. We can see, too, something more positive at work: Disraeli is widely considered to have

developed a kind of Conservatism with which working men could identify;
Salisbury incorporated the interests of the new suburban middle class,
Macmillan tempered his style of Conservatism to the aspirations of the
1960s affluent working-class consumer and Thatcherism was in part a
response by the party to 'populist-authoritarian issues' which concerned
'Essex man'. Commentators such as Brian Walden[65] claimed that middle-
class leaders such as Tebbit and Major destroyed the 'old boy networks' in
the party and were 'insidiously destructive' of its values. Walden believes
that they had thus brought the party closer to the people. The research
discussed in this chapter lends little justification to this claim, and the
collapse of the party in local government in the 1990s and the rout of 1997
indicate that if the power of the 'old boys' was broken (more likely
weakened) it was not permanently replaced by the power of the 'new lads'.
Talk of transformation in the late 1980s became talk of implosion by the late
1990s.

Commentators in the late 1980s forgot that a very substantial number of
Conservative voters of all classes – no fewer than 49 per cent in 1983 for
example – were motivated primarily by a fear of Labour; in that election
only 40 per cent of those who voted for the party actually 'liked the
Conservatives'.[66] As 1997 was to show, an electable Labour party could
challenge for the newly dealigned vote with every prospect of success. We
do well to remember that in 1992, on a turnout of 77.7 per cent, the
Conservative party polled over 14 million votes, the largest popular vote
polled by any British party and fully 7 per cent more than Labour. In that
light, then, 1997 was a spectacular fall. Curtice and Stead show that the party
fared worst in the areas where it was previously strongest, and that
warnings of this trend could be observed in local election results from 1993
onwards and again in the 1994 European elections. 'This continued
repetition of the same pattern of loss suggests that the Conservative defeat
in 1997 was but yet another expression of a long-standing nationwide
political disenchantment that almost undoubtedly set in the moment that
the pound fell out of the European Exchange Rate Mechanism in
September 1992.'[67]

To the extent that this conclusion suggests an instrumentalist voting
pattern – 'it's the economy, stupid' – it partly contradicts their previous
argument which pointed to the relatively healthy state of the economy in
1997. It is also counter-intuitive in the sense that few ordinary voters could
have been fully aware of what ejection from the ERM signified, especially
since the economy began soon to improve. What ordinary voters,
especially those natural supporters of the party, would have been aware
of was weak leadership, party divisions, and perhaps above all the
seemingly endless stream of sleaze.

Conclusions

The Conservative party seems to be in the throes of fundamental change. We have seen that the changes that commentators wrote and argued about in the parliamentary party especially from the 1970s pale into insignificance when compared to the changes to the party after the leadership of Margaret Thatcher. I have suggested that in rejecting the notions of consensus, intra-party coalition and compromise Mrs Thatcher changed the historic role of a non-ideological party. She replaced that role with a dynamic, ideological Conservative party that had a mission; she replaced it, that is to say, with Thatcherism – and with Thatcher. What the party failed to realise was that the latter was more important than the former and when it sought, under Major's leadership, to secure the benefits of Thatcherism without Thatcher, it actually finished with the worst not the best of both worlds. Bereft of its great warrior leader, shorn of its traditional self-belief, the party foundered. The parliamentary party lost its cohesion, the leadership became fatally split, the party organisation lost its sense of direction, the historic relationship with capital became much weaker, party members deserted in droves and Conservative voters jumped ship by the hundreds of thousands.

Max Hastings, Conservative editor of the *Evening Standard*, said in a radio interview that his party did not deserve to win the election of 1997; had the government been an old dog, it would have been put down long since out of kindness. A BBC correspondent reported: 'shy and silent Tories stayed at home because they could not bring themselves to vote for a party which, in the public's mind, had become so discredited and so tainted'.[68] Faced with an opponent which had striven so hard and to such good effect to make itself electable, the Conservatives simply imploded. To his substantial credit, William Hague has put his weight behind the effort to rebuild the party. A number of critics have compared the Conservatives' post–1997 position to that of Labour in 1983. This is a simple but important mistake: as we shall see, by 1983 the left had seized control of the Labour party in terms of structure, policy and leadership. The Conservative party is currently in danger of being taken over by right-wing Europhobe 'English nationalists' but this has not yet happened. The Conservatives are in fact where Labour stood in 1979. They have not yet forsaken the centre ground, but they might. If they do then those on the centre-left will become increasingly isolated and disillusioned. There is one difference, however, between the late 1990s and the early 1980s. Unlike Thatcher in 1979 who moved to the right, Blair did not move to the left in 1997 but to the centre. After 1979 Labour in opposition had the option – which they did not take – to adopt the centre ground. Looking for 'clear blue water', however, Hague's Conservatives in 1999 may be forced into adopting a more right-looking stance. If Labour's history is any guide this will mean that the recovery of the Conservative party might be long delayed. In short, if by

1997 the Labour party had shown an enviable capacity to transform itself into a 'catch-all party', then the Conservatives appear subsequently to have begun the unenviable transformation into a 'catch-nothing' party.

Notes

1. Martin Burch and Michael Moran, 'The Changing British Elite', *Parliamentary Affairs*, **38**(1), Winter 1985, pp. 1–15.
2. Colin Mellors, *The British MP*, Farnborough, Saxon House, 1978.
3. *Ibid.*, p. 39.
4. *Ibid.*, p. 71.
5. *Ibid.*, p. 71.
6. S. Haxey, *Tory MP*, London, Gollanz, 1939.
7. *Interim and Final Report of The Committee on Party Organisation*, London, National Union of Conservative and Unionist Associations, 1949, pp. 13–14.
8. Quoted in J.F.S. Ross, *Parliamentary Representation*, London, Eyre and Spottiswood, 1948, pp. 236–8.
9. D. Butler and M. Pinto-Duschinsky, 'The Conservative Elite 1918–78: does unrepresentativeness matter?' in Z. Layton-Henry (ed.), *Conservative Party Politics*, London, Macmillan, 1980.
10. Burch and Moran, 'The Changing British Elite'.
11. *Ibid.*
12. Michael Rush, 'The Selectorate Revisited: selecting party candidates in the 1980s', *Teaching Politics*, **15**(1), January 1986, pp. 99–114.
13. *Independent*, 8 November 1988.
14. D. Thomas, 'The New Tories', *New Society*, 2 February 1984.
15. D. Baker and I. Fountain, 'Eton Gent or Essex Man?', in S. Ludlam and M.J. Smith, *Contemporary British Conservatism*, London, Macmillan, 1996, pp. 86–97.
16. J. Critchley, *Some of Us: People who did well under Thatcher*, London, John Murray, 1992.
17. Quoted in D. Thomas, 'The New Tories'.
18. *Observer*, 10 February 1985.
19. *Observer*, 22 May 1983.
20. Andrew Roth, *Parliamentary Profiles*, London, Parliamentary Profile Services, 1984.
21. *Observer*, 10 February 1985.
22. I. Crewe and B. Sarlvik, 'Popular attitudes and electoral strategy', in Layton-Henry, *Conservative Party Politics*, pp. 244–75.
23. Butler and Pinto-Duschinsky, 'The Conservative Elite'.
24. Baker and Fountain, 'Eton Gent or Essex Man?'.
25. P. Whiteley, P. Seyd and J. Richardson, *True Blues, The Politics of Conservative Party Membership*, Oxford, Clarendon Press, 1994.
26. The following figures, like similar material in subsequent chapters, are extracted from data provided by Colin Mellors of the University of Bradford to whom I am most grateful.
27. *Today*, 14 August 1986.

28. *Guardian*, 9 February 1983.
29. Philip Norton, 'The Conservative Party: "In Office but not in Power"', in Anthony King *et al.*, *New Labour Triumphs: Britain at the Polls*, Chatham NJ, Chatham House, 1998, pp. 75–112.
30. Fresh Start became the title of a staunchly Eurosceptic group of about 80 MPs.
31. Norton's article gives a blow-by-blow account of the passage of the Maastricht legislation and points out how extraordinary a passage of events it constituted in the history of the Conservative parliamentary party.
32. According to the *Guardian*, 25 April 1995, The 'Whipless Nine' were 'feted as heroes in their own constituencies and beyond' and were more generally regarded as the tail that wagged the party dog.
33. *Independent*, 9 October 1996.
34. Norton, 'In Office but not in Power', p. 94.
35. Martin Holmes, 'The Conservative Party and Europe: From Major to Hague', *The Political Quarterly*, **69**(2), June 1988, pp. 133–47.
36. John Ramsden, *An Appetite for Power*, London, HarperCollins, 1998, p. 470.
37. Quoted *ibid.*, pp. 477–8.
38. *Sunday Times*, 4 May 1997.
39. *Sunday Telegraph*, 2 November 1997.
40. *Report of the Enquiry into the Export of Defence Equipment and Dual-Use Goods to Iraq and Related Questions*, HC 15, London, HMSO, 1996.
41. David Willetts 'Conservative Renewal', *The Political Quarterly*, **69**(2), June 1998, pp. 110–18.
42. Ramsden, *Appetite for Power*, p. 176.
43. *The Times*, 16 November 1996.
44. Quoted by Ronald Butt, *Sunday Times*, 16 October 1977.
45. Martin Burch and Michael Moran, 'The Changing British Elite'.
46. See W.J. Guttsman, *The British Political Elite*, London, MacGibbon and Kee, 1963.
47. Baker and Fountain, 'Eton Gent or Essex Man?', pp. 86–97.
48. *Ibid.*, p. 97.
49. Ramsden, *An Appetite for Power*, p. 493.
50. Philip Cowley, 'Just William? A supplementary analysis of the 1997 Conservative leadership contest', *Talking Politics*, **10**(1), Autumn 1997, pp. 91–5.
51. Philip Tether, 'Kingston upon Hull Conservative party: a case study of a Tory party in decline', *Hull Papers in Politics*, no.19, December 1980.
52. Whiteley, Seyd and Richardson, *True Blues*, p. 22.
53. *Ibid.*, pp. 156, 157.
54. *Ibid.*, p. 160.
55. Richard Rose, 'Voting Behaviour in Britain 1945–74', in *Studies in British Politics*, 3rd edn, London, Macmillan, 1976, pp. 208, 209.
56. David Butler and Donald Stokes, *Political Change in Britain*, 2nd edn, London, Macmillan, 1974, p. 181.
57. R. McKenzie and A. Silver, *Angels in Marble*, London, Heinemann, 1968, p. 242.
58. See, for example, Mark Abrams *et al.*, *Must Labour Lose?*, Harmondsworth, Penguin, 1960.
59. Butler and Stokes, *Political Change in Britain*, p. 185.

60. See R. Jowell, S. Witherspoon and L. Brooks (eds), *British Social Attitudes*, Aldershot, Gower, 1988.
61. D. Butler and D. Kavanagh, *The British General Election of 1997*, London, Macmillan, 1997.
62. I. Crewe, B. Barrington and J. Alt, 'Partisan Dealignment in Great Britain 1964–74', *British Journal of Political Science*, **7**(2), April 1977.
63. D. Butler and D. Kavanagh, *The British General Election of 1983*, London, Macmillan, 1983, appendix 2.
64. P. Norton and A. Aughey, *Conservatives and Conservatism*, London, Temple Smith, 1981, p. 175.
65. *Sunday Times*, 8 November 1987.
66. Butler and Kavanagh, *The British General Election of 1983*, p. 293.
67. John Curtice and Michael Stead, 'The Results Analysed', in D. Butler and D. Kavanagh, *The British General Election of 1997*, London, Macmillan, 1997, p. 305.
68. Quoted in Ramsden, *An Appetite for Power*, p. 483.

CHAPTER FIVE

What is Socialism?

Superficially the problem of dating the origins of British socialism seems easier than doing so for British conservatism. The word 'socialist' was used for the first time in November 1827 when Robert Owen's *Co-Operative Magazine* advanced the principle that cooperation was superior to competition and that consequently capital should be 'socially' owned. We shall soon see that this exactitude is more apparent than real, but it is useful to note that Owen's argument encompasses two themes, moral and economic, and that they are related. The moral theme suggests that people should be far more equal than they were in Owen's time and that socially-owned industries and enterprises would both achieve this morally desirable objective and in doing so - in fact, as a direct result of doing so - become more economically efficient (the economic theme). He thus established the main contours of the ideology of socialism, though most socialists speak of ethical rather than moralistic socialism and scientific - a more encompassing descriptor than merely economic - socialism.

The fundamental principles of socialism

Owen was right to establish equality as the *sine qua non* of socialism: it was the one feature about which nearly all socialists agreed.[1] However, major differences were soon to emerge as to the kind of equality to be aimed at and the manner in which it was to be achieved. Two fundamental principles can be elucidated within Owen's socialism - in which they fit together happily - and each encapsulates a different view of human nature and potential.[2] Each evoked a fundamental distaste for the gross inequalities of contemporary society for which capitalism was held to blame. But as we shall see, much divided them. As Dennis and Halsey noted, 'divisions within socialism have been as bitter and crucial as conflicts between socialism and its competing ideologies'.[3]

Ethical socialism

Ethical socialists believe, above all, in 'the good sense of ordinary people'[4] and as a consequence the basis of the good society should be community – what Dennis and Halsey call fraternity – which encompasses the notions of both equality and liberty. It is only in a community of equals which possesses a capacity for collective decision-making that liberty has any meaning. Then everyone could have an equal say in the decisions affecting his or her life. Among early socialists, William Morris[5] could be said to represent this tradition and his Utopian novel *News from Nowhere*[6] offers a vision of the equal, free community of 'ordinary people' that ethical socialists cherished. Here power as well as rewards and opportunities are shared equally. Ethical socialism draws its inspiration from the Judaeo-Christian tradition. In 'Acts of the Apostles' for example, we are told of the early Christian community that:[7]

> Neither was there any among them that lacked; for as many as were possessors of land or houses sold them and brought the price of the things that were sold
>
> And laid them at the apostle's [Peter's] feet, and distribution was made unto every man according as he had need.

Decisions were made collectively and after full discussion, and no hierarchical structure of power existed.

Scientific socialism

Scientific socialists, on the other hand, believed not in empowering ordinary people but in the efficient running of the economy and of society, and in the equitable distribution of goods and services. Thus income, education, health, housing and so on should be made available to all at a similar standard. It was fanciful to imagine, though, that a community along the lines envisaged by the ethical socialists could ever accomplish such a task except for the most primitive of communities. Power should not be dispersed, but aggregated, and used for the benefit of all. 'If you ask me', said Bernard Shaw, ' "Why can't the people make their own laws?" I shall answer, "Why can't the people write their own plays?" '[8]

For the scientific socialists equality does not exist but has to be built, and building is the work of experts. Early exemplars of scientific socialism in Britain were the Fabians, of whom Shaw was one. The Fabians held that the state had to be controlled in the interests of all by a scientifically trained élite. Government was a specialised task, which must be undertaken by a minority or élite on behalf of the majority; it demanded the application of scientific techniques to social and political problems. Scientific socialists attacked the wastes and inefficiencies of capitalist society and believed that a centrally-controlled socialist state run by their scientifically trained élite would be capable of maximising welfare for all. And they put their money where their mouth was: the Webbs founded the London School of Economics and Political Science.

Operational principles

There is another dimension to socialist ideology and, following from the analytical model established in Chapter 2, we may consider this dimension in terms of operational principles: principles, that is to say, which tell us more about the way in which socialism was to be achieved. There are two:

Fundamentalism

Fundamentalist socialists endorsed a programme aimed at creating equality by abolishing capitalism and replacing it with public ownership. Their aim was to break up the existing state which was largely an institutionalisation of the needs of capitalism, by violence if necessary – indeed some argued that the catharsis of violence was essential – and to reconstitute society so that all its assets were socially-owned and equally distributed for the benefit of all.

Gradualism

Gradualists, on the other hand, were concerned chiefly to create equality by alleviating poverty. Their policies entailed a humane concern for the underprivileged but nothing so ambitious as the desire to reconstitute social relations. Gradualists tended to abjure violence and indeed radical change, and to press for reform constitutionally.

Tensions within socialism

So, we may speak of four kinds of socialist: the ethical and the scientific fundamentalist, and the ethical and scientific gradualist. This is not to suggest that we would recognise, say, an ethical fundamentalist if we bumped into one in the street, especially since the various forms tend to coalesce. But we fail to understand socialism – and we fail to understand why socialism appears to have failed – if we underestimate the significance of these distinctions. From its inception British socialism has been an uneasy alliance between these four strands. The tensions at play between them are by no means unique to British socialism and they are not necessarily harmful. Indeed, according to R.N. Berki, socialism is never and nowhere a 'single thing, but a range, an area, an open texture, a self-contradiction'.[9] This is not true simply of socialism; it is true even of individual socialists, as we shall discover if we consider the most influential of all socialists.

Marxist socialism

Marxist socialism presents a crucial mixture of ethical and scientific fundamentalism, though it was always an enemy of gradualism. Although Marx's influence has been far less significant on British than on continental socialism, any analysis of British socialism that omitted Marx would be incomplete. One concept that Marx made common currency among socialists was the (ethical fundamentalist) concept of alienation. Man, says Marx, is unique among animals in that his self-consciousness takes in the whole species: man is a species being. But under capitalism he is prevented from living as a species being, his consciousness being limited by social divisions. Man also has a species activity, labour. To find fulfilment man must 'objectify' his labour in an end product. But under capitalism the worker has no control over the product of his labour, especially in a mode of production that divides labour for specialised tasks. Thus the product of man's labour is independent of its creator and in fact comes to dominate him. What man helps to make becomes more important than what he is. Thus man becomes alienated from the fruit of his labour, alienated from the activity of labour and alienated from his fellow beings, especially from the exploiters of his labour. And the dominating feature of the system which holds men together is capital; men exist only to further the interests of capital.

Why not throw off the capitalist yoke without delay? Here we come to Marx's second major contribution to socialist thought: the essentially scientific concept of false consciousness.[10] As Marx declares, it is not the consciousness of men that determines their existence, but their social existence that determines their consciousness. And what determines man's social existence? The 'relations of production' (that is, the way economic life is organised, especially property relations). This relationship is the foundation – what Marx called the 'base' – of all social and political relations; all other institutions and ideas are dependent – part of what Marx called the 'superstructure'. Now, since the relations of production are dominated by the capitalist class, it follows that the institutions which help to shape people's attitudes – such as the education system, the churches, the mass media, and so on – are also dominated by the values of the capitalist class. Most people's ideas, then, are the ideas of the ruling class[11] whose true purpose is to perpetuate their class's dominance.

So the workers live in a state of false consciousness, knowing that theirs is a life of poverty and hardship but believing this to be inevitable. Marx did not develop this concept of false consciousness as fully as did later Marxists, especially the Italian Gramsci,[12] but its importance is clearly central, especially for British socialists who had to contend with a passive and accepting working class. This is the theme of Robert Tressell's socialist novel *The Ragged Trousered Philanthropists*,[13] which captures vividly the attitude of pre-1914 workers who argue: 'It can't never be altered ... There's always been rich and poor in the world, and there always will be.' The philanthropists of the title are the workers themselves who willingly donate their birthright to the owning class, content to live cocooned in their false consciousness. Little prospect for ethical fundamentalism here.

But this state of affairs would not continue forever, because, according to Marx, a proletarian revolution would inevitably occur. Why? We need look no further than the opening sentence of the *Communist Manifesto*[14] to discover a clue: 'The history of all hitherto existing society is the history of class struggles.' For Marx and his collaborator Engels the nature of this struggle resides in the inevitable emergence of a contradiction between the factors whose relationship constitutes a society's economic base – the productive forces – and the mode of production. We have already considered the latter; productive forces are the processes and tools used in manufacture. The inevitable contradiction between the two occurs because although productive forces develop continuously and sometimes rapidly, the mode of production tends to become rigid and increasingly inappropriate to the changing productive forces. The resulting dislocations tend to be disastrous for the workforce and so the contradiction must be resolved by struggle: the (scientific fundamentalist) class struggle that characterises historical development. Now, because the value of any commodity can only be measured in terms of the labour bound up in it, the interests of the capitalists inevitably conflict with those of the workers, for the capitalists must restrict the worker to a subsistence wage in order to make a profit. Moreover, as a consequence of the intensity of competition, capital increasingly concentrates in fewer and fewer hands. This leads to falling profits, the growing misery of the proletariat and the heightening of class divisions. Any groups trapped between the two increasingly antagonistic classes would join the proletarian camp, leading to – at last! – a growth of 'true' consciousness among the workers. From this growth would come the forces of proletarian revolution.

But who would lead the revolution? Marx believed that the proletariat could hardly manage such a grand objective without leadership, and here is our last (scientific) concept, that of the 'dictatorship of the proletariat'. This is not a concept that Marx himself set out with any precision, though it has played a dominant part in the theories of many Marxists since. For Marx there would have to be a transitional stage between the overthrow of capitalism and the establishment of communism. After all, the existing state, designed to protect the interests of the bourgeoisie, would need to be destroyed and it was quite clear to Marx that a new society so radically different from anything that had gone before would need a good time to be built up. But when would such a dictatorship end? Marx did not say, but the transitional period would be a long one.

Marx's theory of alienation had a profound effect on ethical fundamentalists, especially William Morris. On the other hand, Marx's emphasis on the management of society had an equally significant influence upon scientific fundamentalists in Britain, especially on radicals such as Hyndman, and even on some allegedly moderate Fabians such as Bernard Shaw. For the ethical socialist, Marx's belief in equality, in revolution and in what was later to be called the 'withering away of the state' made him one of them; the scientists, on the other hand, could simply point out that Marx himself saw his socialism as being scientific and not ideological and, after all, firmly believed in the scientific organisation of the economy. No ethical socialist, however, could be very happy with the concept of the dictatorship of the proletariat. For their part, most gradualists had little sympathy for Marx whom they generally regarded, and still do regard, as a dangerous romantic. These then are the main principles and tensions within socialism.

Socialism emerges

The anarchist Prince Kropotkin was of the opinion that the individual principally responsible for the emergence of socialism in Britain was an American land reformer named Henry George. Properly speaking, George was not a socialist at all; but his highly successful lecture tours of Britain and even more successful pamphlet *Progress and Poverty*[15] were instrumental in encouraging the establishment of political groups which were soon to become overtly socialist. George was instrumental in creating a general climate conducive to the growth of socialist ideas. The intellectuals who were attracted to George's theories and who joined one of the many groups formed to discuss them were soon introduced to another writer of far greater erudition and analytical skill, Karl Marx. Men and women of genuine intellectual stature were drawn towards socialism in one of its many forms. They shared to varying degrees distaste for contemporary social and political arrangements, disenchantment with mainstream liberalism and a sympathetic understanding of Marx's economic analysis.

During this period four avowedly socialist groups grew up. First was the Social Democratic Federation (SDF) which had begun in 1881 as the Democratic Federation. It developed as a Marxist group and was dominated by H.M. Hyndman, the best known of the early British Marxists. It was, however, principally a scientific fundamentalist movement intent upon establishing a Marxist state, and though it was prepared to 'use' parliament,[16] it regularly drilled its members and preached revolution. Second was a breakaway group known as the Socialist League (SL), founded in 1886 by William Morris, Marx's son-in-law Aveling, and Belfort Bax. Ethical fundamentalist, anti-parliamentarian, anti-authoritarian, the SL quickly acquired a reputation for anarchism and when, in 1891, Morris withdrew to form the Hammersmith Socialist Society, the SL disintegrated into factions and eventually disappeared. The influence of the SL was slight, that of the Hammersmith Socialist Society considerably greater; but Morris's personal influence was always substantial. One of his 'converts' was the journalist Robert Blatchford whose Clarion movement, based primarily on a newspaper of that name, flourished in the North of England. Blatchford wrote a tract called *Merrie England*[17] explaining the benefits of socialism to a symbolic John Smith of Oldham. It was said that for every convert Marx brought to socialism in Britain Blatchford brought 50,000: the most effective propagandist of socialism that Britain had produced.[18]

The third group was the scientific gradualist Fabian Society. Taking its title from the Roman general Fabius Cunctator whose characteristic tactic was to refuse to give battle until he was certain to win, the Fabian began to develop in an expressly political way in 1884. Among its earliest members was one of the foremost polemicists and propagandists of the age, the playwright Bernard Shaw, and he soon introduced his friend Sidney Webb,[19] the future Labour Cabinet Minister. Intellectually the Fabian was – and remains – the most influential of the socialist groups, but it always abstemiously avoided a large membership, preferring to see itself as an intellectual vanguard.[20]

The fourth of the groups, founded in 1877 by Stuart Headlam, was the ethical fundamentalist Guild of St Matthew. The guild represented the involvement of the churches in socialist politics. It has often been said that British socialism owed more to Methodism than to Marxism, but in fact churchmen of all denominations – Headlam himself was an Anglican – were very active in the socialist movement. This, then, was the intellectual foundation of British socialism.

Socialism and the unions

The popular foundation of socialism was to be provided by the trade union movement. During the 1880s unions representing unskilled workers such as the matchmakers, the gas workers and the dockers undertook successful strike action, thus increasing the confidence of the labour movement generally. Union representatives, moreover, were standing for parliament, and the miners (who took the Liberal parliamentary whip) were highly successful. In 1893 at Bradford, a meeting of trade unionists and representatives of the socialist societies was called specifically to advance the parliamentary representation and political visibility of labour. The result was the establishment of a group whose task would be to coordinate support for labour parliamentary candidates and for socialism generally (though the word was not actually used): the group was known as the Independent Labour party (ILP). The next step was the creation in 1900 of the Labour Representation Committee (LRC), which sought to establish a cohesive unit in parliament, thereby acknowledging the socialists' acceptance of parliament as their main sphere of activity. This made strategic sense: by the turn of the century the working-class man had the vote, indeed working-class men had already been elected to the House of Commons. The unions had made provision for financial support for LRC candidates.[21] These factors tended to reinforce the natural disposition of most of those who claimed to speak for the British working class to opt for parliamentary influence and not popular agitation, which was never used as a strategy by the LRC or the broader labour movement. Keir Hardie's definition of labourism (not socialism) was: 'The theory and practice which accepted the possibility of social change within the existing framework of society; which rejected the revolutionary violence and which increasingly recognised the working of parliamentary democracy as the practical means of achieving its own aims and objectives'.[22] So the LRC was precisely what its title implied: a body dedicated to enlarging labour – not specifically socialist – representation at Westminster. The LRC was an alliance between the 'new unionism' (representing generally the less skilled) and the socialist societies who by now numbered chiefly three – the ILP, the SDF and the Fabian. In its early days the Labour party was a coalition with the socialist wing a distinct minority. In short, far from having 'arrived', the pre-war Labour party represented, in Coates' words, an 'expression of trade union aspirations which involved no coherent programme and no officially accepted socialist commitment'.[23] It is doubtful if socialists would have agreed, anyway, what socialism was. As one of H.G. Wells' characters remarked: 'To understand socialism ... is to gain a new breadth in outlook: to join a socialist organisation is to join a narrow cult.[24]

Socialism in action

It was the electoral pact with the Liberals that brought Labour's first electoral successes in 1906. Prior to the pact only two candidates had been successful in the 1900 general election, though three by-electoral successes had followed in the next two years. But in 1906 all of the LRC's leading figures were elected – Hardie, Ramsay MacDonald, Henderson, Snowden and Clynes. The decision of the Miners' Federation in 1909 to take the Labour whip and join what in 1906 had become the Labour party was decisive. In the two elections of 1910 the party returned forty and then forty-two members. It would be a mistake, though, to believe that by 1910 the Labour party had arrived. Although it played a useful role in the repeal of anti-union legislation and supported the Liberals' welfare legislation, it was hardly a major force. Moreover, in the period between 1910 and the First World War it lost five seats in by-elections.

And yet within ten years a Labour government was in office. Coates ascribes this reversal of fortune to the party's own efforts, to its acceptance of 'some sort of socialist faith' which established Labour as the militant class party that Coates feels was appropriate to the post–1918 world. An alternative explanation would be that Labour's greatest advantage after 1918 was not so much its socialist faith as the irreparable split within the Liberal party. Labour's weakness before 1914 was, paradoxically, to prove to be its strength after 1918. It had been too peripheral to be rent by major public schisms or personality clashes, too unimportant to feel obliged to empty the pockets of its conscience publicly in the search for justifications for conscription, as did the Liberals in 1916. The party survived the war intact; the Liberals, despite (or perhaps because of) Lloyd George's dominance, survived it in tatters.

Labour after the Great War

If the new position was to be built on, it was important for Labour to establish itself as an independent force with an identity separate from that of the Liberals. Reforms undertaken by the party in 1918 saw the trade union movement and not the socialist societies becoming the dominant force in party policy-making, both at the annual conference and at the governing National Executive Committee (NEC) level. Local constituency parties were set up, replacing the old ILP branches. The main thrust of policy was set out in *Labour and the New Social Order* in which, says Coates, Labour 'appealed to the working-class electorate for the first time in its history as a socialist party: one, that is, that claimed to be in battle not simply with discrete problems but with a total social system'.[25] But any programme worth its salt would have been clear exactly how and in what priority its policies would be put into effect. Even Labour's capital levy, said to have struck fear into the middle classes, emerged as little more than totemic. Yet perhaps totems were what the emerging party needed.

In the general election of December 1923 Baldwin's Conservative government was returned with 259 seats compared with 159 for the Liberals, briefly reunited, and 191 for Labour. Liberal leader Asquith let it be known that the Liberals would not keep Baldwin in office nor deny Labour the right to govern. The prospect of a socialist administration filled many with alarm: red revolution, according to the Conservative press, would destroy the army and the civil service. The Duke of Northumberland prophesied the introduction of free love! To others a Labour government

111

offered the prospect of a new way of life, no less. The Labour party was a working-class party with many working-class leaders uncontaminated by failure.

Labour in power

Baldwin was defeated on a Labour amendment to the king's speech and on 22 January 1924 Ramsay MacDonald kissed hands as Britain's first Labour Prime Minister. To many people's surprise, the sky did not fall in. Although the key Cabinet positions went to party stalwarts, there was a leavening of experience. The Cabinet contained two old-guard Fabians and seven trade unionists (including three ex-miners), but also a former Liberal Minister, an ex-Viceroy of India and several middle-class and aristocratic recruits from the two older parties. The new ministry, as Asquith said, constituted no new departure and the great institutions of the state (and indeed the institution of marriage) remained unravaged.

MacDonald's problems were considerable. To maintain a separate identity meant no coalition with the Liberals, no pact, no deal. This still left scope for some informal understanding: after all there was much that the two parties had in common in terms of policy. However, so great were the mutual antagonisms between the leaders that this was not seriously contemplated. Perhaps the Labour leaders believed that if they made a good show of actually administering the nation's affairs and were forced into an election prematurely, the voters would respond by turning on the Liberals. But Labour had to do more than act tactically; it had also to convince the fundamentalists (especially the ILP) that it was attempting, within its limited scope, to implement some of the party's socialist programme. Both of these objectives were achieved to some degree. First, running the country and 'dishing' the Liberals: Haldane, with considerable Ministerial experience himself, believed that the Cabinet comprised at least six men of first-rate administrative ability.[26] The government's major piece of legislation, its budget, was described as a political masterstroke.[27] Moreover, although Labour was defeated when it went to the people in 1924, the Liberals were totally routed. Second, 'squaring' the fundamentalists: although not enthusiastic about the government's performance, the fundamentalists (especially the militant Clydesiders) tolerated it; after all, the Cabinet presided over the establishment of public works schemes, and Wheatley's Housing Act, providing housing for the poor through the local authorities, was also generally popular.

The government was brought down finally by a motion of censure. Any hopes of winning an overall majority at the ensuing election were dashed by the Zinoviev letter,[28] which purported to be from a senior Russian leader, calling upon British communists to prepare for armed insurrection. The letter was obligingly published by the Conservative *Daily Mail*.

MacDonald calculated that no sane voter would take the letter seriously, but he could scarcely have been more wrong.

Labour spent five years in opposition. MacDonald maintained his personal dominance over the party despite criticisms from the Clydeside militants, who were acquiring a firm grip on the ILP and turning it into that regular Labour ulcer, the party-within-a-party. Labour did not yet possess a clearly prioritised programme for when it came back into power. True a new recruit to the party, the dashing aristocrat Oswald Mosley, advanced a platform for combating unemployment that drew some support, and the ILP had similar proposals. But Mosley was thought by party leaders to be naïve and the ILP proposals were seen as part of a general challenge to MacDonald's leadership. In 1928 a new programme, *Labour and the Nation*, emerged. If it was more specific than its predecessor, it was no more realistic, with over seventy proposals but no priorities: implementation, according to future leader and Prime Minister Clement Attlee, would prove 'nothing short of a miracle'.

Labour's second ministry

For all that, in 1929 Labour formed a minority government for the second time. MacDonald's second spell in Downing Street was to last much longer than the first, though once again there was to be no arrangement of any kind with the Liberals. Unfortunately for the Labour party, it was to confront a world slump and a collapse of the international money market, in response to which it offered nothing but conventionally deflationary economic policies. It rejected the Keynesian public works programme of the Liberals and the radical strategy of Mosley. To paraphrase Keynes, the government promised nothing and kept its word. Treasury orthodoxy – no devaluation – together with chancellor Snowden's opposition to protectionism were MacDonald's guiding principles, though none of his advisers could have known what lay ahead. Anticipating a trade deficit in 1931 a deflationary package, based upon massive cuts in public expenditure, the most severe being in unemployment benefit, was discussed in Cabinet but finally rejected. A crisis developed. Gold reserves were dwindling rapidly and a foreign loan tied to severe cuts in public expenditure became a necessity. But the government could not agree on a package. MacDonald decided to resign but was persuaded by King George V to stay and head a national coalition government instead.[29] The following month MacDonald was expelled from the Labour party and shortly after found himself fighting a general election against most of his former colleagues. He remained Prime Minister but the party he had helped so conspicuously to build was reduced to only fifty-two MPs in the election of 1931.

All the same, the Labour government had achieved some successes before its demise: Greenwood's Housing Act of 1930 inaugurated a programme of slum-clearances; Addison's Land Utilisation Act helped with the problems of rural unemployment; the Coal Mines Act provided some sort of *modus vivendi* for miners and owners; and a bill to raise the school-leaving age was passed (though subsequently defeated in the House of Lords). Yet few would say that this second Labour government advanced the socialist cause one jot: the tension between fundamentalism and gradualism, or ethical and scientific socialism, had never been resolved; in fact it had never been addressed. And now the parliamentary party had been reduced to a rump and the government was dead; dead, as Tawney said, not from murder or misadventure, but pernicious anaemia.

Labour and the collectivist state

In how different an atmosphere did the Labour party next come into office. The party's overall majority in the 1945 election was 146. Its leadership was known to the public but was not tainted by the failures of the 1930s. The Labour Cabinet was dominated by men with solid ministerial experience, powerful and respected figures from the wartime coalition administration like Attlee himself, Bevin and Morrison; but it contained imaginative appointments too, none more so than the Minister of Health, the mercurial fundamentalist Aneurin Bevan. The war had impoverished Britain, with exports and overseas investments particularly badly hit, and collapse of the infrastructure and facilities of all sorts was widespread. Yet there were also major advantages for the incoming Labour government. The machinery established during the war to plan and control all major aspects of the nation's economic life was still in existence and people had grown accustomed to it. Investment was controlled by licence, consumer spending severely restrained by rationing, and the balance of payments shored up by import controls. This degree of central management was something that scientific socialists could only have dreamed about earlier.

The Attlee government

The new government was not going to miss this unique opportunity. The coalition government had planned major programmes of social reform in health, education and housing. They were there ready for Labour to amend and implement. The government enjoyed the goodwill of the majority of the population, who recognised that recovery was dependent upon planning. A secure platform existed for the implementation of a socialist programme and very soon the Bank of England, coal, electricity, gas and much of inland transport were nationalised. A comprehensive system of insurance based upon the Beveridge report was established; the provisions of Butler's Education Act were implemented and the minimum school-leaving age raised to fifteen; new controls were established over the development of land; a programme of council house building was initiated; and finally - and probably most important - in 1948 a comprehensive health service was established, free to all at the point of use. In foreign policy the government had taken the first steps towards dismantling the empire by granting independence to India, Burma and Ceylon.

To what extent did this, the most celebrated of Labour governments, resolve successfully the conflicting demands of fundamentalism and gradualism, ethical and scientific socialism? The machinery for the central control of the economy was in the hands of the state and most aspects of the nation's public life were planned. Most of the major reforms were aimed unambiguously at improving the quality of life of the citizens. Yet the emphasis of this Labour government was not, as the ethical fundamentalists would have wished, on providing a framework in which ordinary people could direct their own lives, but on the government's acting on behalf of ordinary people; in George Orwell's terms this socialism was 'what "we", the clever ones, are going to impose upon "them", the lower orders'.[30] The Labour government was pursuing a form of scientific socialism that comprised elements of both fundamentalism and gradualism, resulting in the heavily centralised structure of the nationalised industries. In foreign affairs the dismantling of the empire and the strong support for the United Nations (fundamentalism) was balanced by membership of the North Atlantic Treaty (gradualism) and eventually, with the outbreak of the Korean War, the most costly peacetime rearmament programme in history. By this time, however, Labour had fought and very narrowly won the 1950 general election and was facing many other problems.

The deteriorating economic climate and the rearmament programme caused the government to increase taxation and to implement charges for spectacles under the supposedly free National Health Service (NHS). This was anathema to many fundamentalists as indeed to some gradualists, and it undermined confidence in the party's future. The general public had become tired of scarcity and regimentation, and the government, some of whose leading lights had retired or died, was being harassed by the opposition in such a way as to make life intolerable. Attlee went to the people and in 1951 Labour's period of office came to an end.

The desert years: 1951-64

Parenthetically, though defeated, Labour secured more votes than any party before, but the British electoral system gave victory to the Conservatives. Labour leaders must have left office with some anxiety; if Labour could not succeed with the world it inherited in 1945, could it ever succeed? Labour was to spend thirteen years in opposition contemplating this question, and they were years of division and bitterness. Ethical fundamentalists could not be satisfied with the programme of the previous government; it had basically not shifted the balance of power in society. New and more radical forms of socialisation were called for. Scientific fundamentalists, too, were dismayed that their planning had not been more effective and argued that it had been half-hearted. More nationalisation, more control, was the answer. Some scientific gradualists, too, argued for more refined ways of controlling the economy.

The new party leader, Hugh Gaitskell, basing his case on the writings of Anthony Crosland,[31] Richard Crossman[32] and John Strachey,[33] argued that modern industry had produced a new breed of enemies of socialism, managers who did not own the businesses they managed. This new enemy might be found in state-run industries just as in private industry, so nationalisation offered no easy road to socialism. 'The main aim of socialism today', said Crossman, 'is to prevent the concentration of power in the hands of either industrial management or state bureaucracy.' Crosland believed that socialist ideals could more readily be achieved by taxation policy than by further nationalisation. Matters came to a head after Labour's third successive, and heaviest, defeat in 1959. At the party conference of 1960, Gaitskell argued that not to modify the traditional policy on nationalisation (embodied in Clause Four of the constitution) would be to condemn the party to permanent opposition. So began one of the most acrimonious conference debates since the 1930s which was to end in defeat for Gaitskell and his supporters. As the next election began to impinge on politicians' thinking, Labour appeared to be a spent force, riven on major issues, indecisively led and pursuing unpopular and outmoded policies.

It is both feasible and helpful to suggest that by the 1950s scientific socialism of the Shavian variety had become less of a force; after all many of its aims had apparently been achieved. Ethical socialism, too, had become less influential. The divisions in the post-1951 party were really now between the fundamentalists and the gradualists. But with the collectivist state in place it is more appropriate to substitute 'social democracy' for gradualism. This phrase better described the traditionally limited objectives of the gradualists, as embodied in the writing of Crosland *et al*. Modern journalists settle for the simpler left versus right dichotomy, but it is more accurate and useful (since it alludes both to their history and their objectives) to stick to fundamentalists and social democrats.

Technology and managerialism: 1964–70

Within two years the situation had been transformed, not because these issues had been resolved but because opposition to two government policies brought the party together: Britain's proposed entry into the European Economic Community (EEC) and the 1962 Commonwealth

Immigration Act, which terminated the traditional rights of Her Majesty's Commonwealth subjects to settle in Britain. Party unity was aided further by the untimely death of Hugh Gaitskell and his replacement by Harold Wilson. With considerable acumen, Wilson circumvented the debate concerning the future of socialism, and indeed the whole debate between the fundamentalists and the social democrats, by revamping Robert Owen's faith in the application of science and technology. The 'white heat of the technological revolution' would be harnessed; science and technology would be used to create the conditions for the burgeoning of a modern socialism that would incorporate the best features of fundamentalism and social democracy. Simply stated, by achieving a rate of growth in the economy of twenty per cent over a five-year period a Labour government would transform the lives of all citizens. It was on this policy that Labour won the 1964 general election, though by the slender margin of five seats overall.

Simple to state, twenty per cent growth proved more difficult to achieve. A Department of Economic Affairs was created with the task of wresting macro-economic control from Treasury and drawing up and implementing a five-year plan. Labour intended to involve the trade unions and the employers in collaborative planning with the government, and an early fruit of this policy was the National Board for Prices and Incomes whose task would be to examine price increases and wage demands. In 1966 Labour sought to strengthen its hand by appealing to the electorate again; it was rewarded with an overall majority just short of a hundred and returned to its task with new vigour. However, within two months a seven-week seamen's strike led to a dramatic collapse in the value of sterling. Once again a Labour government found itself obliged to introduce a policy of deflation, including a wage and dividend freeze. The five-year plan was thus effectively torpedoed and the unity that had existed for four years was severely shaken. And things got worse. In November the pound was devalued and drastic cuts in public expenditure were to follow, including re-imposition of NHS prescription charges. (Ironically Prime Minister Wilson, who introduced the charges, had resigned from the Cabinet when charges were originally imposed in 1951.)

However, the government's strategy was not completely deflected. An Industrial Reorganisation Corporation was created in 1966 to encourage and assist the restructuring of industry. The following year iron and steel were renationalised. Welfare spending increased substantially in real terms and so did the number of house completions. The government also began to dismantle the selective system of secondary education, promoting comprehensive schools and discriminating positively in favour of inner-city schools. Labour sought to improve the lot of the underprivileged by a new supplementary benefits scheme, by paying family allowances directly to mothers, and by redundancy payments, rate rebate schemes and new allowances for the long-term sick and disabled. If these policies mollified fundamentalists within the party, Wilson's attempted reform of the trade unions did the opposite. Wilson was obliged to give way after six months of a struggle that, like Gaitskell's attempt to reform, left a legacy of bitterness. Labour's unexpected defeat in 1970 led to the customary period of recrimination. In the words of one fundamentalist, a middle-class Conservative government had been replaced in 1964 by a working-class conservative government. Moreover, the inability to prevent damaging strikes and to plan effectively was a major indictment.

The swing of the pendulum

The four years of opposition were characterised by attempts by fundamentalists within both the parliamentary party and the movement to 'democratise' the party structure. The fundamentalists believed that they could prevent the leadership betraying them – as so often before – only by capturing the party organisation so that they might exercise some control over the leadership in matters such as drawing up the manifesto, selecting the Cabinet and electing the party leader. When the party came back to office it was divided not only on major issues of policy but on the general direction in which the party appeared to be moving. Worse, the Party came to office in the middle of a state of emergency, with British industry working a three-day week and the population experiencing regular power cuts, both consequences of the dispute between the Conservative government and the miners over pay policy. Labour's majority in February 1974 was four.

During the summer of 1974 the government outlined the policies it planned to pursue, including devolution of power to Scotland and Wales, the public ownership of development land and greater government involvement in industrial development. On this platform Labour called for another election in October, which it duly won though with an overall majority of only three. The narrowness of its success did not prevent Labour governments under Wilson and then Callaghan from implementing many of their policies, including the establishment of the Advisory, Conciliation and Arbitration Service (ACAS), the National Enterprise Board and the British National Oil Corporation. A new earnings-related state pension scheme was introduced, the push towards comprehensive schools was intensified and steps were taken to abolish pay beds in the NHS.

Referendums were used to decide whether Britain should continue to belong to the EEC and whether executive and legislative powers should be devolved to elected assemblies in Scotland and Wales. By allowing a national referendum on the EEC and absolving Cabinet members from collective responsibility the government secured two objectives: its own survival and continued membership of the EEC. That the referendums both in Scotland and Wales failed to produce a sufficient majority was, to be cynical, the ideal solution for Labour, but by that time (1979) its days were numbered anyway. Labour had been sustained in office for eighteen months by a pact with the Liberals. From the government's point of view this period of comparative stability helped them to pursue their anti-inflation policies based upon wage constraint negotiated with the TUC, a key example of Labour's ability to control the modern economy with union support (social democracy). However in 1978 the government insisted on a wage-rise norm of five per cent – the rate of inflation was then of the order of eight per cent – and the TUC refused to cooperate. There followed a series of damaging strikes involving, among others, lorry and petrol-tanker drivers and public service manual workers. Ambulancemen struck, with a consequent direct threat to human life. This was the 'Winter of Discontent'. The social contract had been shattered and with it Labour's claim to managerial competence. In the general election in the spring of 1979 Labour was decisively defeated. In a sense the 1974-19 government represented the failure of social democracy. No small wonder that the fundamentalists thought that enough was enough.

Back to the desert: 1979–97

After the debacle of 1979 the fundamentalists began to achieve notable victories in their campaign to 'democratise' the party, and this worried some social democrats so much that four of the most prominent left the party to found the Social Democratic Party (SDP). The immediate consequence of both was that in the general election of 1983 Labour faced serious competition for the non-Conservative vote and opted for a fundamentalist manifesto, based upon its radical Alternative Economic Strategy. This programme envisaged sweeping reflation, the extension of public ownership to encompass profitable firms, the introduction of planning agreements with other major companies, price controls, import controls and the introduction of ill-coordinated schemes of industrial democracy.[34] The party sustained its most humiliating defeat since 1931 and as a direct consequence the resignation of the fundamentalist party leader Michael Foot and the election to the leadership of the social democrats' 'dream ticket' of Kinnock and Hattersley.

Kinnock's early years as leader were consumed by the need to re-establish the party's credibility and in 1985 a new economic strategy began to emerge with the launching of the Jobs and Industry campaign. This campaign sought to emphasise that Labour was more concerned with creating and not redistributing wealth and stressed the desirability of a partnership between Labour and the private sector.[35] Labour government would intervene in the market only to correct its systemic failures, such as short-termism. The party fought the 1987 election with considerable confidence. Its leadership was progressive, its policies modern and the party no longer anti-European. Moreover, public support for its rival for the left-of-centre vote, the Alliance, had peaked. However, despite a widely acclaimed campaign the party was defeated again.

For the second time since 1945 Labour had lost three successive general elections. For a party that was spoken of in the late 1940s and again in the 1960s as the new natural party of government, this represented a worrying failure. It is in the very nature of failure to drive the defeated to introspection; winners seldom indulge in post-match inquests. Labour's progress in modernising its policies had not been matched by organisational modernisation, and as we shall see later it was to this problem that Kinnock now turned his attention. By the 1992 election, however, significant steps had been taken in this area too and victory seemed to be within the party's grasp, especially after the Shadow Chancellor John Smith's studied policy of 'cosying up' to the captains of industry – the so-called 'prawn raids'. But the party lost in 1992 despite his best labours and Kinnock must have felt not so much like a Hercules as a Sisyphus. Many commentators said after the 1992 election that if Labour could not win then, they never would.

The world in which socialism grew up and flourished had changed. Towards the end of the 1980s socialism nearly everywhere imploded. The Soviet Union ceased to be either socialist or united and the command economies of Eastern Europe, one after another, simply collapsed. The toppling of the Berlin wall exposed the limitations of these states, naked, to all; as an economic, social and moral system socialism was simply no longer taken seriously by many. Twenty years or so previously Joseph Schumpeter had predicted the imminent demise of capitalism and the world-wide triumph of centralised socialism,[36] yet by 1993 Francis Fukayama (perhaps with equal prescience) would be writing about the final, absolute and irreversible triumph of liberalism and the market economy.[37] So the demise in Britain of a party whose commitment to socialism had always been problematic anyway was seen to be just a part of a worldwide process. Chameleons adapt by changing the colour of their skin to fit new environments; what was required of the Labour party as the 1990s approached was something far more radical. David Marquand, reacting to the 1987 election, suggested that in order to win the votes that could give it electoral victory, Labour would have to abandon its three most distinctive aspects: its opposition to the EU, its close relationship with the trade unions and its attachment to socialism. To do so, he thought, required it to 'cease to be the Labour party'. How unwittingly prophetic.

The post-socialist Labour party

While Kinnock's efforts to modernise the party were chiefly organisational, the accession to the leadership of Tony Blair, following the untimely death of John Smith, brought a new dimension and a new urgency to modernisation. Blair could scarcely have signalled his intentions more clearly. Within a year of succeeding to the leadership he sought the removal from the party constitution of Clause Four. This was in many senses the kernel of Labour's traditional ideology. What it sought was:

> To secure for the producers by hand and by brain the full fruits of their industry, and the most equitable distribution thereof that may be possible, upon the common ownership of the means of production ...

Although nationalisation is not mentioned or even necessarily implied here, Clause Four came to be seen as a symbolic commitment to public ownership through nationalisation. When he had attempted to reform it in 1959-60, Hugh Gaitskell unleashed a torrent of hostile opposition from fundamentalists and had to beat a hasty retreat. Neil Kinnock did not challenge Clause Four directly but more deftly undermined its salience for the party. Blair announced his intention to reform Clause Four to a silent conference in 1994. Crucially he managed finally to gain the support of Prescott and indeed no senior figure openly opposed him. Blair appealed to the ordinary party members, touring the country in the first three months of 1995. It was estimated that at the outset 90 per cent of constituencies and the great majority of the affiliated unions were against the change, but Blair stuck to his guns and refused to compromise. He eventually won a comfortable victory: of 470 constituency parties that balloted on the change no fewer than 467 voted in favour.[38] Clause Four now reads that the party should work for a 'dynamic economy ... the rigour of competition ... a just society ... an open democracy'.[39] Justin Fisher described his victory as relatively easy, largely because of the skill with which the campaign was organised,[40] but its symbolic significance for Blair's modernising project cannot be over-stated.

Blair coined the phrase 'New Labour'[41] to capture the flavour of his project. Briefly the main constituents of New Labour can be summarised as follows: a rejection of the usefulness of the traditional distinction between state and market, public and private; a scepticism concerning the virtues of state enterprise and a sympathetic attitude towards those of private ownership – and thus to the process of privatisation; a willingness to experiment with the application of market disciplines in the provision, management and delivery of 'public' services; a rejection of the traditionally close relationship between Labour and the unions; a belief in the virtues of devolved government and of creating a new style of 'inclusive' (as opposed to adversarial) politics involving further constitutional reform, and a general sympathy towards more individualistic, consumer-orientated values rather than the traditional collectivist ones.

To take the economic aspects of New Labour first, New Labour would claim to be responding to changes in the international economy – globalisation – which nowadays 'strictly circumscribe the capacity of the nation state to control its own economic destiny'.[42] Thus the rejection of traditional Labour policies can be seen as drawing a realistic conclusion concerning the circumscribing of 'sustainable macro-economic policy options open to states'.[43] But there is more at work than international economic theory.

Almost two decades of Conservative government – in which exchange controls had been abolished, public services deregulated and privatised, the powers of trade unions drastically reduced and labour protection laws dismantled – a 'new conventional wisdom, a cultural … and institutional transformation' had been cumulatively created.[44] New Labour has, to all intents and purposes, accepted what amounts to a consensus about what is possible for modern governments acting independently to achieve. Andrew Gamble has described this new post-Keynesian consensus as Margaret Thatcher's greatest achievement.[45] It has accepted that Thatcher's electoral dominance was based upon her ability to articulate the needs of the aspiring working class and that Labour too must win the trust of this group. As Eric Shaw says, 'in a new, more individualistic and consumer-orientated world what mattered most to voters was the freedom to dispose of their income as they chose' and this meant, as Radice and Pollard conclude,[46] projecting an image of Labour as a party representing individual citizens and not just a particular class or group.

Among the groups most affected were the trade unions, Labour's founder, paymaster and ally. Blair went out of his way to tell the unions in the run-up to the 1997 election that they could expect 'fairness and not favours' from an incoming Labour government. Unions were no longer able to mobilise sufficient electoral support to ensure good prospects for a Labour victory. In fact quite the reverse: strong links to the unions were perceived as a positive electoral liability for Labour. The historic link was not severed but it was weakened almost beyond recognition or repair.

In many respects Blair's politics are now to the right of social democracy. It is principally on matters of constitutional reform that his government adheres to a social democratic tradition – indeed here his policies are so radical as perhaps to be considered fundamentalist. The cynic might consider that in committing itself to constitutional reform Labour was simply seeking to win the votes of Liberal Democrat supporters but after its victory in 1997 it showed no inclination to ditch its commitments. Indeed constitutional reform is seen by some as the only policy area in which the Labour government has acted radically.[47] The government moved swiftly to incorporate the European Convention on Human Rights into British law, fulfilled its pledges on devolution to Scotland and Wales, instituted proportional representation for European elections and prepared legislation on freedom of information. Shortly afterwards the government established an independent enquiry on voting reform for Westminster elections. A Cabinet committee on constitutional reform was established; it included senior Liberal Democrats.[48] We might charitably say that these reforms represent the re-emergence of ethical-fundamentalist socialism: the empowerment of local (and national) communities so as to give people greater control over the decisions which affect their lives. But that is by no means how the government has sought to portray them.

New Labourism?

How are we to characterise Labour ideology in the late 1990s? Unmistakably it is not socialist. The rejection of Clause Four was symbolic but nothing that the party has done since has been done in the name of any form of socialism. Some have argued that Blair's government is not even social democratic but simply Thatcherism with another name: it has done nothing to halt the casualisation of labour or what Marquand calls 'the hollowing out of the public domain'.[49] The government does not entertain the idea that public authorities imbued with a spirit of public service should provide public goods. Nevertheless Marquand sees fundamental differences between Blair and Thatcher: the former is 'inclusionary', talks of 'the people' and seeks to act through consensus, whereas the latter was 'exclusionary' referring to a body of citizens as 'the enemy within', and was seeking always new battles, new missions. Marquand observes that Blair draws his inspiration not from European social democracy but, like Thatcher, from the United States. Labour's social welfare policy, Workfare, is based largely on US experience and rhetoric (though it also reflects the sentiments of early Fabian scientific socialism). Means testing and the targeting of benefits, though different terminology might be used, are increasingly forming the cornerstone of Labour's attempts to modernise and make more effective the provision of welfare services. Marquand himself admits that Labour's social vision is 'closer to Thatcherism than to any other tendency'.

But what really distinguishes 'New Labour-ism', says Marquand, is its attitude to constitutional reform. Well, we know what the government has done and is planning to do in this area but we do not know its attitude towards a truly decentralised state whose logical concomitant might be a written constitution. Labour seems to have achieved constitutional reform in the way that Britain acquired its empire, in a fit of absence of mind. Marquand admits that the 'Blairite right hand seems not to know – dares not to find out – what the left hand is doing.' Constitutional change clearly has its own dynamic; it might transform British politics in unimagined ways. Given this we may doubt if even the Blairite left hand knows what *it* is doing! The policies of the Blair government are not constrained by either fundamentalism or social democracy; New Labour can best be seen as following the old Tory tradition of abjuring ideology for pragmatism.

Conclusions

Socialism developed as an intellectual critique of nineteenth-century capitalist society. It had an ethical dimension, which drew heavily upon Judaeo-Christian values, and a 'scientific' dimension, which concentrated on capitalism's alleged inefficiencies and inhumanity. Some socialists sought a fundamental, even revolutionary, transformation of society but others were concerned to seek a more gradual and controlled change. Given the manifestly ideological nature of socialism these tensions played an important part in its development. The Labour government of 1945–50 created what foreign commentators referred to as a collectivist state;[50] this represented scientific socialism's greatest achievement. During the following forty or so years, however, Labour governments were elected to manage their collectivist state for only ten. From the late 1950s onwards Labour leaders sought to reposition the party, to 'modernise' to meet voter aspirations in a generally more affluent society. They enjoyed little success. Finally the challenge of reform was taken up by Neil Kinnock after Labour's third successive defeat in 1987. But only when Labour lost its fourth successive election in the most propitious circumstances (in 1992) did party leaders John Smith and especially Tony Blair make the kind of changes which could truly be described as transformative. Out of their efforts was born New Labour.

Although Blair's efforts to transform the party have been signally successful he has been far less successful in identifying an ideology which we might call New Labourism. When he became leader he was identified as an ethical socialist and journalists wrote about the number of Christians in the Shadow Cabinet and the pervasive influence of Christianity within the party. But ethical socialism was to be replaced as a possible Blairite ideology by 'stakeholding',[51] based in part on the writing of the economist Will Hutton.[52] This sought to describe an ideology whose aim was create a society which was neither collectivist nor individualist but inclusive and cooperative, cohesive and productive. It would be based upon dialogue between owners, managers and workers in industry, between the providers and recipients of all state services. All would have rights and responsibilities. Hutton acknowledges his debt to the New Liberalism of the turn of the twentieth century, but these theories were also reflected in the policies of the post-war Liberal party – such as co-ownership and co-partnership.

His critics considered Hutton's theories to lack formal coherence, to represent an exhortation rather than an ideology. Talk of stakeholding (an unprepossessing word) gave way to talk of 'the third way', associated with the writing of the political sociologist Anthony Giddens.[53] What distinguishes the third way from stakeholding is primarily the emphasis in the former on the development of the notion of economic and personal responsibility as a fundamental of welfare institutions. 'Welfare systems', writes Giddens, 'need to contribute to the entrepreneurial spirit, encourage the resilience to cope with a world of speeded-up change, but provide security when things go wrong.'[54] Giddens also gives more emphasis to the virtues of decentralising government (subsidiarity) and to what he calls the upward devolution of power – that is, to transnational agencies. Others take talk of the third way with a pinch of salt. According to John Lloyd we can be sure of only three aspects of the third way. It will be 'light on its ideological feet, opportunistic on policy matters and obsessed by image'.[55]

These theories – ethical socialism, stakeholding and the third way – have a lot in common. They emphasise a commitment to performance rather than ideology, and it is known that Labour has a 'Domesday Book' of state assets which might be either privatised or put in the hands of public/private partnerships. (They range from Air Traffic Control to the car park at Ipswich Town FC!)[56] From these theories may well emerge something we can call New Labourism. For the present we can say of New Labourism that it is not socialism. As to what it is we can do no better than this: it is what the New Labour government does.

Notes

1. See M. Beer, *A History of British Socialism*, London, Bell and Sons, 1920, esp. vol. ii.
2. These views are contrasted by example in Stephen Ingle, 'William Morris and Bernard Shaw', in B.C. Parekh, *The Concept of Socialism*, London, Croom Helm, 1975, pp. 73–83.
3. N. Dennis and A.H. Halsey, *English Ethical Socialism*, Oxford, Clarendon Press, 1988, p. 4.
4. *Ibid.*, p. 5.
5. See for example A.L. Morton (ed.) *The Political Writings of William Morris*, London, Lawrence & Wishart, 1973.
6. William Morris, *News from Nowhere*, London, Lawrence and Wishart, 1973.
7. Acts of the Apostles 5(34, 5).
8. See Bernard Shaw, *Everybody's Political What's What*, London, Constable, 1944, and *Prefaces By Bernard Shaw*, London, Odhams Press, 1938.
9. R.N. Berki, *Socialism*, London, Dent, 1975, p. 13. The account of Marxism which follows is loosely based upon Berki's longer and more detailed analysis.
10. *A Contribution to the Critique of Political Economy*, 1859, p. 67.

11. Marx explores this idea in, for example, *German Ideology*, written in 1845.

12. See Gramsci's *Selections from Prison Notebooks*, London, Lawrence & Wishart, 1971.

13. Robert Tressell, *The Ragged Trousered Philanthropists*, St Albans, Panther Books, 1965.

14. Karl Marx and Friedrich Engels, *Manifesto of the Communist Party*, Moscow, Progress Publishers, 1952.

15. Henry George, *Progress and Poverty*, printed in London, Manchester and Glasgow, 1882; this very popular 87-page document did not make easy reading.

16. The SDF sought parliamentary representation, to the extent even of fighting a by-election (unsuccessfully) against the Liberals in 1895 with clandestine financial support from the Conservative party (the so-called Tory gold scandal).

17. At first serialized in the *Clarion*.

18. See P.P. Poirier, *Advent of the Labour Party*, London Allen & Unwin, 1958, p. 57

19. Sydney and Beatrice Webb were later enthusiastic supporters of the Soviet Union and wrote *Soviet Communism: A New Civilisation?* London, WEA, 1935.

20. Margaret Cole has written a detailed history of the Fabians: *The Story of Fabian Socialism*, London, Heinemann, 1961.

21. The LRC had contested the general election of 1900 with funds of only £33!

22. Quoted in J. Saville, 'The ideology of labourism', in R. Benewick *et al.*, *Knowledge and Belief in Politics*, London, Allen & Unwin, 1973, p. 215.

23. D. Coates, *The Labour Party and the Struggle for Socialism*, Cambridge, Cambridge University Press, 1975, p. 12.

24. H.G. Wells, *The New Machiavelli*, Harmondsworth, Penguin, 1970, p. 243.

25. Coates, *The Labour Party and the Struggle for Socialism*, p. 13.

26. R.B. Haldane, *An Autobiography*, London, Hodder & Stoughton, 1929, p. 330.

27. R.W. Lyman, *The First Labour Government, 1924*, London, Chapman & Hall, 1957, p. 148.

28. For a brief account of these events see C.F. Brand, *The British Labour Party*, London, Oxford University Press, 1995.

29. For a full analysis of these developments see H. Berkeley, *The Myth That Will Not Die*, London, Croom Helm, 1978.

30. George Orwell, *The Road to Wigan Pier*, Harmondsworth, Penguin, 1963, p. 157.

31. Anthony Crosland, *The Future of Socialism*, London, Cape, 1956.

32. Richard Crossman, *New Fabian Essays*, London, Turnstile Press, 1953.

33. John Strachey, 'Tasks and Achievements of British Labour', in Crossman, *New Fabian Essays*.

34. See Mark Wickam-Jones, *Economic strategy and the Labour Party*, Basingstoke, Macmillan, 1996.

35. See, for example, Neil Kinnock's *Making Our Way*, Oxford, Blackwell, 1986.

36. Joseph Schumpeter, *Capitalism, Socialism and Democracy*, London, George Allen & Unwin, 1976.

37. Francis Fukuyama, *The End of History and the Last Man*, London, Penguin, 1993.

38. Peter Mandelson and Roger Liddle, *The Blair Revolution*, London, Faber and Faber, 1996, p. 217.

39. *Labour into Power: A Framework for Partnership*, London, Labour Party, 1997.

40. Justin Fisher, *British Political Parties*, London, Prentice Hall/Harvester Wheatsheaf, 1996, pp. 83–5. Jones, on the other hand, ascribes Blair's victory to astute tactics. See Bill Jones, 'Clause Four and Blair's Brilliant Campaign', *Talking Politics,* **8**(1), 1995.

41. The term New Labour was not in fact new. A party with this name had been formed by a group who had resigned in the mid-1980s from the New Zealand Labour party. They, however, were rebelling against their party's move to the right. Confusingly the New Labour in the Antipodes equated much more closely to Old Labour in the United Kingdom.

42. Eric Shaw, 'The Determinants of the Programmatic Transformation of the British Labour Party', a paper given at the APSA conference in Boston, 1998.

43. David Andrews, 'Capital mobility and state autonomy: towards a structural theory of international monetary relations', *International Studies Quarterly*, **38**(2), p. 193.

44. Stephen Wilkes, 'Conservative Government and the Economy', *Political Studies*, **45**(4), 1997, p. 692.

45. See Andrew Gamble, 'The Legacy of Thatcherism', in M. Perryman (ed.), *The Blair Agenda*, London, Lawrence & Wishart, 1996.

46. G. Radice and S. Pollard, *More Southern Discomfort*, London, Fabian Society, 1993, p. 16.

47. For example, G. Holthsam and R. Hughes, 'The State of Social Democracy in Britain', in R. Cuperus and J. Kandel (eds), *European Social Democracy*, Amsterdam, Friedrich Ebert Stiftung, 1998, pp. 171–3.

48. The party's rules forbid local parties to cooperate formally with other parties. However a number did so in the south of England from the early 1990s. *Guardian*, 10 May 1995.

49. David Marquand, 'The Blair Paradox', *Prospect,* May 1998, pp. 19–24.

50. For example *Modern British Politics* by S.H. Bear, published in the 1960s, was titled *British Politics in the Collectivist Age* elsewhere.

51. See for example *Stakeholding and its Critics*, Will Hutton *et al.*, London, Institute of Economic Affairs, 1997.

52. Especially Will Hutton's influential *The State We're In*, London, Jonathan Cape, 1995.

53. Anthony Giddens, *The Third Way: The Renewal of Social Democracy*, Oxford, Polity Press, 1998.

54. Anthony Giddens, 'The Future of the Welfare State', in Michael Novak, *Is There a Third Way?*, London, Institute of Economic Affairs, 1998, pp. 25–9.

55. *The Times*, 12 February 1998.

56. *Scotland on Sunday*, 14 June 1998.

CHAPTER SIX

Who runs the Labour Party?

In organisational and leadership terms the Labour party has always been a quite different animal from the Conservative. Moreover, as we shall see, the reshaping of the party under the leadership of Kinnock (and briefly Smith) but especially of Blair has created what is in effect a new party. This means, among other things, that we will not be able to follow the pattern of Chapter 3 very closely; even the position of the party leader has not, in the past at least, been directly comparable. Nevertheless leadership is one discrete feature of both parties that is amenable to comparison, even if the situations in which it has been exercised have been different. So we shall begin here.

Leadership in the Labour party

It is safe to assert that the Labour party has traditionally required far more of its leader than has the Conservative party. The actual structure of the party, more federal in nature, poses problems for a leader. Like the Conservative leader, the Labour leader heads not just a party but a movement. Although the Conservative party has always comprised three fairly disparate sections (the National Union, Central Office and the parliamentary party), the leader was undisputed head of each. For Labour leaders, however, the federal structure comprised a parliamentary party which prided itself on being its own master, an autonomous party organisation whose efficiency was less than legendary, an ideologically active party outside parliament and a large number of affiliated trade unions which paid the piper and sometimes liked to call the tune. But there was always more to it than structures. Loyalty has played a great part in Labour party politics, but not loyalty to the leader. Loyalty has traditionally been owed to a concept: not socialism as such, but rather, the interests of the working class. No statement existed of what precisely these interests were, and to equate them with socialism was no help since, as we have seen, there was no precise statement of what that was either. What resulted was a permanent and growing tendency to sectarian division, with the leader finding his time and energy taken up attempting to keep all the faithful within the 'broad church'. So nobody has sought to describe Labour leaders as monarchs, leviathans or soccer managers!

Leaders in action

The first comparison to be drawn between Labour and Conservative leadership in action is that since the Second World War both parties have had eight leaders. Of the eight Conservatives seven have been Prime Minister and one still hopes to be; of the eight Labour leaders only four (including the current incumbent) have been Prime Minister. To lead a party without the prestige and responsibility of leading the nation is altogether a more difficult task; you are not a winner. But this is not the only disadvantage under which many Labour leaders have had to work. Until 1922 the leader of the party was designated as chairman of the parliamentary party, an elected post; thereafter he was referred to as chairman and leader. Between 1906 and 1922 there had been no fewer than six chairmen, and the position commanded little of the loyalty owed to the leaders of the other parties. The prospect of power, though, brought a new emphasis on the independence of the parliamentary party, especially its leader. So when MacDonald became Prime Minister he formed his own Cabinet without official party consultations, thereby rejecting the precedent set by the Australian Labor party and conforming instead to the practice of the other British parties.[1] In 1931, however, MacDonald formed a national coalition, thereby selling his party out and leaving what has been referred to as a permanent scar on the party's psyche.[2] The cult of individualism is still an emotive and powerful charge levelled at any party leader who seeks to assert his own authority unduly.

The most successful of Labour's leaders in achieving a legislative programme resembling socialism was Clement Attlee. Yet Attlee clearly saw one of his most important functions as preserving the unity of his government despite its apparent success.[3] He tenaciously held on to power amid considerable Cabinet intrigue, and thereby managed to hold the party together. Attlee's successor, Hugh Gaitskell, was of quite a different cut, as his assault on Clause Four was to show. As the ensuing conference debate demonstrated, Gaitskell's modernising aspirations were deeply offensive to the fundamentalists and worrying to all those concerned with party unity. Religious terminology shaped the debate, with Clause Four referred to as 'The Tablets of Stone' and 'The Thirty-Nine Articles', and Gaitskell concluded the debate by wishing that 'he led a political party and not a religious movement'.[4] Within a few months he abandoned any attempt to change the party constitution; it had proved impossible to lead the party, united, down the path to modernisation and electoral success.

Elected leader on Gaitskell's untimely death, Wilson sought to make socialism synonymous with technological change and its underlying ethos of managerialism, and in wholeheartedly promoting the latter to appear to be promoting the former. In reality he was attempting to reconcile the fundamentalists and the social democrats within the party. For a while he appeared to succeed but in major policy areas decisions were taken which offended the fundamentalists: for example, the attempt to join the European Economic Community (EEC), the retention of Polaris submarines and the acceptance of the 1962 Immigration Act. In his second administration Wilson single-mindedly addressed himself to what he took to be the major problems facing the country. Against the advice of a Royal Commission he decided to attempt to reform the trade unions by law, but when it became clear that he could not persuade the parliamentary party (or indeed the cabinet) to support him Wilson simply abandoned the proposals. When he returned in 1974 for a third term, Britain had joined the EEC and party policy was to withdraw. Wilson and a number of senior Ministers thought that this was against the nation's interest. What was the Prime Minister to do? Wilson called for a renegotiation of Britain's terms of entry, held a national referendum on the outcome and allowed all individuals within his divided government to campaign as they saw fit. As a consequence Britain remained within the EEC, the Labour government remained in office and Wilson remained party leader and Prime Minister. All in all, however, Wilson failed to modernise Britain or Labour, though he did succeed in keeping the party together. Just.

Wilson left the party in the hands of the solid, experienced James Callaghan. The problems confronting the government were as great as ever and the success of the Scottish and Welsh nationalist parties obliged Callaghan, whose parliamentary majority was slender, actively to pursue plans to devolve powers to Scotland and Wales, although this was not generally popular with the party, nor were his government's deflationary economic policies, nor was the attempt to control wages which produced the Winter of Discontent. Callaghan left the party defeated, demoralised and in considerable disarray when he resigned in 1979.

Michael Foot came to the leadership with his early reputation as a Robespierre-like figure, 'bitter, intolerant and humourless',[5] counting for less than his potential as a force for stability. Foot was highly regarded by many within the parliamentary party though his accession to the leadership owed much to the fact that it prevented an open confrontation between the fundamentalists (led by Benn) and social democrats (led by Healey); owed much, that is, according to backbencher Austin Mitchell, to his ability 'to obscure issues'.[6] However, Foot was unable to prevent a divisive contest for the deputy leadership between Healey and Benn which the former won narrowly, nor to prevent Benn from attacking his leadership. Foot's failure to recreate stability within his party might suggest that the task had become an impossible one. Foot was never fully able to slough off his otherworldly zeal. According to Ken Livingstone, 'his basic humanity and compassion played a part in preventing the destruction of the Labour party by our enemies'.[7] Unfortunately he was to prove less successful in defending the party against its friends.

His successor, Neil Kinnock, was elected according to the procedures established by Labour's special conference in January of 1981. Kinnock's greatest advantage on becoming leader was his general popularity – he was the candidate most preferred by Labour supporters (56 per cent); Foot, by contrast, was only fourth choice of Labour supporters when he became leader.[8] By any standards Kinnock's task as leader was enormously difficult. What made matters worse was the outbreak in spring 1984 of the miners' strike, led from Yorkshire by Arthur Scargill. This was a Morton's fork for the Labour leaders: should they side with Scargill and suffer general popular opprobrium or denounce Scargill and be accused as class traitors by their more radical supporters? Kinnock rode out these storms and by 1986 began to stamp his authority on the Labour movement. He set in train a revamping of traditional Labour policies, for example substituting 'social ownership' for nationalisation as the major objective. Other important changes in Labour's policy profile included a moderation of the party's proposals for reforming the Conservatives' trade union legislation, a muted acceptance of council house sales, no pledge to leave the European Community, and a strong commitment to conventional defence spending. The 1987 campaign was a personal triumph for Kinnock. Over the next five years he strengthened his hold over the party, pushing it decisively towards social democracy and away from fundamentalism.

Kinnock's resignation after the unexpected election defeat of 1992 brought his erstwhile Shadow Chancellor John Smith to the leadership. In the short time that he held the post – before his death in 1994 – Smith followed Kinnock's lead. For example he reduced the union's voting strength at conference, removed their block vote for candidate selection and pressed for the principal of 'one member one vote' (OMOV) in all party elections. These steps together 'effectively broke the power of the unions in the party'.[9] Smith's task was to adapt Labour's traditions to a new world, but he died before being put to the test.

Smith was replaced by Tony Blair, whose friend and ally Gordon Brown allowed him a free run against the more traditional John Prescott. He won comfortably with 58 per cent of the votes. Blair saw his task differently than Smith had: it was simply to transform the party. The reform of Clause Four, which we considered previously, marked not the end but the beginning of Blair's programme of transformation. Ensuring party unity was of major importance and Blair ran his Shadow Cabinet, then his Cabinet and the parliamentary party with a firm control which critics have described as autocratic. He changed procedures for selecting the chief whip from election to appointment (he appointed Donald Dewar), set up new standing orders to minimise left-wing opposition within the PLP, downgraded the policy-making powers of the NEC, weakened decisively the link with the unions and exercised far greater central power in candidate selection. It is no exaggeration to say that, taking into account the policy changes outlined in Chapter 5, Tony Blair – building on the foundations laid by Kinnock and Smith – has constructed a new party.

This potted history shows that the personality and ideological disposition of Labour leaders have important consequences, but it also shows their influence (even Attlee's) to have been constrained by the party structure. Only in the case of Kinnock and, more especially, Blair have leaders been able to take the party down paths of their own choosing. Circumstances were propitious but personality and ideology were decisive.

Labour party organisation

The Labour party was born out of the bowels of the trade union movement. It represented an attempt by organised Labour to secure the active representation of its interests in the House of Commons. To describe the structure of the party as federal is to encapsulate the essence of these origins and traditions, not just to reflect on the structure of its organisation. The most visible party of that traditional, federal organisation is the Parliamentary Labour Party (PLP).

The parliamentary party

Strictly speaking there is no Labour equivalent to the Conservative backbench 1922 committee. For Labour the whole party, including the frontbench, meets twice weekly; once very briefly to set out forthcoming business and once for more general debate on issues and policy. We have accounts of these meetings, in Ministers' memoirs, from when Labour was last in office (1974–79). They tell of bitter debates, with the fundamentalists using the opportunity to hold the frontbench to account. The shift in the ideological balance under the Blair government has so far prevented the re-emergence of this bitter hostility. In any event, Brand is right to argue that such meetings do not provide 'a satisfactory forum to explore policy'.[10] In addition to the full PLP meetings the party is organised into regional and departmental committees. Party Standing Orders require frontbenchers to attend the relevant departmental committee, though in fact they seldom do and neither do the whips. In fact when Labour was in power the committees sought to 'cooperate' with the relevant Ministers in shaping policy and Ministers shunned them accordingly. Members are free to join three such groups and to elect their own officers. Backbenchers may attend any group meeting but may only vote on those to which they belong. The committee chairmen have a status within the party and will be called by the Speaker at an early stage in any relevant House debate. Committee positions are contested by the factions within the party.

From the earliest days fundamentalists in the PLP had sought to pressurise the leadership into adopting policies to transform the economic and social structure. Even after the apparently triumphant administration of 1945–50 a number of left-wing MPs formed themselves into a group called Keep Left under the chairmanship of Harold Wilson. By 1958 a larger and better-organised group, Victory for Socialism, was formed which coordinated the struggle against Gaitskell's revisionism. Traditionally the largest of the left-wing parliamentary groups has been Tribune, named after the famous house journal of the Labour left, founded in 1937. The group itself was founded in 1964 and is the oldest surviving 'faction' within the parliamentary party. It grew steadily in numbers over the years and frequently contained frontbench members in its ranks; indeed Michael Foot and Neil Kinnock had both been members. In the 1979–83 parliament Tribune was particularly influential, achieving a membership of more than seventy, though twenty members eventually left the group, feeling it to be insufficiently radical. Although the group has traditionally enjoyed considerable political visibility, especially in periods of opposition, its achievement in actually influencing the policies of Labour governments has been modest. When Kinnock became leader he effectively drew Tribune into an anti-fundamentalist alliance and it lost the political idealism, some would say innocence, that had been its hallmark.

In the meantime, however, fundamentalist influence grew. The Campaign Group, founded in 1982 by MPs leaving Tribune, put up its own slate for elections to the NEC, though with decreasing success as the 1980s wore on. After 1987, Kinnock attempted, with increasing success, to isolate the 'hard left' and build an alliance (including Tribune) against them. When later Blairites began to dominate the ideological debate, the left as a whole had simply lost influence. By the late 1990s the Campaign Group, in fact the left at large, had become largely of symbolic importance, with its charismatic champion, Tony Benn, a John the Baptist figure. But it had not gone away.

Many social democrat MPs were represented by the Manifesto Group, established in 1974. The group, open only to backbenchers, never revealed its membership numbers but it was generally considered to have been influential despite the fact that its first two chairmen subsequently deserted to the SDP. Indeed the defection from the party of some leading social democrats to become Social Democrats in 1981 provided both a severe blow and a call to arms to those who stayed. Historically speaking, though, the right has never had the same need to organise as the left simply because it has usually dominated the party leadership.

A significant number of Labour MPs have traditionally been sponsored by trade unions, under the financial arrangements set down in the Hastings Agreement (1933) which allowed for the subsidising of up to 80 per cent of election expenses (though usually less was given). Sponsorship nowadays is not actually of an individual but of a constituency party and it is clear that the relationship is not anywhere near as strong as it once was.[11] When elected however, sponsored MPs form the Trade Union Group, now largely uncoordinated, but once an important agent for the social democrats in the ideological struggle. Of the 180 or so candidates who are regularly sponsored, around 130 are usually elected, with the T&GWU sponsoring over thirty MPs. It would be unconstitutional for unions to attempt to exercise direct influence over their sponsored MPs, and indeed sponsored MPs have frequently voted in a way contrary to union policy, though few have had their sponsorship withdrawn.[12]

The PLP also includes the Co-operative party, which is officially the electoral partner of the Labour party. In the 1980s some 140 co-operative societies subscribed to the Co-operative party. The party sponsored around twenty-five candidates, mostly in safe seats.[13] Typically, though, the House contained between fifteen and twenty such MPs and they formed a Co-operative parliamentary group with a chairman and vice chairman. Nowadays the party is not a sponsoring organisation and its significance is chiefly historical. In 1997 twenty-six 'Labour and Co-operative' candidates fought the election and each won.

It was a number of years before the Labour group in the European parliament made any impact in Brussels (still less in domestic politics), hardly surprising given the party's official opposition to membership. In the elections of 1984 thirty-two were successful and their frequently disruptive tactics led to comparisons with English soccer hooligans.[14] Almost entirely as a reflection of growing Conservative unpopularity, the Labour presence in Brussels has grown. In 1994 Labour's representation rose from forty-five to sixty-two (the Conservatives representation fell from thirty-two to eighteen). The left-of-centre grouping at Brussels was now firmly in control and Prime Minister Major was speaking fearfully of a 'socialist super state' though most commentators concentrated only on what these elections presaged for any British general election. Although MEPs now have recognised status within the party structure they are not an influential group. Two, Ken Coates and Hugh Kerr, who would happily describe themselves as old Labour, voiced opposition to the closed party list system which the Labour government introduced for the 1999 elections; they were expelled from the party and so will not be re-selected, though in truth age may have prevented them from standing again.[15]

There are over 130 Labour peers in the House of Lords and, since they and the nearly eighty Liberal Democrat peers, together with cross-benchers, could potentially outvote Conservative peers, they have become rather more active than formerly, especially after 1983 when numbers of Conservative peers were prepared to vote against their own government on such matters as the abolition of the metropolitan counties, the introduction of the 'poll tax' and the abolition of free dental and optical checks. Under a Labour government they have become less active again, though a number voiced opposition to the imposition of differential university fees for other-UK students studying in Scottish universities and indeed to the closed-list system of proportional representation adopted for European elections. The commitment of Labour peers to the House of Lords has never been great, given their party's declared intention, likely to be enacted by the present Labour government, to abolish the House.

The movement

Nowadays constituency parties (CLPs) comprise a number of branches, usually based upon local government wards and whose tasks are primarily electoral, and Women's Sections and Young Labour groups. Trade unions, and indeed socialist societies and co-operative societies may also affiliate to the constituency party at branch level. Members of affiliated organisations acquire rights as individuals in party matters, for example the right to vote. The party claims that the principle of affiliation is underpinned by the principle of consent. Unions must ballot their members every ten years for approval to continue to affiliate, and individual members have the right to claim exemption. The CLP is administered by its elected general (management) committee which represents the branches, runs the party locally, appoints a campaign committee to coordinate campaigning activity, chooses its delegates to the annual conference and elects an executive committee which has the day-to-day running of the constituency party as its responsibility. The important task of selecting a parliamentary candidate had traditionally been in the hands of the general management committee, but this will be discussed fully a little later.

Above the CLP are nine regions (including Scotland and Wales). Each possesses an executive elected by a regional conference composed of CLP delegates and women's and youth groups and also by the affiliated organisations. The executive too mirrors in its composition the conference's 'federal' structure, and it is responsible for the day-to-day administration of the regional party between conferences (annual for the Scottish and Welsh parties, biennial for the English regions). Regional conferences were traditionally responsible for determining policy, according to the constitution. With the development of the party's policy forums, soon to be discussed, they lost this 'power'.

At the national level there are six institutions which, together, run the party. Two of them, the leadership and the parliamentary party, we have already discussed. That leaves the National Executive Committee (NEC), the party headquarters, the annual conference and the newly created policy forum.

Celtic Socialism

The Scottish and, to a lesser extent, the Welsh Labour parties have held a symbolically important position in the history of Labour which finds no echo in Conservatism. Keir Hardie founded the party; its first Prime Minister was Ramsay MacDonald. In good days and in bad over the last forty years Scotland and Wales have continued to return Labour MPs in proportions unmatched in England (in 1997 for example, fifty-six of Scotland's seventy-two and thirty-three of Wales' forty were Labour). Even in 1983 Labour secured forty-two Scottish seats – twice as many as the Conservatives, and twenty Welsh seats – almost 50 per cent more than the Conservatives did. In structural terms Scotland and Wales are counted as regions, but the establishment of a Scottish parliament and a Welsh assembly will, as we shall see later, give them far greater autonomy.

Until the referendum on devolution in 1997 the Scottish party owned no buildings, employed no staff, had no members and no leader – all belonged to the national party. By the time of the first elections to the Scottish parliament, however, the Scottish party had built a framework for autonomy, though not without some difficulty. The Scottish Labour party now has a procedure for electing its leader and deputy leader; it is the same as the national party's. The Scottish party will comprise exactly the same components as the national party, with an annual conference (in March) organised by a five-member committee representing conference (three members, including a woman) and the constituency organisations (two members, including a woman), a Scottish Policy Forum, a Scottish Executive committee, mirroring the NEC. The focus of the party will be principally on Edinburgh, not Westminster, though Westminster MPs will be represented on the SEC. One of the SEC's chief early responsibilities was the allocation of seats and list places for the 1999 elections. Dual membership of Edinburgh and Westminster or a local authority is not permitted by the party (allowing for a transitional period). A selection board of fifteen oversaw the selection procedures: five SEC members, five prominent 'independent' members appointed by the SEC and five non-voting advisers. Those not selected had a right of appeal – to a committee dominated by the party hierarchy. Fundamentalists criticised the SLP leader Donald Dewar for treating the structure as if it were his fiefdom.[16] They saw the failure of Falkirk West MP Dennis Canovan to secure nomination for an

Edinburgh constituency as a clear indication of the SLP's following Millbank instructions and ridding its ranks of potential fundamentalist critics. We shall return to this later.

The Welsh Labour party has gone down much the same route as the SLP, though it must be understood that Wales' focus will remain as much on Westminster as on the Welsh Assembly because the powers of Cardiff are in no way comparable to those of Edinburgh. Selections disputes have not been so fierce, though the campaign to elect a leader was hard-fought and, following the subsequent political demise of the successful candidate (and Secretary of State) Ron Davies, Millbank was again accused of interfering to try to ensure that the independent-minded Rhodri Morgan did not secure election. All in all, the recent flourishing of Celtic socialism as a result of the Labour government's devolution legislation has not been unproblematical.

National Executive Committee

The National Executive Committee (NEC) is described in the party constitution[17] as 'the administrative authority of the party', subject to the control and directions of the conference. It would be a mistake, though, to believe that the NEC was ever concerned solely or even primarily with administration, for the constitution also gave the NEC the duty to confer with representatives of a Labour government 'prior to the formulation of legislative proposals'. The NEC, then, has traditionally been a crucial body not simply advising on the formulation of legislation but in deciding the content of the policy package upon which a Labour government would hope to legislate. It was, moreover, the hub of a network of policy advisory committees and so oversaw the development of party policy in the longer term.

Kavanagh wrote that the NEC 'defies any coherent theory of representation'.[18] When the constitution was drawn up it comprised sixteen members, representing the unions, the socialist societies, local trades councils and the treasurer. As women's sections and individual constituency parties developed, so the NEC grew to reflect the new structure. After 1918, these positions were elected by the whole conference (thus effectively decided by the union block votes) and it was not until 1937 that CLPs gained the power freely to elect their own representatives. In reality however the constituencies were represented by MPs. Indeed, for half a century after 1945 MPs provided more than half of the membership of the NEC including nearly all constituency and women's representatives. Cabinet Ministers frequently sat on the NEC and used the NEC as a forum within which to attack the policies of their own government (for example Callaghan and Prime Minister Wilson's trade union reforms, Benn and Prime Minister Callaghan's economic policies).

The position of the NEC in policy matters has traditionally been pivotal, hence the perennial struggle between fundamentalists and social democrats to secure dominance. Nevertheless NEC's influence began to wane when Kinnock established the strategic Shadow Communications Agency in 1986 under the direction of the party's first director of campaigns and communications (an NEC appointment) Peter Mandelson and gave it such a large role in election and public relations strategy. As the red rose replaced the red flag as Labour's symbol in the late 1980s, the NEC became more or less an echo chamber for the leadership, with only Tony Benn and Dennis Skinner providing opposition from the fundamentalists.[19]

The NEC currently comprises thirty-two members: the leader, deputy leader and leader of the European party who sit ex officio; the treasurer; twelve trade union representatives (minimum quota of women: six); six constituency representatives (three women); three government representatives (one woman); three PLP and EPLP representatives (one woman); two local government representatives (one woman); a representative each of the socialist societies and Young Labour; and – potentially – a representative of the Black Socialists Society (depending on the size of its membership). This membership is said to represent the party's 'stakeholders' and its 'key' members enjoy regular meetings with the party leadership in Blair's No. 10 policy unit. The Prime Minister chairs a pivotal Joint Policy Committee including equal membership from the government and the NEC, with responsibility for the 'strategic oversight of policy development … and the rolling programme'.[20] The NEC is also represented on a Joint Campaign and Elections Committee, with strategic responsibility for 'campaigns and message delivery'. To enable the NEC to undertake these newly focused duties, its responsibilities for parliamentary and local government candidate selection and re-election has been devolved to a senior committee. In other words, the leadership has tightened its grip in this key area. Moreover, with their own sections on NEC for the first time, MPs, MEPs and Ministers may no longer stand in other sections.

Despite the curtailing and sharper focusing of its responsibilities,[21] representation on the NEC – and particularly the constituency section – remains an important target for the fundamentalists. There was much rejoicing among their ranks when Ken Livingstone defeated Peter Mandelson in the 1997 elections.[22] In 1998 the leadership ran a powerful campaign, at an estimated cosy of £100,000,[23] to ensure the defeat of the slate put up by the so-called Grass Roots Alliance, whose election leaflet 'Members First' was produced at a cost of £2500. But to no avail: four of the six Grass Roots candidates, including Liz Davies who had earlier been deselected as a parliamentary candidate in Leeds North East by the leadership, were elected on a turn-out of only 35 per cent.[24] As Seyd concluded, apathy rather than docility seems to characterise the new, larger membership.[25] And apathy, so social democrats have always said, is fruitful ground for fundamentalists.

The annual conference

Symbolically the role of conference in the politics of the Labour party was crucial;[26] because Labour MPs represented 'the movement' their role was ambiguously balanced between that of representatives and that of delegates. Moves to control the parliamentary party through the annual conference gained strength after MacDonald's 'betrayal'. In 1937 the leader, Clement Attlee, wrote that conference 'lays down the policy of the party and issues instructions which must be carried out by ... its representatives in parliament ... the Labour party conference is in fact a parliament of the movement'.[27] After he became Prime Minister Attlee had a change of heart but the relationship remained ambiguous. Gaitskell's defeat on the policy of unilateral nuclear disarmament at the 1960 conference was reversed in 1961 and this caused *The Times* to conclude that the party leader had 'exploded the theory that the Party conference is the policy-making body which issues orders to the MPs and their chosen leader'.[28] But Gaitskell did not ignore conference; he overturned the 1960 resolution only through another conference resolution the following year.

There were always three limitations upon the status of conference as a parliament of the party. First, as Gaitskell pointed out to conference *à propos* the nuclear issue, the majority of MPs could hardly be tied to a policy with which they were fundamentally at odds. 'So what do you expect them to do?' he asked delegates, 'change their minds overnight? ... What sort of people do you think we are?'

Second, the unions' block vote. This procedure allows the conference to reach decisions, in Coates' and Topham's words, 'as a confederal organisation':[29] affiliated unions commanded a block of votes that represented the number of members paying the political levy to the party. The 'block vote' originated as a device to thwart the fundamentalists at the TUC conference of 1894 and the practice was carried over into the Labour Representation Committee and hence into the party itself. In 1922 a constituency attempt to abolish the block vote was defeated, the leadership pointing out that it was a small price to pay for the (then) 95 per cent of party funds contributed by the unions. Thereafter the block vote was used to control fundamentalist constituency delegates. The block vote helped to defeat Stafford Cripps and the Socialist League in the late 1930s; it defeated Bevan's left-wing challenge in the 1950s. But when the Campaign for Labour Party Democracy (CLPD) challenged the leadership in the late 1970s the block was no longer solid. The unions had begun to elect a more left-wing leadership but, more important, after 1966 the Labour government had initiated a series of assaults on union autonomy, through incomes policies and trade union reform. For these reasons the block vote ceased to be solid.

The block vote was always open to corruption, and since it traditionally accounted for 90 per cent of the conference vote, this was a crucial consideration. Moreover it gave the major unions a dominant role in party deliberations. In 1992, however, the block vote was reduced to 70 per cent and in 1997 to 50 per cent. Party leaders, who could usually count upon the support of the major unions, were reluctant to abolish the block vote altogether because they were usually able to rely upon the support of the major unions in any dispute with fundamentalist constituency representatives. Only as the party membership grew did leaders feel sufficiently confident to limit block voting. As deputy leader Hattersley once remarked: 'We are not going to get rid of the block vote and find ourselves at the mercies of the constituencies'.[30]

The third limitation on conference's power is that it became far less representative of the movement (and thus less of a 'real' parliament) than it ought to have been. In 1973 the Labour party decided to abolish its list of proscribed organisations, and several groups of activists previously banned entered the party. These new 'hard-left' groups began to coalesce around existing fundamentalist groups. Tony Benn, the acknowledged leader of this alliance, sought to reopen the whole issue of the relationship between the conference and the PLP by attempting to shift the balance of power towards conference and in particular towards the constituency representatives. Through his chairmanship of the NEC's home policy sub-committee he enjoyed considerable influence; indeed he had his eyes on the leadership.[31]

The fundamentalists' first target was to oblige sitting MPs to seek reselection.[32] The conference of 1978, however, voted against giving constituencies the power to deselect their MPs (though only because the Amalgamated Union of Engineering Workers 'forgot' to cast its vote). In 1979, however, mandatory re-selection was reconsidered and passed this time, as was a motion calling for NEC control of the election manifesto, though a motion to allow the party membership rather than the PLP to elect the party leader was defeated. This last setback, however, proved not to be final. Pressure was put upon the NEC to appoint a commission of enquiry to consider proposals for constitutional reform and one of the results was an electoral college, representing all the party, whose function would be to elect the leader and deputy leader.

The leadership hoped that the subsequent conference in 1980, with the major unions playing a key role, would vote down these proposals. But union leaders were no longer able to control their delegations and mandatory re-selection and some form of collegiate election for the leadership were passed, though the proposal to give the NEC control of the party manifesto was lost: union votes were becoming difficult to call.[33] A special conference was held in 1981 to decide on the shape of the electoral college, and the outcome comprised 60 per cent of the college votes shared equally between the constituencies and the PLP and 40 per cent of the votes to the unions. Far from representing an example of party democracy, the whole exercise was Byzantine and divisive. Subsequent attempts by Kinnock, when he became leader, to persuade conference that candidate re-selection should be the responsibility of all constituency members and not the general management committee were defeated, again because the important unions proved unreliable. The struggle had not been about democracy versus oligarchy but about whether an 'unrepresentative grassroots elite [could] seize power from the ruling parliamentary elite'.[34] Labour conferences in this period, for those of the general public who bothered to watch, were not so much a parliament as a pantomime of the party with many opportunities to cry out to party leaders: 'Behind you!'

However, the pendulum was to swing once again. Following the electoral defeat of 1987 the leadership obtained conference support for some sweeping constitutional changes affecting, among other things, conference itself. Most important was the requirement that delegates were to be elected by party members in the constituencies on a 'one-member, one-vote' basis (OMOV). Moreover, constituency delegates were obliged to ballot their members on party leadership and NEC elections before casting their votes at conference. These moves made it much more difficult for well-organised fundamentalist groups to dominate and the consequences of OMOV were soon apparent. In 1991 Gerald Kaufman became the first social democrat MP to be elected in the constituency section of the NEC for sixteen years.[35] In the leadership elections of 1992, moreover, John Smith received 90 per cent of the CLP vote; it is hardly conceivable that activists would have supported him to anything like this extent.

Conference's role as the parliament of the party was further challenged by the proposal to create a National Policy Forum (NPF). The activities of the NPF have decisively curtailed conference's influence on policy-making. Issues that are not within the purview of NPF may form the subject of the one resolution which CLPs and affiliated groups may submit. These resolutions are then sifted by the Conference Arrangements Committee and presented to a delegates' ballot to decide on priorities for subsequent debate. But these debates are not intended to deflect attention from the policy debates emanating from CPF. All in all the modern Labour conference is simply a different animal from the many-headed beast that stalked the television screens during autumn in the 1970s and '80s.

Though Labour leaders would vehemently deny any such thing in public, conference is now under control, for the time being. In the 1998 conference, for example, large coloured screens backed speakers which coordinated with their ties: red for Gordon Brown, green for Peter Mandelson and royal purple for the leader. But for the fundamentalist union leader Rodney Bickerstaff, a disjointed patchwork of conflicting colours provided a 'suitable' context. At the close of conference the comrades used to sing the socialist anthem 'The Red Flag'. By the late 1950s it was clear that few on the platform knew the words and in Wilson's day 'Auld Lang Syne' was substituted for it. Under Blair 'The Red Flag' came back, and all on the platform know the words. Resurgent socialism … or clever stage management?

Faucher's recent study of Labour conferences tends to be more positive, arguing that the new policy-making procedures offer 'genuine possibilities of democratic participation' as ordinary members respond to the opportunities for consultation.[36] But she concedes that the process is a tightly controlled one.

The National Policy Forum

This body, whose establishment was approved in principle by the 1990 conference, originated in the policy review undertaken earlier which exposed flaws in party policy-making procedures.[37] NPF membership comprises the following: fifty-four CLP representatives from Scotland, Wales and the English regions (with five ordinary and one youth representative from each, two of whom must be women); eighteen from the regional Labour parties (two from each, one of whom must be a woman); thirty trade unionists (fifteen women); nine from the PLP (four women); six from the EPLP (three women); eight from the government (three women); three from the socialist societies (one woman); two from the Co-operative party (one woman); four from the Black Socialist Society Conference (two women); nine representatives from local government including the unions (four women); and finally thirty-two from NEC (twelve women) sitting ex officio.

The chief task of this large (175 members) body is to set up and oversee the development of party policy in the so-called rolling programme. It would first establish standing commissions on each of the broad areas of policy: economic, social, educational, health, environmental, democratic and international/security. The commissions operate on a two-year cycle, the first year given over to reviewing existing policies and their context and the second to setting out proposals for developing policy, to be discussed at the relevant annual conference. Branches, CLPs and regions are kept informed of developments and encouraged to contribute. NPF meets twice a year to review progress, and each year it presents a report for inclusion in the general NEC report.

The party claims that the reformed NEC and the new CPF are 'stakeholder' organisations – a New Labour word for truly representative – and so provide a more democratic and participative procedure for developing policy than ad hoc conference decisions. They are also easier for the leadership to contain.

The movement in action

The important task of selecting a parliamentary candidate had traditionally been in the hands of the CLP general management committee whose executive may draw up a short list. These arrangements were to be conducted after consultations with the NEC but constituencies could be their own masters, and until the mid-1980s some selected known supporters of the Trotskyite Militant tendency. However, Kinnock, acting through the NEC, was prepared to overrule local parties regarding candidate selection. As the 1980s wore on the NEC decisively reasserted its power to overrule constituency selections. The idea behind these changes was to bypass 'unrepresentative' activists, and the leadership's best method was to empower all rank-and-file members. In 1993 electoral colleges were abolished and all candidates were chosen by a postal ballot of all members and not by delegates. Since that time affiliated trade unions have lost their role in selection, and only individual members may participate. This procedure applied to all party elections and in 1994 the leadership ticket of Blair and Prescott was elected in this way; indeed all NEC constituency elections were reformed. Commenting on this use of balloting (and it was to be used in policy decisions too – for example Clause Four reform), Tony Blair concluded that the party had 'freed itself from the vanguardism of the eighties'.[38]

At constituency level the party experienced a clash of competing values during the 1980s involving traditional Labour supporters and younger radicals. It would be an over-simplification to identify the radical forces as Militant tendency; there were other groups at work within the constituencies, including the unemployed, tenants, gays and blacks. There was one ingredient binding these radical forces together: a belief in the efficacy of extra-parliamentary activity, a belief that did not endear them to the party leadership. Of these groups only the blacks made specific constitutional demands upon the party: for independent black sections. Black sections were formed in over thirty constituencies in the 1980s,[39] and were given delegates' status on a number of general management committees. The party took a stand against separate black representation and nowadays the Black Socialist Society is guaranteed representation on the NEC if its membership exceeds 2500. After more than five years membership is still counted in the hundreds.

Another perennial problem for the constituencies was infiltration from the far left. Although infiltration, or entryism, was a great cause for concern in the 1980s, it was not new. Neither was militancy among constituency parties generally: in 1930 Sidney Webb said that 'the constituency parties were frequently unrepresentative groups of nonentities dominated by fanatics and cranks'.[40] Later, Crossman observed that the party constitution was designed to 'maintain their enthusiasm by apparently creating a full party democracy whilst excluding them from effective power'.[41]

The party had first acknowledged the existence of Militant tendency in 1975, in a highly critical committee report, but no action followed; indeed the findings were not made public. After the electoral defeat of 1979,

Militant became more active in the crusade to save the party for socialism and in 1982 the party established another committee whose report recommended the expulsion of Militant.[42] Yet the leadership needed active assistance from the constituencies, and this neither Foot nor Kinnock got. Toward the end of 1985 a third enquiry was set up, looking specifically into the activities of the Militant-dominated Liverpool district party. The report roundly condemned a number of alleged Militant supporters by name, calling for their expulsion. By an overwhelming majority the district party refused to comply. Nevertheless in 1986 the NEC established a National Constitutional Committee (NCC) entrusted with the task of maintaining party discipline, in effect hearing cases of members charged with breaches of the rules. In 1988 some 100 Militant supporters were expelled with little or no press coverage. The battle against Militant and the hard left generally was waged vigorously and with no little success but it was a long and tedious battle fought on a wide front.[43]

The youth organisation, as well, traditionally fell regular prey to the extreme left. In 1964 the then Young Socialists had been reconstituted because they were thought to have been controlled by Trotskyists; in the early 1980s the position was broadly similar, with the Labour Party Young Socialists (LPYS) organiser an acknowledged Trotskyist and all fourteen members of the national committee believed to be supporters of Militant tendency.[44] In 1988 the annual conference was cancelled by the leadership and the NEC decided to establish a new youth structure under a National Youth Campaign Committee (NYCC), bringing together LPYS, the Organisation of Labour Students, and young representatives of affiliated trade unions. In 1993 conference established Young Labour, with an upward age limit of twenty-seven. At its inauguration Young Labour had some 23,000 members. By 1999 membership stood at around 30,000 and the organisation of Young Labour, keyed into the overall party structure, has so far proved immune to entryism.

Because of the party's origins in the unions, it was not until 1918 that it became possible under the new constitution to take out direct individual membership. Within ten years there were 215,000 individual party members, and this figure grew to a peak of over 1 million in 1951, declining thereafter. By the 1980s membership stood at 288,776.[45] Falling membership was not the only indication of hard times. There was also a steady decline in the number of paid agents. By the 1987 general election there were only sixty, a number of whom worked in two constituencies. Kinnock's attempts to boost party membership failed but, with the advent in 1989 of a national membership database, he at least knew he was failing. Blair's efforts, in contrast, were initially highly successful: from 1994 to 1997 membership rose from 305,000 to 405,000. Seyd has argued that Blair sought an expanded membership because it was believed that it would counterbalance activist fundamentalism (hence the leadership's championing of OMOV) but, additionally, members are campaigners and fundraisers.[46]

One aspect of constituency politics that made Labour distinctive was its use of women-only short lists. The 1993 conference agreed that women should fight 50 per cent of the most winnable Labour seats and those where Labour MPs were retiring. This decision caused considerable controversy and was dismissed as a gimmick by the Conservatives, and as an attack on their liberty by some male party members especially in the North of England.[47] In 1996 a Leeds industrial tribunal declared that the policy contravened the Sex Discrimination Act (1975) and the policy was discontinued. Nevertheless women-only short lists had already been drawn up by a considerable number of local parties. Others chose women in the normal way. In the event 159 women stood for Labour, and no fewer than 101 of them were successful.

The trade union connection

As we have often had reason to note, the feature that most distinguished the Labour party was its close relationship with the unions. The unions played a very obvious part in the founding of the party, providing both an organisational infrastructure and a social base;[48] but they also had an influence on ideological development, moving Labour decisively away from socialism, making it very much a trade union party and causing MacDonald to refer to the unions as that 'terrible incubus'. The influence of the unions has frequently been decisive in the party's history. It was primarily the TUC's opposition to cuts in public expenditure which brought down MacDonald's government in 1931 and it was the two union leaders Bevin and Citrine who took control of the Labour rump after the 1935 election, through the Joint National Council. Especially important was the Transport and General Workers' Union (T&GWU). One commentator has written: 'The historic role of general secretaries of the T&GWU has been to make or break Labour party leaders. To that end they have often acted with brutal decisiveness.'[49] Though unions leaders expected transformative policies from the Labour party, they did not intend to allow left-wing infiltration to radicalise the party. So secure was the union hold that in 1937 they felt able to agree to an increase in constituency representation on the powerful NEC and to allow these representatives to be elected not by the whole of conference (in effect by the union block vote) but by the constituency delegates themselves.

The demise of the patently undemocratic union block vote should not necessarily be considered a triumph for democracy. It was replaced by a series of smaller block votes often used capriciously. In the 1987 conference, moreover, more block votes were cast than individual votes for Labour in the preceding general election! In 1988 the T&GWU general secretary defeated the leadership's attempt to allow its policy review a free hand in the area of defence by the use of his union's block vote, without bothering to seek the views of his members. He was called a dinosaur by the popular press. All the same, the Labour leader could not dispense with the block vote nor do battle with the dinosaurs until he became confident of support from the constituencies; and they had always been less reliable, from the leader's perspective, than the unions.

Constrained by Conservative laws but even more by the changing nature of employment generally, membership of the TUC has halved since 1979. As we saw in Chapter 5, from Labour's point of view the unions are as much a liability as an asset in electoral terms. From the TUC's point of view, too, the relationship with Labour was bound to change. The areas of expanding employment in recent years have not been within the traditional union strongholds of full-time, male, manufacture but in part-time, often female, service industries where union recognition was spasmodic. Whereas the traditional relationship between Labour governments and the unions was 'voluntarism' – keeping the government out of industrial relations – any new relationship would need, given the changed circumstances, to be based on the creation of a new framework of labour law representing the interests of the 'new' workers. And the best prospect of securing such legislation was via Brussels not Westminster. Thus in 1994 the TUC relaunched itself as a non-partisan pressure group. Several unions began to shift funds away from Labour and into the provision of Brussels offices. The Transport and General Workers' Union (T&GWU), for example, had reduced its funding of Labour by 50 per cent by the 1997 election.[50] The Amalgamated Engineering and Electrical Unions (AEEU), so concerned at Labour's 'pro-middle-class' candidate selections, has diverted funds from the party to promote the candidacy of working people.

This is not to suggest that Labour and the TUC are no longer allies. The party still receives substantial financial support, and in return the government introduced a national minimum wage (if not at the level sought by the TUC) and signed up to the European Social Chapter. But the Fairness at Work legislation, offering a 'framework of decent employment legislation for the 21st century',[51] may well represent Labour's final major repayment on its debt to the unions. As Howell argues, New Labour and the unions now inhabit separate cultural universes. The party has alternative sources of funding and the unions seek to wield influence elsewhere. The rationale for their alliance – one of the decisive ingredients of twentieth-century politics in Britain – no longer exists. 'It is simply not clear', Howell concludes, 'that there is anything that trade unions can offer a Labour government that it both wants and cannot achieve in other ways'.[52]

Brief mention must also be made of the existence of a plethora of socialist intellectual groups, the largest and most formidable of which is the Fabian Society. Founded in 1884, the Fabian has had innumerable illustrious members many of whom have gone on to the highest office. Today the Fabian has an active branch in most cities and publishes a substantial number of books and policy documents. Its influence on Labour policies over the years has been considerable and it has no real counterpart in the Conservative party, or indeed anywhere in the world. In August 1988 a left-wing 'think-tank', the Institute for Policy Research, was established. Modelled on the Thatcherite Centre for Policy Studies, the Institute is funded partly through the Labour party and is sympathetic to its aspirations. Other 'think tanks' such as Demos and Charter 88 have also been influential in the 1990s in shaping Labour thinking. On becoming Prime Minister, Tony Blair sought to secure for himself an intellectual group based upon these and other groups. Two regular contributors from the then dead (but now resurrected) *Marxism Today*, Geoff Mulgan and Charles Ledbeater, joined Blair's advisers.

The party bureaucracy

In comparison with that of the Conservative party, Labour's administrative machine has not been the creature of the party leader. Indeed it has always represented that notion of federalism which has provided the central theme to so much of what has been discussed in this chapter. Whether that federalism is as strong today is an issue that we shall be exploring by considering both the party's head office and party financing.

Head Office

The NEC has traditionally played a key role in the party organisation. Originally it operated through ninety sub-committees overseeing all aspects of party affairs. When he was leader Kinnock and the general secretary of the day managed to reduce this number to fewer than twenty with consequent efficiency savings. One of the new committees, the campaign strategy committee, set up a review in 1984 to consider the structure of party organisation, and its recommendations were acted upon. Traditionally the Labour party headquarters had been characterised by ineffective leadership and an amateurish approach to public relations generally. Many of its electoral campaigns prior to 1987 had been considered failures, none more so than that of 1983.[53] In 1985, however, first fruits of the review, the NEC appointed two key new officers, Larry Whitty as general secretary and Peter Mandelson as head of communications and campaigns. What was needed, it was agreed, was to change the profile of headquarters by shifting resources into campaigning. Headquarters was to give more attention to recruiting and training than to 'serving the constitutional bodies of the party', said the committee. Indeed the committee spoke of the organisation as being less efficient, less adventurous and less flexible than that of the Conservatives. The party's new general secretary was concerned to change the atmosphere of headquarters from neighbourly anarchy to task-oriented professionalism. It is not certain that the NEC knew just what it was doing when it appointed Whitty and Mandelson, but Kinnock knew.

The committee suggested a strategic management structure, which was put into effect in 1986. The resulting structure proved far more efficient if less cosy than its predecessors: the selling of 'socialism' went on to a business footing, with power in the party bureaucracy moving away from the amateur (the politician) and toward the professional administrator. As Mandelson said, the days when a general secretary could declare that Labour would not present politicians 'as if they were a breakfast food or baked beans' were long over.[54] Early fruit of Labour's new approach was the Labour Freedom road show which toured nine holiday resorts in the summer of 1986, giving free (red!) balloons to children and Labour sun visors to parents. A mobile circus with jugglers, tumblers, buskers and magicians – and fire-eaters – spread the message. The new emphasis on packaging and presentation was never more in evidence than in Kinnock's unambiguously presidential-style election campaign of 1987. What Keir Hardie would have made of all this scarcely bears thinking about, but it represented the shape of things to come. To put it bluntly, Peter Mandelson was the shape of things to come.

Eric Shaw has charted the rise of Mandelson through the Shadow Communications Agency, explaining this apparently most unsocialist of phenomena as follows: 'The grim toll of apparently endless electoral defeats … most traumatic of all [being] 1992 … was to precipitate a collapse of morale, a loss of … political and ideological self-confidence … and offer a virtual carte blanche to anyone who appeared to possess the secret of electoral success.'[55] Although its is true that the Agency failed to deliver in 1992 and was disbanded by John Smith when he became leader, it had made its mark. The mark was simply this: parties exist to win elections and they do so largely, as Blumler says, through winning a 'competitive struggle to influence and control popular perceptions … through the mass media'.[56]

In the 1997 election Labour planned its campaign from Millbank Towers, which then became official party headquarters. It was described as 'the most sophisticated, efficient, authoritarian election machine ever used in Britain'.[57] The prize asset was a database of press cuttings, speech texts and the like, known as Excalibur, which served the 'attack and rebuttal' unit. This technology became permanently available to the administration after the election, though the party, at an annual cost of £250,000, could not afford to run Excalibur on a daily basis.[58] Moreover, the high-powered team which had helped to plot Labour's 1997 victory began to break up, especially with the appointment of Margaret McDonagh as general secretary.[59] Headquarters staff was reduced to seventy, morale was said to be low and senior posts were not filled.

Party funding

We have seen the closeness of the traditional relationship between the Labour party and the trade union movement, and nowhere was this more important than in party funding. The unions contributed in a number of ways, with affiliation payments, grants and donations, with the sponsorship of parliamentary candidates and with indirect help such as the provision of resources and personnel. In recent years however, the party has sought successfully to diversify the sources of its funding so as to limit its dependence upon the unions. Justin Fisher has shown the increasing importance of Labour party business plans, which are financed largely by individuals rather than by institutions. Labour has been impressively successful in garnering donations through, for example, 'high-profile dinners'[60] arranged by the Thousand Club: the late Chelsea FC director Matthew Harding donated £1 million. Substantial donations were also received from David Sainsbury, Lord Puttnam, Chris Haskins (Northern Foods), Lesley Silver (former chairman of Leeds United), and – famously – Bernie Eccleston of Formula One motor racing.[61] This is not an entirely new phenomenon. Wealthy men have donated substantially to socialism – William Morris being an excellent early example – but more recently Oswald Mosley, Stafford Cripps and Robert Maxwell exercised generosity to the party. The offices of both Clement Attlee and Harold Wilson benefited from donations, as has Tony Blair's and some of his Ministers'.[62] The loan of over £300,000 from Geoffrey Robinson to Peter Mandelson in 1998 to assist him in buying a house, however, is probably not to be construed as a donation to socialism. Numbers of celebrities such as Eddie Izzard, Lisa Stansfield, Ben Elton and Richard Wilson also donated to Labour. Seven donors were subsequently made life peers; others have been given prestigious jobs.[63] Overall, between the general elections of 1987 and 1997 trade unions contributions declined from some three-quarters to about 40 per cent, and in the pre-election year of 1996 private business donations provided £15 million for the party; standing order payments raised over £10 million.[64] This new funding was diversified and largely predictable.

Estimated annual party income in 1997 was £24 million, an increase of 75 per cent over the previous election. Individual and corporate donations provided 55 per cent (28 per cent in 1992) and the trade unions 40 per cent (66 per cent in 1992).[65] Since 1995 the party has published an annual report identifying all who have donated above £5000. In 1996 there were twenty, in 1997 there were 135. In short, the Labour party is relatively secure financially. Moreover in no area of party activity more than in its financing can we see the transformation that the party has undergone. It is no longer a party financed chiefly by and therefore beholden to the organised working class.

Conclusions

In 1960 the general secretary of the party identified three centres of decision-making within the movement: the parliamentary party, the NEC and the conference. 'None of these elements can dominate the others', he said. 'Policy cannot be laid down: it must be agreed.'[66] The charmingly disingenuous omission of any specific reference to the party leader or the unions notwithstanding, this overview of the party remained generally valid for a further twenty-five years. By then, however, the moles had begun tunnelling and after 1987 the walls of the federalist citadel began to topple. It is probably true that Kinnock, Smith and Blair would not have been able to modernise the party without the support of a membership despairing of electoral victory. Nevertheless it was the leadership that transformed the party, recreating it eventually in its own image. Two processes were at work and, though they may at first seem to be in conflict, were in fact two sides of the same coin: centralisation and the empowerment of ordinary members. As Peter Mair wrote, 'democratisation on paper may ... actually coexist with powerful elite influences in practice'.[67] We have seen how the leadership has sought to control the PLP, and indeed Cabinet Ministers (especially through the head of the revamped Cabinet Office, Jack Cunningham);[68] how it controls policy development through the Joint Policy Committee and the process of policy review; how the wings of the NEC and of Conference have been clipped and the influence of the trade unions curtailed. All in all these changes constitute a minor revolution in Labour party politics. Tony Benn has concluded that these structural reforms will vest 'all effective power in the party ... in a new elite around the leadership'.[69] The strengthening of the political and policy units at 10 Downing Street and the boosting of the Cabinet Office allow Blair an executive authority and strategic grasp that previous leaders would have envied.[70]

The empowerment of ordinary members, however, is potentially even more revolutionary because it overturns one of the collectivist traditions of British working-class politics: delegatory democracy. Delegatory democracy, very briefly, allows ordinary members to participate through attendance at branch meetings at which delegates are mandated to national bodies that decide policy. This was how trade unions worked and how the Labour party was supposed to work.[71] The abandonment of delegatory democracy was a response by the reformers to the 'capture' of the party by fundamentalist activists in the 1970s and early 1980s. What the leadership sought, according to Mandelson and Liddle, was to: 'ensure that the party's mass, grass roots membership, rather than unrepresentative groups of activists, has the greatest say in the agreement of policies and the election of its leaders'.[72] Mair, however, has shown that the empowerment of individual members can often enfranchise those who are 'more likely to endorse the policies (and candidates) proposed by the party leadership',[73] and indeed Mandelson and Liddle conclude their description of Labour's reforms by stating unambiguously: 'the leadership must lead'.

After the revolution comes the post-revolution, a period in which the revolution is either firmly established or overthrown. The modernisers have gone much further in transforming the party than the fundamentalists did in the 1970s. Nevertheless only electoral success will fully establish the New Labour revolution, and that means achieving what no Labour government has ever achieved in Britain (though reformist Labo(u)r governments in Australia and New Zealand have): two consecutive full terms of office. After its 1997 victory the omens are good.

Notes

1. See R.T. McKenzie, *British Political Parties*, London, Heinemann, 1955, pp. 426-31.
2. See 'Changing styles of Labour Leadership', in Dennis Kavanagh, (ed.), *The Politics of the Labour Party*, London, Allen & Unwin, 1982.
3. See Francis Williams, *A Prime Minister Remembers*, London, Heinemann, 1961, p. 535.
4. For an account of this debate, see P.M. Williams, *Hugh Gaitskell: A Political Biography*, London, Cape, 1979.
5. Alan Watkins, *Observer*, 16 November 1980.
6. See Austin Mitchell, *Four Years in the Death of the Labour Party*, London, Methuen, 1984. p. 51.
7. *Guardian*, 4 June 1984.
8. See Ivor Crewe, *Guardian*, 30 September 1983.
9. David Butler and Dennis Kavanagh, *The British General Election of 1997*, London, Macmillan, 1997, p. 49.
10. Jack Brand, *The Power of Parliamentary Parties*, Oxford, Clarendon Press, 1992, p. 48.
11. L. Minkin, *The Contentious Alliance*, Edinburgh, Edinburgh University Press, 1991.
12. *Ibid.*, pp. 262-7.
13. In 1981 four Co-operative-sponsored MPs left to join the SDP.
14. During one debate in Brussels, for example, Leslie Huckfield, who had exhausted his time and thus had his microphone cut off, produced a megaphone to continue his speech. See *Guardian*, 23 November 1984.
15. Hilary Wainwright (editor of *Red Pepper*), in *The Times*, 7 January 1998.
16. *Scotland on Sunday*, 31 May 1998.
17. *Labour Party Year Book 1984-5*, London, Walworth Road, 1985.
18. 'Representation to the Labour Party', in Kavanagh, *The Politics of the Labour Party*, p. 206.
19. Justin Fisher, *British Political Parties*, Hemel Hempstead, Prentice Hall, 1996, p. 47.

20. *Labour Party, Partnership in Power*, London, 1997, p. 8.
21. It was always Blair's intention to reform the NEC as a key to wider reforms. *Guardian*, 1 January 1995.
22. *The Times*, 30 September 1997.
23. *Daily Telegraph*, 26 September 1998.
24. *The Times*, 28 September 1998.
25. Patrick Seyd, 'New Parties, New Politics? A Case Study of the Labour Party', *Party Politics*, no. 4, 1999 (forthcoming).
26. See L. Minkin, *The Labour Party Conference*, London, Allen Lane, 1978.
27. C.R. Attlee, *The Labour Party in Perspective*, London, Odhams Press, 1937, p. 93.
28. See R.T. McKenzie, 'Power in the party: intra-party democracy', in Kavanagh, *The Politics of the Labour Party*.
29. K. Coates and T. Topham, *Trade Unions in Britain*, Nottingham, Spokesman Press, 1980, p. 319.
30. *Independent*, 30 September 1988.
31. See Terry Coleman, *Guardian*, 6 October 1983.
32. Their reasons for doing so are set out in Tony Benn, *Parliament, People and Power: Agenda for a Free Society*, London, Verso, 1982.
33. For example, a member of the Boilermakers delegation, mandated to vote against reselection, chose to be absent when the vote was taken and his union's vote was cast in favour. An AEW delegate changed his mind on the electoral college issue and switched 900,000 votes to the pro-college lobby.
34. Peter Jenkins, *Guardian*, 22 October 1980.
35. *Guardian*, 1 October 1991.
36. Florence Faucher, 'Is there room for democratic debate at British Labour party conferences?' Paper presented to the PSA annual conference, 1999.
37. Eric Shaw, 'A better way to make policy', *New Socialist*, December 1989/January 1990, pp. 30-3.
38. *Guardian*, 1 May 1995.
39. *Sunday Times*, 9 March 1986.
40. Quoted in McKenzie, 'Power in the party'.
41. *Ibid.*
42. *Guardian*, 19 June 1982.
43. *Sunday Times*, 31 January 1988.
44. See *Campaign Guide*, London, Conservative Research Department, 1983.
45. *Sunday Times*, 9 March 1986.
46. Seyd, 'New Parties, New Politics?'.
47. Simon Jenkins described the process as 'evil, profoundly undemocratic'. *The Times*, 27 May 1995.
48. See R. McKibbins, *The Evolution of the Labour Party 1916-24*, London, Oxford University Press, 1977, especially Ch. 7.
49. J. Torridge, *Independent*, 6 October 1988.
50. John Leopold, 'Trade Unions, Political Fund Ballots and the Labour party', *British Journal of Industrial Relations*, **35**(1), March 1997, pp. 23-38.
51. *Fairness at Work*, Government White Paper, London, Cm. 3968, May 1998.
52. Chris Howell, 'From New Labour to No Labour? The Blair Government in Britain. Paper delivered to the APSA conference, Boston, 1998.

53. *Guardian*, 30 June 1983.
54. *Guardian*, 25 November 1985.
55. Eric Shaw, 'The Determinants of the Programmatic Transformation of the British Labour Party'. Paper given at the American Political Science Association annual conference, Boston, 1998.
56. Jay Blumler, 'The Modern Publicity Process', in M. Ferguson (ed.), *Public Communications: The New Imperatives*, London, Sage, 1990, p. 103.
57. *The Times*, 21 April 1997.
58. *The Times*, 26 September 1997.
59. *Daily Telegraph*, 4 October 1998.
60. Fisher, *British Political Parties*, p. 80.
61. *Scotland on Sunday*, 16 November 1997.
62. *The Times*, 22 April 1998.
63. *The Times*, 31 August 1998.
64. Butler and Kavanagh, *The British General Election of 1997*, p. 55.
65. Source: *The Labour Party: Membership, Structure and Finances*, 1997.
66. Quoted in the *Guardian*, 22 October 1980.
67. Peter Mair, *Party Systems: Change: approaches and interpretations*, Oxford, Clarendon, 1997, p. 150.
68. *The Times*, 8 July 1998.
69. Tony Benn, *Tribune*, 3 April 1998.
70. *The Times*, 29 September 1997.
71. Minkin, *The Contentious Alliance*, p. 291.
72. Mandelson and Liddle, *The Blair Revolution*, p. 215.
73. Peter Mair, *Party Systems*, p. 149.

CHAPTER SEVEN

Who are the Socialists?

This chapter leads with a question which many would feel to be inappropriate to the Labour party as we move into the twenty-first century. It is arguable whether the party was ever truly committed to socialism or whether the majority of its representatives or supporters could have been classified as socialists. Nowadays the question 'Who are the socialists?' might prompt the same response as the traditional Scots question 'Wha's like us?' – i.e. 'guy few and they're all deid'. Nevertheless there is no more appropriate form of the question to hand, and so we shall retain it in this traditional form while acknowledging that it is short-hand, and that we are really concerned with those who have represented and supported the Labour party over the years.

The parliamentary party

The Labour party was established expressly to represent organised labour directly in parliament, and so it will be no surprise to discover that in its early years (between 1906 and 1918) no fewer than 89 per cent of Labour MPs came from the working class; indeed even after the party assumed government for the first time the proportion was 71 per cent.[1] The great majority of Labour MPs were workers representing working-class constituencies. But politics is a middle-class profession, and it was always going to prove difficult for Labour to retain such strong links with the class it claimed to represent when the first cohort of MPs began to lose preponderance, especially with the great wave of new MPs who entered the House after Labour's triumph in 1945. To what extent does the party these days represent its original constituency?

The backbenches: social background

Perhaps the first distinctive feature that would strike a student of parties when looking at the post-war parliamentary Labour party (PLP) would be its age profile: it tended to be an older party than its rivals. For example, before the influx of new members in 1997 nearly two-thirds of Labour MPs elected since the war were over fifty. Indeed a typical parliament would comprise more than 20 per cent over sixty. Although the landslide victory of 1966 brought an increase in younger MPs, the safer seats still were held by older members – largely because a safe seat was often the reward for lengthy service to the movement – and so when times subsequently became electorally hard these older, usually working-class members, tended to dominate. The election in 1997 changed all that, at least in the short term. The average age of the new cohort was forty-four, whereas the average age of incumbents was fifty-three; and the new cohort comprised the largest intake by far of new MPs since 1945.

In terms of educational background, around three-quarters of Labour MPs in the inter-war period had been to school only for the minimum period prescribed by the state; in the next thirty (post-war) years less than one-third of Labour MPs were in this category. But a closer scrutiny of the statistics for the whole post-war period reveals a rapid transformation that the averages hide: by the mid–1970s the proportion of Labour MPs with a minimal formal education stood at only 16 per cent. There was no doubt in Mellors'[2] mind that this represented an important shift away from working-class representation. In particular, 'elementary school' children were being replaced by the grammar school/university products, who formed what he described as 'the meritocracy'. Mellors' statistics show that while the proportion of MPs with minimal formal education had dropped from 43 per cent to 16 per cent by the mid–1970s, that of MPs with a university education rose from 34 per cent to 56 per cent. In part this process was the result of a conscious effort by the leadership to improve the 'quality' of Labour MPs. As one Fabian put it, 'With all the education there is about these days Labour must show that its candidates are as well qualified as the Tories.'[3] Even the holders of safer Labour seats – represented by older members, invariably sponsored by a union and almost equally invariably having left school at the earliest opportunity – tended, in time, to be replaced by younger, better educated members. Moreover, around 19 per cent of Labour MPs up to the 1970s had been educated in public school, more than might have been expected.

Moving on now to the 1990s, we can see that the unmistakable 'embourgeoisement' of the party continues apace. While the percentage of public-school-educated MPs has declined to 14.7, the percentage of university-educated MPs has risen to 72 per cent, with a further 16.8 per cent educated at polytechnics or colleges. While the percentage of university-educated Conservative MPs has remained constant since 1945, that for the PLP has more than doubled.

Consonant with the changing educational background of Labour MPs is the changing occupational background. The expansion of graduates has been matched by the expansion of professionals. By 1966 the number of professionals within the Labour party had outstripped that in the Conservative party. By the mid-1970s more than half of Labour MPs were professionals, whereas the proportion of manual workers in the PLP had been more than halved. Mellors characterised this process as the 'displacement of workers by teachers',[4] and we shall be considering this trend in greater detail later. Not only were there more professionals in the Labour party than in the Conservative party by the mid-1970s but they tended to be different kinds of professional. For the Conservatives the armed forces and the diplomatic service formed the core of professional recruitment; for Labour it was law and medicine and – increasingly – teaching. Studies of graduate employment have indicated that it is predominantly the graduate children of manual workers who moved into teaching,[5] and thus the increase in Labour's professionals is another manifestation of the march of the meritocrats. The proportions of this relatively short march are significant: teachers and lecturers have more than doubled their representation since the war. Burch and Moran, tracing these developments after 1983, suggested a modification to this dominant trend, though since the numbers of Labour MPs elected in 1979 and 1983 were the lowest since 1935, they were rightly tentative about their conclusions.[6] Kavanagh pointed out that, after all, the trend towards a predominantly middle-class meritocratic PLP reflected similar changes in society as a whole and was therefore unlikely to be reversed.[7]

Another important feature of the make-up of the PLP during the 1970s and 1980s was the substantial number of trade union officials, 12 per cent. This was a relatively elderly group who did not often go on to achieve office. In many senses they provided a kind of ballast for the PLP. The importance of trade union sponsorship to candidates is clear: the success rate of such candidates since the war has been of the order of 70 per cent, and in the case of the National Union of Mineworkers (NUM) it has traditionally been substantially higher. Originally union sponsorship was a reward for active participation in the affairs of that union, but increasingly it became a kind of status symbol for unions and they would actively compete to sponsor promising candidates.

Since the war, then, the PLP could be said to comprise three principal occupational groups: professionals (comprising two sub-groups: the older-established professions, such as the law or the military, and the newer professions, especially teachers), 'politicals' (i.e. trade union officials, political organisers and researchers and journalists, broadcasters, and publishers) and workers. What we have been talking about is the transformation of what used to be a working-class party into something quite different, and evidence suggests that – Burch and Moran's misgivings notwithstanding – by the mid-1970s that transformation had happened. With the 1992 intake and, more particularly, the substantial new intake of 1997, we are able to confirm the extent of change. The PLP in 1992 comprised 42.5 per cent professionals (in addition, 8.1 per cent were businesspeople), 13.6 per cent 'politicals' and 21.8 per cent manual workers. By 1997, however, 49 per cent of the PLP were professionals, an astonishing 26.8 per cent 'politicals' and only 8.9 per cent manual workers. Those in education, as a separate category, comprised 25.1 per cent of the PLP – almost three teachers for every manual worker. Finally there were more businesspeople than manual workers – more company executives than miners – in the workers' party; indeed the new intake contained as many millionaires as it did manual workers.[8] This New Labour government is less representative of organised Labour than was the Liberal party of Campbell Bannerman and Asquith.

There is another aspect to the 1997 entry that merits some discussion. We saw the steps that the Labour leadership took to increase the number of women MPs. They were successful. In 1983 thirteen Conservative and ten Labour women sat in the House; in 1997 there were still thirteen Conservatives (though not the same ones!) but 101 Labour women. Were they in any sense different in terms of social background to their male counterparts? In educational terms they were hardly distinguishable, but they were somewhat younger: 68.3 per cent were under fifty compared with 53.7 per cent of men. They were even less working-class: a slightly higher proportion had been professionals, teachers and 'politicals' but a lower proportion had been in business. Fewer women had had experience in local government, though they nevertheless formed a majority. In short they were very much like their male colleagues – but even more in the New Labour mould.

The backbenches: ideological background

We need to consider the kind of changes in ideology[9] that might be said to have resulted from this transformation, but we will have to start with the obvious caveat that influxes into the parliamentary party in the years prior to 1997 have not been very great. Even the landslide victory of 1966 brought only sixty-seven new MPs. In 1974 and again in 1979 the party acquired only thirty-nine new recruits and in the calamitous election of 1983 a mere nine. The influx of over seventy new members in 1987, however, did have an ideological impact, though with the party remaining in opposition it was less noticeable.

In terms of ideology MPs from the older-established professions have been traditionally associated with liberal attitudes towards, for example, humanitarian and third-world issues, and by their nature these professions have made it possible to combine careers, perhaps giving a broader perspective to the PLP's political attitudes. The 'new' professionals, though, tended to be full-time politicians and 'much more strongly associated with the wider issues and principles of socialism'[10] than either the traditional professionals or – more importantly – the group which they are replacing, the manual workers. Traditionally the manual workers have been 'strong on the bread and butter issues and more moderate on ideological positions'.[11] So the changing structure of the PLP, according to Mellors, would be certain to have substantial effects upon the party's ideological stance. The former senior backbencher Jack Ashton argued that there was little likelihood of such newcomers making a major impact anyway: 'The House of Commons has been taking in rebels for centuries and most of them turn out just to be rascals. Some will get bought off, some will be sold off, some will end up in the bar, and others will get their heads down and become good constituency MPs.'[12] Rebels however tend to be individuals; Mellors was speaking of a social trend.

Fundamentalist opposition to the parliamentary leadership is as old as the party. James Maxton and the 'Red Clydesiders' brought debates to a halt on occasions in the 1920s by singing 'The Red Flag'. Much later, Tony Benn set out how he saw his parliamentary task:[13]

> I see our job ... as being to use the statute book to redress the balance in a way that allows the bubbling up of socialism from beneath to take place. I see a Labour House of Commons as ... a liberator unlocking the cells in which people live. If you do that, you find you have actually created socialism ...

This was not how the parliamentary leadership saw its task. Indeed Kinnock believed that his job was to bring the so-called soft left round to support him precisely to limit this radical notion of Labour's legislative possibilities. To attempt anything resembling Benn's programme, the party first had to achieve power and that, Kinnock thought, could only be done by defeating the fundamentalists. He was successful to an extent that would have been considered impossible at the time of the miners' strike, and this altered the balance of power in the parliamentary party, perhaps crucially. In terms of the perennial debate between social democracy and fundamentalism, the advances appear to confirm that the social democrats were once again beginning to gain the upper hand. In replacing nationalisation by social ownership as the party's goal (without even referring to Clause Four), Kinnock posted notice of what had been a considerable success for the social democrats. All the same, among the new intake in 1987 was ex-leader of the Greater London Council, Ken Livingstone, described once as the Borgia of the hard left,[14] and a number of other more vociferous if less able new MPs who found Kinnock's leadership too right-wing. The Target Labour Government group declared: 'We are not interested in reforming the prevailing institutions ... through which the ruling class keep us "in our place". We are about dismantling them and replacing them with our own machinery of class rule.'[15] All the same, Kinnock, who had acquired personal kudos from his creditable election campaign, did manage to marginalise the unconvertible in a way that might have proved impossible had Labour won in 1987. (A survey of 121 of the 130 marginal seats in the 1987 general election[16] showed that a Labour government would have been younger, more middle-class, better educated and almost certainly more radical than any of its predecessors: 70 per cent, for example, belonged to the Campaign for Nuclear Disarmament). This is not to suggest that Kinnock experienced no problems as leader of Her Majesty's loyal opposition, as his inability in 1988 to prevent forty-four Labour MPs from defying the party line on the Prevention of Terrorism Bill, with two resignations from the shadow cabinet, indicates.

Kinnock and his allies made a concerted attempt to move the party towards the perceived interests of those whose votes it had lost. At the party conference in 1987 support was given for a wide-ranging policy review which resulted in the publication of *Aims and Values: Statement of Democratic Socialism*. It was this evident shift to the centre-right which prompted Benn and Heffer to contest the leadership and deputy leadership of the Labour party against Kinnock and Hattersley. These champions of fundamentalism were badly beaten in the PLP, the constituencies and the unions. Labour's own research showed the electorate to be less anxious about Labour's policy review than were fundamentalist MPs.

Defeat in 1992 strengthened the leadership's hand still further against the fundamentalists and the PLP was swept along, like much of the rest of the movement, by the Blairite 'project' of modernisation. Nevertheless, as Cowley and Norton have shown, between 1994 and 1997 Blair did not 'lead a party where dissent is rare, or where the prospect of government imposed a discipline of which Government whips can only dream. Rather the reverse ... these rebels are not going to go away'.[17] The authors show that between 1992 and 1996 there were thirty-eight MPs who had dissented from the party line on more than twenty occasions. Cowley and Norton believed that since only a handful of these were to retire in 1997 Blair, with a small majority, would be at risk. They did not envisage a New Labour majority of 179!

Neither did they envisage that Labour's new recruitment process would produce a predominantly middle-of-the-road cohort including no fewer than 101 women. Attitude surveys of the 1997 cohort indicate[18]

a clear and unambiguous shift away from traditional socialist values ... The principle of state ownership of public services was endorsed by ... 70 per cent in 1992 but by ... 48 per cent in 1997 ... moreover the proportion of Labour members who believed that it was the government's responsibility to provide

> jobs fell from two-thirds to one half ... the last five years have seen a significant
> shift towards abandoning Keynesianism and embracing the market economy.

Norris concludes that Blair's project has not been foisted upon a reluctant
party as Cowley and Norton hinted but in fact 'seems to reflect the attitude
and values of most backbench Labour MPs'. And women generally are
among New Labour's firmest supporters.[19] Indeed fundamentalist MP Brian
Sedgemore compared the new intake of women, which we discussed
earlier, to the Stepford Wives with 'chips inserted in their brains to keep
them on message'.[20] From what we saw of their background we would
have expected them to be loyal supporters of New Labour ideology.

Some fundamentalists slipped through the tight selection procedures –
the *Independent* identified seven in the new cohort[21] – hardly enough to
worry the leadership. Nevertheless over eighty MPs signed an early-day
motion opposing the government's cuts in benefits to single parents
(though only nine were women). Forty-seven went on to vote against the
government and a further fourteen abstained.[22] In 1998 thirty-four Labour
MPs voted against the government on an amendment to the Teaching and
Higher Education Bill. Seven of the thirty-four were new members. Twelve
of these MPs had participated in two previous 'rebellions' (on single-parent
benefits and support for air strikes against Iraq), including five new
members. It is unlikely that the Cabinet was shaking at the knees.

Party leadership

Moving up the PLP hierarchy to the Cabinet, we encounter a problem: the
numbers are small because there have been few Labour Cabinets. It would
not be helpful simply to substitute Shadow Cabinets because traditionally
these have been elected by the parliamentary party for a range of reasons
and not chosen by the leader for their leadership qualities, and to that
extent they represent a rather different phenomenon. For obvious reasons
there are no developments between 1979 and 1997 to analyse. Nevertheless, earlier trends were clear enough. The student of parties will
immediately observe that, in Kavanagh's words, 'the higher one ascends the
political hierarchy, the more socially and educationally exclusive it
becomes'.[23] All the same, Labour cabinets traditionally comprised nearly
50 per cent of ministers with elementary education; more than half of
Labour ministers had not been to university though just over 25 per cent
had been to public school. Moreover, 55 per cent were from working-class
families. Many of Labour's 'great names' of the past came from this
background, including its first Prime Minister, Ramsay MacDonald, and
leading members of Attlee's 1945 administration, such as Ernest Bevin and
Aneurin Bevan. More recently that tradition has tended to be eroded, with
Harold Wilson's deputy George Brown being the last senior working-class

Cabinet figure before John Prescott. It was during Wilson's period as leader that the trend of the replacement of workers by meritocrats gathered momentum. When Wilson left office in 1970 only three cabinet ministers came from the working class. It is true that Callaghan's ministry contained four but none was senior. Burch and Moran agreed that there had been a 'changing balance in favour of those who have practised a middle-class profession, at the expense of those who were, at some stage of their adult life, manual workers'.[24] Party leader Neil Kinnock was of working-class origins, though not himself ever a manual worker.

Burch and Moran pointed out that the influence of aristocratic and upper-middle-class families, by way of contrast, has been in decline from pre-war cabinets; since 1970 Labour Cabinets have contained not a single Harrovian or Etonian, not a single aristocrat. Kavanagh, on the other hand, uses the term 'patrician' rather than aristocrat, thereby including upper-middle-class professional families, and in this classification he finds a continuing tradition, including such figures as Attlee, Dalton, Cripps and Gaitskell in the 1940s and 1950s and Crossman, Gordon-Walker, Jay, Benn (and Owen) in the 1960s and 1970s, to which can be added Foot and Williams. It is hard to refute the argument that these individuals were disproportionately influential in the development of the party.

Our attention is drawn by Burch and Moran to what they take to be 'the most striking long-term alteration at the top of the Labour party': the substantial number of those meritocratic Cabinet Ministers who were actually born into the working class but who rose, through education, into the middle class – and often, of course, into the new professions. These meritocrats are the beneficiaries of the improved state education system – the scholarship generation – and include many senior figures, such as Wilson, Kinnock, Hattersley, Shore, Healey, Castle (and Jenkins and Rodgers of course). It is they who ran the Labour party for a quarter of a century before the advent of the Blair project. At first sight this category might appear set to play, as Burch and Moran seem to imply, an important part in the party's long-term future. Indeed, in a sense these leaders might be thought to bring the best of both worlds: to put it crudely, humane working-class hearts and educated middle-class heads. This line of reasoning looks less persuasive on closer examination. The left-wing Labour MP Dennis Skinner has written rather scathingly of the 'smooth-tongued, generally tall, dark, handsome men … percolating and permeating their way around the slag-heaps … and into the miners' welfare to … weave a series of ten-minute speeches out of a concoction of the 1926 strike; the beauty of pigeon and whippet racing … and grandfather's long-cherished pit helmet and safety lamp!'[25] This phenomenon, the ex-working-class meritocrat, is 'of the people' only by ascription; certainly he or she is seldom considered as such by the people themselves. Moreover, the post-1944 Education Act meritocrat has to be part of a 'one-off' generation; he or she is being replaced by second-generation meritocrats, and no future education change is likely to prove as socially profound as the 1944 Act. These men and women, then, are a temporary phenomenon. Perhaps some senior figures in all parties find that a consoling thought.

When Kavanagh analysed the background of the fifty-eight ministers who have held a post in a Labour cabinet since 1964 he concluded that exactly half could be classified as meritocrats, a quarter as working-class and a fifth as patricians. He then went on to ponder the emergence of a definable Labour establishment and concluded that it was possible to discern the emergence of such an establishment 'based on dynastic and kinship ties'. He gives as examples those sons and daughters of former Labour MPs who sat in the 1974 parliament; they numbered nine. 'If we took account', he concludes, 'of MPs who were the sons and daughters of trade union officials, of Labour councillors, or nephews and nieces of Labour politicians, then membership of a political family would emerge as an important factor'.[26] This is no more than an interesting aside: there are no grounds to suggest that these families held any disproportionate sway in the councils of the Labour party, the influence of Herbert Morrison's grandson Peter Mandelson notwithstanding. All the same, each of the three left-wing contenders for the party leadership in 1980 was the product of political dynastic families.

Tony Blair's Cabinet does not have the ideological divisions that bedevilled its Conservative predecessor, yet it does seem to be torn by personal rivalries that might prove equally damaging. Thus although, for example, Mandelson and Brown were both ardent Europhiles, this did not prevent a headline in *The Times* reading: 'Brown Rules Out Single Currency for Life-time of This Parliament', though in fact nothing in the speech which the paper reported seemed to support this statement. The explanation was that the interpretation was the result of a briefing by Brown's press secretary Charlie Whelan attempting to wrong-foot Mandelson.[27] Worse was to follow when, in December of 1998, it was disclosed that Peter Mandelson had accepted a loan of £300,000 from fellow Cabinet Minister Geoffrey Robinson, whose business activities were the subject of an enquiry by Mandelson's own department. It was generally believed that Whelan was involved in the disclosure, though he denied it. In any event it caused Mandelson to resign – a great blow not simply to Mandelson's career but also to the Prime Minister, who relied greatly upon his advice. The rivalry dates from the succession to the leadership after the death of John Smith when Mandelson, unknown to Brown, is said to have kick-started Blair's campaign even during an agreed moratorium.[28] Blair has sought to contain these rivalries by instituting the role of Cabinet 'enforcer' at the head of the revamped Cabinet Office with the formal responsibility to 'cajole departments, co-ordinate policy and initiate cross-departmental action'.[29] The Prime Minister's press secretary Alastair Campbell also acts as a less official enforcer, writing to two Cabinet Ministers for an explanation of why they chose to give interviews to *Woman's Hour* and *The World at One* without clearing them with his office. It is a remarkably controlled environment, said one commentator, when an 'unelected hireling, a mere press officer [can] write to a Cabinet Minister with such peremptoriness'.[30] Coincidentally, both Ministers were later sacked from the Cabinet.

What does set Blair's Cabinet apart, however, is the extent to which the Christian Socialist movement is represented in its ranks. No fewer than eight were members, with others claiming a religious affiliation. This distinguishes the present Cabinet from any in recent times.[31]

All in all, there is overwhelming evidence that the PLP, including the leadership, has become far less of a working-class party in any measurable terms since the war, and the most recent intake of 1997 tends only to consecrate this transformation. As the PLP became more middle-class so it became more ideological, more fundamentalist, until Kinnock sought, with increasing success, to re-establish the social democratic hegemony. With the influx of Blairites in 1997 this process, too, seems to have been consecrated. And if, nowadays, any backbenchers step too far out of line then the Chief Whip will send a report to the NEC and the constituency party that will include all their unauthorised absences and all disloyal votes.[32]

Party members

Labour's constituency activists have always had a reputation for funda-mentalism and, as we have seen, the leadership traditionally sought the support of the union leadership to contain their radicalism. We need to examine whether this assumption has had any foundation.

In a detailed study of Labour constituency parties in the 1960s, Janosik[33] analysed the background of local activism; in many respects, although it was not his intention, he explained the genesis of the problems which came to beset many constituencies in the following two decades. He began by distinguishing between 'strong' and 'marginal' constituency parties. In terms of occupational background, unlike the Conservative party, there was not an overwhelming preponderance of businessmen and professionals, but much more of a balanced mixture, in both strong and marginal constituencies, with a powerful trade union presence, and this had no equivalent in the Conservative party. In educational terms, though, the general pattern was not so dissimilar: the more important the position, the more likely it was to be held by somebody with post-secondary education. In some Labour constituency parties this apparently meritocratic tradition was leavened by a substantial component of manual labourers with a basic state education, and this was particularly true of the 'strong' constituencies. We find the typically 'strong' party in the 1960s to have been led by older men, many of whom were workers without much formal education. As the 1960s turned into the 1970s, an increasing number of these constituencies were to provide easier pickings for determined groups of young well-educated activists than did the marginals.

Although the role of the trade unions in the constituency parties was widely acknowledged to be crucial, especially in a typical safe seat, one aspect of trade union dominance was frequently overlooked: the unions put up much of the money. This meant that in many safe seats the constituency party did not need to engage in fund-raising activities to the same extent as Conservative or Liberal Democrat constituency parties. Fund-raising tends to bring people together, not divide them; it produces camaraderie and, equally important, a formal and an informal network of communications. It is possible that the absence of this kind of continuous communal activity, with specified and attainable goals set periodically, was one of the reasons why Janosik's strong parties did not compare in membership or enthusiasm with many of the marginals.

Janosik went on to consider the political attitudes of his constituency activists and discovered that, on the whole, they were by no means as extreme as was generally depicted. Martin Harrison had earlier drawn attention to the exaggerated contrast between extremist constituency associations and moderate trade unions, pointing to the considerable extent of overlapping membership between the two groups.[34] When asked to assess the party's policies, more than half of Janosik's local activists in both strong and marginal constituencies were generally supportive of the leadership, though around 40 per cent in both were in favour of moving 'slightly to the left'. However, 11 per cent in the marginals favoured a move 'sharply left' as compared with only 2 per cent in the strong constituencies. All who favoured moves to the left thought this would prove electorally advantageous and bring greater unity to the party.

Janosik emphasised the imprint of the socio-economic character of the constituency on the values of local parties, a point that emerges even more forcefully from Turner's study of three London constituencies.[35] Safe Labour seats are almost invariably in stable working-class communities and activists tend to remain associated with the party over a long period of time. 'As veterans in a party that is never threatened by the opposition, they develop routinised ways of dealing with problems ... [and] the party's goals remain unchanged',[36] leading to traditional socialist policies with a strong 'bread and butter' focus being favoured. Marginal constituencies, on the other hand, usually have to contend with a higher rate of mobility and thus a more rapid turnover of personnel with a consequent continuous influx of 'new ideas'. These constituency parties, he says, 'can hardly escape the intellectual jousting and sharp clash of ideas, with the likelihood that ideological splits will be interwoven with personal rivalries'.[37] It is ironic that one of the constituencies which Turner studied was the 'safe' seat of

Bermondsey where 'the crisis threats of an opposition were but memories'. Five years later Bermondsey fell to the Liberals at a by-election. If we remember Turner's analysis of an ageing leadership rooted in 'bread and butter' issues, and bear in mind the overall picture that Janosik built up of such constituencies, we begin to understand how a determined minority of able, better-educated young activists, whose political vocabulary and imagery were more global and more ideological than those of the old guard, could take control of such a seat. After all, the old guard presided over a closed and largely non-participatory system; any change of leadership would represent not a social but a palace revolution. In Bermondsey, though, the old guard hit back and the consequent split allowed the Liberals to win the seat.

What was true of Bermondsey was true of a considerable number of seats in London, Liverpool, Manchester, Glasgow and other large cities. An elderly, often out-of-touch, well-entrenched leadership did little to encourage new members who wished to participate in the constituency's affairs and so, when the palace revolutions came, the old guard could muster little support. Many marginal constituencies, by contrast, made a virtue of necessity and possessed organisational structures that were far more open and more receptive to new activists and new ideas. They, too, were influenced by the move towards greater militancy but were not such easy prey for take-overs. The consequences of these differences became apparent in, for example, the kinds of candidates adopted by the Labour party for general elections in 1979, 1983 and, to a lesser extent, 1987. The fundamentalists won strong representation in many of the safer seats, but in many of the marginals it was soft-left or indeed social democrat candidates who tended to be selected. Collectively these fundamentalist constituency activists and their parliamentary representatives had a much more profound impact upon the party than did their predecessors, especially in securing the constitutional changes which, so they believed, democratised the party, but which the social democrats systematically began to reverse after 1987.

The growth of fundamentalist influence took place at a time when, as Paul Whiteley showed,[38] Labour party membership was falling substantially. Whiteley argued that the failure of the Labour governments of the 1960s to solve the various 'bread and butter' problems that affected many traditional supporters had a disproportionate effect upon working-class activists. These men and women had been motivated to join the party by what Whiteley called instrumental aims: for example, to provide ordinary people with better social services. The predominantly better-off and better-educated, by contrast, had been motivated by more 'diffused and generalised' considerations when becoming active: for example, to build social justice. The instrumentally motivated would clearly be more likely to become disenchanted by what they considered to be the failure of their party in government, whereas the more generally motivated would be likely to take a longer perspective and probably be more concerned with the next and not the last Labour government. The difference was really between those who thought instrumentally and those who thought ideologically. In some respects this difference corresponds to that between social democrats and fundamentalists.

Equally important, said Whiteley, the working-class activists began to find themselves at odds with a party that was becoming increasingly middle-class and ideological. Whiteley did not take much account of additional factors differentiating the middle- and working-class activists alluded to above. Nevertheless we can hardly disagree with his conclusion: 'Thus a small articulate group of middle-class activists may paradoxically drive out working-class activists.'[39] It is not at all clear why Whiteley considered this to be a paradox.

It was not until the late 1970s that the general shift towards the left produced fruits, and we have already looked at most of these. As far as the constituencies were concerned, mandatory reselection of MPs was clearly the most important. In January 1981 the Campaign for Labour Party Democracy produced a booklet entitled *How to Select and Reselect Your MP*. This booklet contained an analysis of how every Labour MP had voted in eleven divisions so that a judgement could be made of the extent of their socialist commitment. It also listed the names of MPs who had signed the statement organised by the social democrats opposing the outcome of the Wembley special conference of January 1981 on the fundamentalists' programme of constitutional change. Only eight MPs were de-selected in this first round (for 1983), though a number of those who joined the SDP were certainly 'jumping before they were pushed'. Criddle gives brief accounts of the de-selection of the eight which tell much the same story:[40] that of a 'take-over' by groups of left-wing ideologists – 'public sector middle-class activists – caricatured as "the polyocracy"'. One de-selected MP in East London was specific, blaming his defeat on 'the bed-sit Trotskyists from the North East London Polytechnic, the usual lefties, community relations officers, people who have only been in the party a few years'.[41] Denis Healey was moved to declare his opposition to the replacement of MPs by 'professional ideologues', but others painted a rosier picture of the new fundamentalists who, in alliance with the traditional 'sources of resistance and radicalism', would become an important force in British politics.

Of the various groups of ideologists who helped to 'fundamentalise' the Labour party in those years, driving out working-class activists as it did so, none received more attention than the Militant tendency. We have already considered the impact of Militant upon the party organisation; its effects, real and symbolic, upon the constituency parties have been equally profound. The Militant tendency was nationally organised, with a ruling central committee (many of whom were members of the Labour party), with, so it was claimed, about 200 full-time workers – approximately the same number as Labour[42] – and a regional and district structure. The movement published not only *The Militant* but also a number of papers aimed at specific groups of workers, such as *Militant Miner*. One of its principal objectives was to infiltrate the Labour party and the trade union movement. It enjoyed a considerable measure of success particularly in the north-west of England, more specifically in the Liverpool district party. As we have seen, the Labour party was sufficiently concerned to establish three major enquiries into the activities of Militant and, as a result of the third, to take action to expel Militant supporters from the party. The principal charges against them were that they were in breach of the constitution in belonging to a party-within-a-party and that in achieving their influence, for example in Liverpool, they acted in a grossly irregular manner, by the 'swamping' of delegate meetings by unelected members, selective notification of meetings, false accounting of membership and, most serious of all, intimidation of ordinary members.

After the 1987 election the NEC established new procedures for dealing with Militant supporters. The NEC annual report for 1988 showed that membership of the Militant tendency was sufficient, if proven, for expulsion. More general was the charge of 'sustained course of conduct prejudicial to the party', though again, if substantiated, this also incurred expulsion. Equally important, the NEC successfully intervened to prevent a number of fundamentalist prospective candidates from standing for local election, some of whom unsuccessfully sought protection from the courts. But it was not all plain sailing. Militant and hard-left activists were able to devote themselves full time to politics because numbers of them were employed by neighbouring councils. Most famous of these was the Militant deputy leader of the Liverpool council, Derek Hatton, who was employed by the neighbouring Knowsley council. The Widdecombe report uncovered 'a web of patronage' in which up to 200 councillors in London, nearly all Labour, were provided with jobs in neighbouring authorities which enabled them to be full-time politicians at ratepayers' expense. In Glasgow almost one-quarter of the council was employed by the Strathclyde region.[43] The fundamentalists, including Militant, were well entrenched.

The steps taken after 1987 halted the flow of Militant influence and the reassertion of control by the leadership, through the NEC, began to have an increasing effect. What is not so often acknowledged in Labour circles, publicly at least, is the defeats inflicted on fundamentalist activism by the Thatcher government. It was Thatcher's resolve (and perhaps even more their own strategic incompetence) which led to the defeat of the miners in 1985 and the subsequent loss of influence and prestige of Arthur Scargill; it was the Thatcherite press which exposed the so-called extravagances of 'loony left' local authorities and the Thatcher government which confronted them through rate-capping. What Kinnock and his advisers, and later Smith and then Blair, sought to do subsequently was to limit the influence of 'unrepresentative' fundamentalist activists by both strengthening the centre and, as we have seen, moving from delegate democracy to representative democracy, thereby giving the greater say to the party rank-and-file.

But are the rank-and-file of the parties any different nowadays? The most detailed study of Labour party members in recent times was undertaken by Seyd and Whiteley.[44] Their findings reinforce everything that we have observed regarding the 1970s and early 1980s: the changing character of local parties, especially in the inner cities, from a situation in which, according to Goss, the local party was part of the local community, a 'centre of social and political life',[45] to an increasingly middle-class group divorced from the local community. Labour party members at this time were disproportionately male (61 per cent), disproportionately middle-aged (average age forty-eight) and middle-class (only 26 per cent were classified as working-class). Although over half (58 per cent) had only the minimum state education, 29 per cent held a degree. Seyd and Whiteley found a 'very sharp divide' between these two groups.[46] Almost two-thirds of Labour members held a public sector job in local government, the local health authority or college, or a public corporation. Manual workers, in contrast, comprised only a quarter of members. On the other hand 70 per cent of this patently middle-class-dominated group considered themselves to be working-class. Seyd and Whiteley concluded: 'The "new model" Labour party of the 1990s may perhaps be in danger of becoming too responsive to the demands of the affluent radical rather than the poor proletarian,'[47] and thus further excluding working-class membership. In all respects, at any rate, the party membership was substantially more middle-class than the voters.

Given their self-ascribed class status, it is not surprising that 66 per cent of them thought that the struggle between capital and labour was the central issue in British politics. (What they would have made of the fact that their security passes at the 1998 conference advertised the Somerfield supermarket chain is not difficult to guess.) Indeed they exhibited a strong commitment to what the authors describe as four socialist touchstones: they believed in public ownership (71 per cent wanted further nationalisation), they were strong defenders of the legitimacy of trade unions, they were sceptical about the benefits of defence expenditure (66 per cent were unilateralists) and, almost unanimously, they believed in high public expenditure even at the cost of higher taxation. Yet the local parties were atrophying at an even faster rate than the working-class communities in which they were located. The downgrading of local government, the changes in the party structure were leaving the local party 'increasingly "de-energised", an organisation in which members are increasingly passive rather than active, disengaged rather than engaged'.[48]

Kinnock's plans to increase rank-and-file membership as a balance to 'unrepresentative' activists had failed, but Blair's did not. Despite the dispiriting picture that Seyd and Whiteley painted, by the time of the 1997 election the Labour membership attracted more new members than the entire membership of the Liberal Democrats, from whom it regained a number of ex-SDP members, including several ex-Labour-ex-SDP MPs. The average age of new members was thirty-nine. Over 62 per cent of new members were under forty-five and just under half were women. The largest single age category were the under twenty-sevens – a group that Seyd and Whiteley had felt obliged to write off – and thus members of Young Labour. The bulk of these, according to Mandelson and Liddle, were 'university-educated and professionally employed, as much in the private as in the public sector'.[49] (A survey of new members showed that 47 per cent described themselves as professional, 25 per cent as retired, 9 per cent as students, 9 per cent as unemployed and – significantly – only 10 per cent as manual workers). No doubt the party took comfort from the fact that 60 per cent of new members came from the Midlands and South of England.

A significant factor in the growth of membership was certainly the change in method of applying. Previously, to become a member one made written application. The application was then scrutinised by the branch before being formally endorsed by the management committee. Normally one would have to be a member of a trade union. 'The system', say Mandelson and Liddle, 'seemed designed to keep people out rather than recruit them'.[50] By 1995 a national membership scheme was in place which allowed people to join directly, for example by simply answering a newspaper advert. Prescott promoted a 'recruit a friend' campaign which was responsible for 28 per cent of new recruits. Less successful has been individual recruitment from the affiliated trade unions, though if other forms of membership continue to grow it is hard to see Labour leaders being too disappointed at this.

Mandelson and Liddle refer specifically to changes in the way that New Labour perceives local government. With more local councillors than ever, they say, the days of 'loony left' councils are over.

> In London (for example in Lambeth), and in Liverpool, Manchester and Sheffield and many other cities where problems previously existed, there has been a sea change in attitude among Labour councillors. Where once they were out of touch ... they are now pragmatic and innovative ... involving the local communities ... advocating close partnership with the private sector, and prepared to take tough decisions ...[51]

It is not easy to disentangle the confusion of ideas here, which conflate innovation with representation, involving local communities with involving the private sector and so on, but a more serious criticism is that the authors fail entirely to address the reality of that 'other' Labour party represented, for example, in the traditional Labour heartland of the West of Scotland or the West Riding of Yorkshire. In these and other parts of the United Kingdom, Labour operates almost as a one-party state and charges of corruption and nepotism are more rife today than ever. And when the party in London seeks to discipline these rebellious outposts they earn the abuse of the locals: they are the modernisers, the Millbank apparatchiks, the Blairites, the class traitors. Unlike in other parts of the country, in these areas Labour was not all-but-destroyed in the 'bad days' of the early 1980s.[52] With only the briefest of interludes Labour has been running John Prescott's Hull, for example, untroubled, since 1935: a typical city council membership would comprise fifty-eight Labour councillors, one Conservative and one Liberal Democrat. The Hull Labour party, like many others in Scotland and the North of England, was not 'saved' by the New Labour knights-in-shining-armour. While such areas are not, by and large, in the pockets of hard-left fundamentalists, they remain proudly Old Labour. The voting turnout in the local elections in Hull in 1998 was 18 per cent: not much sign of the green shoots of a New Labour revolution here. Labour had 10,417 councillors in 1998,[53] the bulk of whom came from its heartland. Bearing in mind that party activists have been estimated to number some 70,000[54], the importance of Old Labour councillors should not be underestimated. According to Marqusee this group, which he calls the 'constituency Left', remains anxious to build support behind the party's traditional commitments to full employment, progressive taxation and strong union links, for example, thus fitting in with Seyd's and Whiteley's earlier findings.[55]

In the elections for the NEC in 1996, although the average vote for the leadership's NEC slate was 81,500, the Socialist Campaign group's slate received a healthy 42,000. A number of Old Labour's heroes continued to outperform New Labour hopefuls in NEC elections. Dennis Skinner, Ken Livingstone and Diane Abbott always record strong support. The following year, as we have seen, Livingstone defeated Mandelson, and one year later four of its slate of six constituency representatives were elected. So the fundamentalists may be down but they are not out.

To pick up on a point made earlier, the constituency Left shares its fortresses with some less salubrious companions. In 1997 the NEC suspended the entire Doncaster district party for corruption and abuses of privilege.[56] The government's plans for a major shake-up of local government is largely aimed at ending the apathy, incompetence and corruption which are so often bedfellows in these one-party states. Yet the task is not easy. In Blair's own Sedgefield constituency, for example, three elderly Labour councillors were deselected. One, a seventy-two-year-old with twenty years experience was replaced by a young female trans-sexual. They complained of New Labour 'ageism'.[57] However, during 1998 the Labour party conducted enquiries into 'irregularities' in Glasgow, Paisley,

South Tyneside, Doncaster, Birmingham, Coventry and Hackney.[58] In Hull the police investigated the expenses of one councillor who, in his year as Lord Mayor, managed a civic hospitality bill of £342,000 – double the previous mayor's bill.[59] Clearly the work had to be done.

Labour voters

Karl Marx was absolutely convinced of the eventual political triumph of the working class, given universal suffrage, and he was equally convinced that the triumph of the working class would be synonymous with the triumph of socialism. Other commentators expressed a similar view more prosaically, pointing out that Labour had only to mobilise its natural class support to win every general election. It has been clear for some time that this is no longer true; in any case, Labour has seldom managed to do so in the past. We have already discussed some of the more important reasons for this failure in a previous chapter but a general point needs to be made here. The history of the Labour party, over nearly a hundred years, shows that the preponderance of party support, organised labour, was not strictly socialist: Hardie's description of their ideology was 'labourism'. However, until the Labour governments of the 1960s a clear identity of interest existed between socialism, labourism and the interests of the working class in general. Each camp, for example, would have supported policies designed to promote greater equality. This was because a very substantial section of the population considered itself underprivileged; indeed, enough to vote in a Labour government. But to the extent that the Labour government of 1945 actually succeeded in creating greater equality, it diminished its bedrock of natural, instrumental support (i.e. those who saw it as being in their interests to vote Labour). The interests of the recently elevated no longer necessarily coincided with those who remained underprivileged; they now have something to lose and so their votes cannot be taken for granted. The interests of a generally better-paid, fed and housed workforce are not necessarily the same as those of the unemployed. A Labour government committed to egalitarian policies will therefore not necessarily be representing the interests of the majority of workers.

In Chapter 4, other factors were considered which tended to loosen Labour's hold on the working-class vote: the success of Thatcherite Conservatism in representing 'populist-authoritarian' values which, research tells us, are considered important by the majority of ordinary people. Labour's policies on these issues were not shaped by the perceived interests of the working class but by humanitarian considerations or simply by socialist ideology. All parties will feel morally obliged to pursue policies that they consider to be 'right' even if the electoral consequences are damaging in the short term. But if they are wise they will ensure that the damage is limited by a comprehensive explanation of what they are doing and why; if they are wise they will listen to what those whom they claim to represent have to say; if they are wise they will also pursue policies favourable to their supporters. A party which purports to speak for the mass of ordinary people must, when it is departing from their perceived interests, take care fully to explain why it is doing so.

The Labour party, in the 1970s and 1980s, moved increasingly away from its traditional voter without taking any of these precautions. In his report to the annual conference in 1982, for example, general secretary Mortimer said: 'It is not the party's policy, but public opinion, which needs to be changed. No socialist worthy of the traditions of the Labour movement should refuse, on occasions, to go against a strong current of public opinion if ... he believes that such a course is necessary for the purpose of social progress.'[60] The election manifesto of 1983 which Mortimer helped to prepare produced what Butler and Kavanagh referred to a 'spectacular retreat' from Labour among working-class voters: only 38 per cent of manual workers and 39 per cent of trade unionists voted Labour, while 32 per cent of trade unionists voted Conservative. Moreover, as Kellner demonstrated, many who did vote Labour did so in spite of and not because of party policy.[61]

A failure to persuade the working class to support it was highly damaging to Labour but, to return to a point made earlier, partly as a consequence of the success of the Attlee government in building a platform for comparative prosperity in the 1950s and 1960s, the working class – 47 per cent of the electorate in 1964 – had shrunk to 34 per cent by 1983, whereas the middle class had grown from 36 per cent to 51 per cent in the same period.[62] Some commentators calculated that by 1987 Labour's 'natural' constituency comprised no more than 37 per cent of the electorate and was still shrinking.[63] Kinnock and his advisers, especially Mandelson and Philip Gould, realised that although the loss of some of its natural constituency was a blow, recapturing the working–class vote would never again be enough to secure electoral victory. Defeat in 1987 only strengthened their conviction. When he became leader Kinnock signalled his intentions to broaden Labour's appeal to voters by 'gaining votes from the home owners as well as the homeless, the stable family as well as the single parents, the confidently employed as well as the unemployed, the majority as well as the minorities'.[64]

Despite what was widely acknowledged to have been a very effective campaign, Labour was defeated in 1992. Nevertheless that election did something to reverse the regional trend through which Labour secured strong support in 'the North' (Scotland, Wales and the North of England) and the Conservatives in the South. In fact the Conservative vote declined in the South and rose in the North (by 2.5 per cent in Scotland, for example). This was generally explained as constituting a response to economic experience: unemployment had actually fallen in 'the North' and risen in 'the South'; house prices had been fairly stable in 'the North' but, after a spectacular rise in the late 1980s had fallen far and fast in the South-east. Nevertheless Labour failed to reap the full benefit of the ailing economy. In 1992 the only social groups in which Labour enjoyed a clear lead over the Conservatives were council house tenants and the unskilled working class (social classes D and E), Scots and the Northern English. Nevertheless the party substantially improved its share of the professional and managerial classes (A and B) and among homeowners, and also gained more votes among the skilled manuals (C2), though it still narrowly trailed the Conservatives in this important group. Finally in 1992 not only did Labour secure the support of fewer women than the Conservatives did but the Conservative lead had actually doubled (to 8 per cent). All in all, then, despite its disappointment in defeat, Labour had gained what Butler and Kavanagh called 'a modest reversal of the long-term [regional and social] pattern that dates back to 1959'.[65]

In 1997 Blair spectacularly reversed Kinnock's failure, making gains among classes A and B (up 9 per cent), and massive gains among the crucial C1 and C2 classes (up 15 and 19 per cent respectively). The party also gained among homeowners (up 11 per cent), actually overtaking the Conservatives (41 per cent to 35 per cent) for the first time ever. Moreover Labour also overtook the Conservatives in terms of support among women. The party made significant gains in all age groups save the over sixty-fives. That these changes reflected a great disillusionment with the Conservatives[66] rather than a new-found love of Labour must be acknowledged, and the great amount of tactical voting is a sure indication of this. Butler and Kavanagh point out that Labour's share of the vote (43.2 per cent in 1997) was lower than that secured by Harold Wilson, after thirteen years of Conservative rule, in 1964 (43.4 per cent) - yet Wilson's majority was not 179 but only five. They conclude that it is therefore too soon to see 1997 as a 'realigning election' but we should want to add that 1997 shows very clearly that Labour can win seats across the whole social and regional spectrum; that voters do not generally fear a Labour victory, and in that sense if no other this election marks a watershed: the long-term trend dating back to 1959 has been reversed. Gaitskell, Crosland, Kinnock and Smith - and for that matter the Gang of Four - could consider themselves vindicated: voters were willing to support a reformist programme run by a party leadership which, for the time being anyway, had routed the fundamentalists. In terms of its supporters, this was indeed a New Labour party.

Conclusions

Accounts of the death of the Labour party, common enough between 1959 and 1992, seem to have been proved much exaggerated. The party is in power with a larger majority than ever before; indeed with such a large majority that commentators speak of second and even third terms of office almost as a matter of course. This chapter has presented a picture of an evolving party, a party that came into existence to redress the balance of parliamentary representation in the interests of organised labour. In so far as it won the votes of ordinary working people the infant Labour party destroyed much of the base of support for the old Liberal party. Whether it would have managed to replace the Liberals without the decisive split which that party endured during World War One is open to doubt, but in the event it did replace the Liberals. However, since its halcyon days of 1945–50 the Labour party has slowly become less of a people's party in terms of those who represent it, those who are active on its behalf and those who support it in the polling stations. The drift towards a middle-class, public sector-dominated party with a more fundamentalist socialist ideology gathered pace during the 1970s and early 1980s, but it found little support in the polls and indeed suffered a series of defections from social democrats who left to found their own party. From the low point of 1983 when Labour received a smaller percentage of the vote than at any time since 1918, modernisers brought the party back towards the centre and, as we have seen, consciously aimed at making Labour more acceptable to all voters. In making the party less of a class-based party Labour came more and more to resemble the Liberal party it was created to replace. The people of Blair's New Labour party in parliament appear to form a party of the centre or even centre-right but the party activists retain more of Labour's traditions. Blair's attempts to build up a mass-membership party, initially very successful, have foundered. His opponents in parliament, and more so in the constituencies and in local government, wait for him to fail. If his government continues to enjoy wide support they may be won over or indeed leave the party, as Arthur Scargill did to found the Socialist Labour party. But if Blair should fail then his ideological opponents, to whom he and his fellow modernisers are little better than traitors, will exact revenge. Fukuyama notwithstanding, social democrats should not be over confident that they have reached the end of the historical confrontation with the fundamentalists, though at the turn of the millennium they are clearly in the ascendancy.

Notes

1. See Dennis Kavanagh, 'Still the workers' party? Changing social trends in elite recruitment and electoral support', in his edited *The Politics of the Labour Party*, London, Allen & Unwin, 1982.
2. Colin Mellors, *The British MP*, Farnborough, Saxon House, 1978, p. 50.
3. Quoted *ibid.*, p. 51.
4. *Ibid.*, p. 74.

5. R.K. Kelsall *et al.*, *Times Higher Educational Supplement*, 25 February 1972.
6. Martin Burch and Michael Moran, 'The changing British political elite', *Parliamentary Affairs*, **38**,(1) Winter 1985, pp. 7-8.
7. Kavanagh, *The Politics of the Labour Party*, p. 103.
8. *Sunday Times*, 4 May 1997.
9. A useful general account of ideological developments within both parties, but especially Labour, is David Judge's *The Parliamentary State*, London, Sage, 1993.
10. See S.E. Finer, H.B. Berrington and D.J. Bartholemew, *Backbench Opinion in the House of Commons 1955-59*, London, Pergamon, 1961, pp. 104-14; and H.B. Berrington, *Backbench Opinion in the House of Commons 1944-55*, London, Pergamon Press, 1963, pp. 7-8.
11. Mellors, *The British MP*, p. 120.
12. *Sunday Telegraph*, 20 July 1986.
13. T. Benn, *Parliament, People and Power*, London, Verso, 1992, p. 70.
14. *Independent*, 27 October 1987.
15. *Sunday Telegraph*, 20 July 1986.
16. *The Times*, 30 July 1986.
17. Philip Cowley and Philip Norton, *Blair's Bastards: Discontent within the Parliamentary Labour Party*, Hull, Centre for Legislative Studies, 1996.
18. Pippa Norris, 'New Labour, New Politicians?', in Pippa Norris and Geoffrey Evans, *A Critical Election: British Parties and Voters in Long-Term Perspective*, London, Sage, 1999, ch. 2.
19. Libby Purves, *The Times*, 2 December 1997.
20. *The Times*, 7 February 1998.
21. *Independent*, 2 May 1997.
22. *The Times*, 12 December 1997.
23. Kavanagh, *The Politics of the Labour Party*, p. 100.
24. Burch and Moran, 'The changing British political elite', p. 10.
25. Quoted in Mellors, *The British MP*, p. 78.
26. Kavanagh, *The Politics of the Labour Party*, p. 103.
27. *Sunday Telegraph*, 26 October 1997.
28. *Sunday Telegraph*, 11 January 1998.
29. Mary Ann Sieghart, *The Times*, 2 July 1998.
30. Libby Purves, *The Times*, 31 March 1998.
31. *Sunday Telegraph*, 30 March 1997.
32. *The Times*, 27 May 1998.
33. E.G. Janosik, *Constituency Labour Parties in Britain*, London, Pall Mall Press for the Foreign Policy Research Institute, 1968.
34. Martin Harrison, *Trade Unions and the Labour Party since 1945*, London, Allen & Unwin, 1960, pp. 238-9.
35. J.E. Turner, *Labour's Doorstop Politics in London*, London, Macmillan, 1978.
36. *Ibid.*, p. 313.
37. *Ibid.*, p. 314.
38. See Paul Whiteley, 'Declining local membership and electoral support', in Kavanagh, *The Politics of the Labour Party*, pp. 111-34. See also his *The Labour Party in Crisis*, London, Methuen, 1983, especially ch. 3.

39. *Ibid.*, p. 123.
40. Byron Criddle, 'The election locally', in D. Butler and D. Kavanagh, *The British General Election of 1983*, London, Macmillan, 1984.
41. *Ibid.*, p. 123.
42. *Ibid.*, p. 223.
43. *Sunday Times*, 22 November 1987.
44. Patrick Seyd and Paul Whiteley, *Labour's Grass Roots*, Oxford, Clarendon Press, 1992.
45. S. Goss, *Local Labour and Local Government*, Edinburgh, Edinburgh University Press, 1988, p. 20.
46. Seyd and Whiteley, *Labour's Grass Roots*, p. 33.
47. *Ibid.*, p. 37.
48. *Ibid.*, p. 202.
49. Peter Mandelson and Roger Liddle, *The Blair Revolution*, London, Faber & Faber, 1996, p. 216.
50. *Ibid.*, pp. 218–220.
51. *Ibid.*, p. 220.
52. *Ibid.*, p. 229.
53. It is unfortunate that Seyd and Whiteley had not been able to differentiate between regions in their party membership analysis: there would have been some interesting comparisons.
54. Colin Rallings and Michael Thrasher, 'The 1998 local election results and democracy', *Talking Politics*, **11**(1), Autumn 1998, pp. 37–42.
55. Mike Marqusee, 'New Labour and its Discontents', *New Left Review*, no. 224, 1997, pp. 127–42.
56. *Ibid.*, p. 131.
57. *Daily Telegraph*, 2 August 1997.
58. *Sunday Telegraph*, 22 November 1998.
59. *Sunday Telegraph*, 2 February 1998.
60. *The Times*, 11 March 1998.
61. K. Roberts, F. Cook and E. Semeonoff, *The Fragmenting Class Structure*, London, Heinemann, 1977, especially ch. 9.
62. Quoted in D. Butler and D. Kavanagh, *The British General Election of 1983*, London, Macmillan, 1984, p. 278. The original is in italics.
63. Peter Kellner, *New Statesman*, 23 June 1983.
64. A. Heath and S. MacDonald, 'Socialist change and the future of the Left', *Political Quarterly*, **58**(4), October–December, 1987, pp. 364–77.
65. Butler and Kavanagh, *The British General Election of 1992*, London, Macmillan, 1992, p. 62.
66. *Ibid.*, p. 279.
67. Butler and Kavanagh, *The British General Election of 1997*, London, Macmillan, 1997, p. 251.

CHAPTER EIGHT

The Middle Ground?

We have spent three chapters on each of the major parties but will be dealing with the Liberal Democrats in one single chapter. This lack of proportion is due to the obvious fact that, whatever part the party may play in the future of Britain, it has played only a minor role in its immediate past. Lloyd George was the last Liberal Prime Minister almost seventy years ago. However, since the 1960s the Liberals have enjoyed a revival, or series of revivals, which has made them once more a force to be reckoned with, especially in local government. Moreover, their alliance with the SDP in 1981 was potentially the most important development in British politics since the advent of the Labour party. If we wish to recount the history of the Liberal Democrats we had better start where all good stories are supposed to start, at the beginning. The difficulty in this case is that there is no clear beginning. Some would want to begin with the founding of the Alliance in 1981, others to go back to the Orpington by-election victory of 1962 when the Liberals showed that the post-war two-party system might not be as permanent and unshakeable as it had appeared. On the other hand, the Liberal party did not spring to life in 1962: indeed, as we discovered in Chapter 1, 1862 would be nearer the mark.

The Liberal party

There is an unbroken thread connecting the Whigs of Charles James Fox, Grey and Russell, through the Liberals under Gladstone and Lloyd George, through the recharged Liberals of the 1960s under Jo Grimond, through the Alliance party of the 1980s, to the Liberal Democrats of today.

Historical development

The Liberals were one of the two great parties of state until 1918. Their sudden decline, the result of a variety of developments – especially the rise of a Labour party better geared to serve the interests of the industrial working class – has been famously accounted for.[1] More directly damaging, however, was the split between Asquith and Lloyd George. The former was party leader and Prime Minister at the outbreak of war in 1914 but the Conservatives would participate in a wartime coalition only under the leadership of Lloyd George. When the latter sought to continue as leader of a peacetime coalition in 1918 he refused to endorse Asquith's supporters who were consequently forced into opposition. Lloyd George in effect broke the Liberal party. 'Dazzled by his own light', said Simon Jenkins, 'he could not see the darkness until it overwhelmed him.'[2] In the face of this irreparable split the party ceded its position as the main anti-Conservative force to Labour in the inter-war years, and Labour's dominance was endorsed by the great victory of 1945 when the Liberals returned only twelve MPs on 1.9 per cent of the national vote. Worse was to follow: in 1950 only nine Liberals were elected and no fewer than 319 deposits were lost. In 1951 and again 1955 there were six Liberals in the House of Commons, elected by around only 1 per cent of voters, and the so-called 'strange death of Liberal England' seemed almost complete. But it did not happen. As the Conservative governments of Eden and Macmillan became unpopular so the Liberals prospered. Derided as a Celtic fringe party, they broke out of their familiar territory with the spectacular by-election victory over the Conservatives in the safe London suburban seat of Orpington. The Conservative vote fell by 18 per cent and the Liberal vote increased by no less than 31 per cent. It was a stunning victory. For the next thirty-five years the Liberals and their successors would garner protest votes with assiduity and increasing tactical nous, though predominantly from unpopular Conservative governments. They were often dismissed by their opponents as ideological scavengers, feeding off the votes of the disgruntled, rather than as representing something that might be called a Liberal tradition.

Liberal ideology

Those who make this claim, however, do not trouble to substantiate it. Even a cursory glance at the history of Liberalism shows it to be somewhat wide of the mark. The Liberal party has a long and on the whole honourable history in British parliamentary politics. Drawing from the philosophical traditions that originally gave them shape, the Whigs and later the Liberals were concerned with the nature and practices of the constitution. Though in many other respects Liberalism can be seen to have changed over the years, with Manchester Liberalism and Lloyd Georgian Liberalism exhibiting almost polar-opposite economic policies, for example, a concern with the protection and enhancement of civil liberties through the constitution has been constant. And this tradition has marked modern Liberal Democracy just as clearly as it marked the Alliance and the Liberal party of Grimond and Steel. It has been, in fact, not simply a prominent but a distinguishing feature of the party, setting it apart from the Conservatives for whom constitutional issues were taken as more or less settled and from the Labour party which traditionally sought a strong central state capable of creating and managing socialism. The Liberal Democrats' concern for constitutional reform and civil liberties did much to set the agenda of change in Britain in the 1990s.

Constitutional reform is not the only debt that Liberals and Liberal Democrats owe to their tradition. They have also been shaped by the forces that emerged in the 1890s. The political currents of the late Victorian period included three distinct but generic traditions on the centre left: the radical liberal, the social democratic and the fundamentalist socialist; distinct but not separate because of overlapping support. There was a fluidity regarding political allegiances at the time, with new groups forming and reforming almost continuously.[3] There were, for example, the 'new Liberals' who claimed to speak in the interests not so much of the traditional nonconformist middle class as of the industrial working class. They argued strongly that the state ought to be prepared to intervene in the economy in the interests of the individual liberties of all citizens. About the same time as the new Liberals were changing the contours of liberalism, socialism was beginning to establish itself. There was much in common between the movements, not least the friendship between the leading members. Indeed several leading Fabians attempted to form a common group with leading 'new Liberals' in 1891, though without success. All the same, collaborative undertakings of an intellectual nature did occur, such as the Rainbow Circle,[4] including Hobson and Herbert Samuel for the Liberals and Ramsay MacDonald and Sidney Olivier for the socialists. The Liberal magazine *The Nation*, declaring that left-wing liberalism merged imperceptibly into socialism, believed that the way ahead would be charted by adherents to a broad progressive platform that it called social democracy.[5]

As time passed clear differences of approach appeared among these various progressive forces, but the most serious separated not socialists from liberals but fundamentalist socialists (of both ethical but especially scientific varieties) from social democrats and radical liberals. The scientific fundamentalists, in contrast with the social democrats (and liberals), had great faith in bureaucratic expertise: it was Beatrice Webb who said that socialism ought to be bureaucratic, bourgeois and benevolent. Hobson, a radical liberal, on the other hand, condemned all socialism that did not represent an expression of popular will, whereas the (especially scientific) fundamentalists were ready to define socialism as what the people needed not what they wanted. The real division was essentially over the proper relationship between political élites and public opinion, and the social democrats were on the side of the Liberals and not that of the fundamentalist socialists. 'It is better to give [the people] what it wants than something "technically better" which it does not want.'[6]

Within a comparatively short time the Liberal party was to cease to be a major force, and social democrats, and indeed many former Liberals, were to join the ranks of the Labour party. But the Liberal tradition lived on, if at times precariously, and it continued to develop its ideology. The Liberals believed in a society in which the individual was able to participate in the decisions which shaped his or her own life; the attempt to build such a society was an essentially radical exercise.[7] But it was more than radical; it represented one of the basic tenets of traditional liberal faith: man's rationality. Jo Grimond argued that men are bound by a common rationality; for him it takes the form almost of natural law. 'What is destructive', Grimond went on, 'is the untimely submission of our will simply to what we are ordered, without any consideration of whether it is right or wrong.'[8] The objectives of Liberalism and Liberal Democracy are not dissimilar to those of John Locke: the creation of opportunities for men and women to become self-directing responsible persons. 'Certainly it is impossible to make men self-directing responsible citizens', says another Liberal writer. 'They must do this for themselves. But society can create opportunities for them to become so, and encourage them to take them.'[9]

Liberal ideologists were never happy with the label of 'centrists', or middle-of-the-roaders. 'By any strict language Liberals are the true Left, the real progressives', said Elliot Dodds.[10] Donald Wade rejected the whole idea of a left–right spectrum based merely on attitudes to public ownership; for Liberals it was more important to measure from libertarian values to totalitarian (more commonly authoritarian) ones, and in terms of this classification the extremes of left and right (in standard terminology) fused into each other. There were only two senses in which the Liberal party was unequivocally centrist: first, its attitude to the 'public versus private ownership' debate was entirely pragmatic, and second, it enjoyed substantial support from the middle classes. Liberals supported the nationalisation of coal and opposed that of steel, they supported the sale of council houses in some areas and opposed it in others. As for middle-class support, it was after all chiefly this sector which sought to become 'self-directing, responsible citizens': that is, to participate.

Participation became the keyword of modern Liberal policies, and it stood in contradistinction to the bureaucratic élitism of fundamentalist socialism and the social élitism of conservatism. But equally important to the understanding of modern Liberalism was the context of participation. At the grass roots that context was provided by the community. Community is defined as a group of individuals with something in common: nationality, neighbourhood, religion, work, workplace, victimisation.[11] Community politics for the Liberals was both a means and an end. It was a means of creating a less unequal society superior to the fundamentalist socialist's public ownership, and it was an end in so far as giving as many citizens as possible a say in the decisions affecting their lives was a goal of traditional liberalism. Liberals rejected the notion of class politics, claiming that Labour discouraged the political participation of ordinary people and that the trade union movement stood in the way of their industrial participation.

The implications of participation were by no means limited to the context of community politics, however. Participation was a basic ingredient of the policy of decentralising government, of giving more not fewer powers to democratically elected local authorities, of inserting a regional tier into the British system of government which would require devolving executive powers to assemblies in Scotland and Wales. Above all, Liberals sought to encourage participation through a fairer electoral system. Although they had long supported reform and it fitted well into the ideology of participation, Liberals realised that they themselves would be the principal beneficiaries of a proportional system of voting: it would be likely to guarantee them an important role in local, regional and national politics.

The Social Democratic party

As we have seen, liberalism was not the only political tradition that looked to the individual or the community for political progress; social democrats within the Labour party had similar aims. However, with Fabians and ex-Fabians dominating the Labour party, faith in the state rather than the community came to characterise the party in power. Given the collapse of the Liberal party, there were good reasons for social democrats to remain within Labour and to continue the struggle for control of party policy-making. Writing before the end of the 1974–79 Labour government, Peter Jenkins[12] drew attention to the divisions between the social democrats and the fundamentalists, and he argued that these social democrats wished to transform their party into a northern European-style social democratic party. Jenkins suggested that their success would depend upon Denis Healey becoming party leader after Callaghan, a development he thought likely at the time. He assumed, that is to say, that the struggle would take place, as it always had, *within* the Labour party.

We know that it did not. Michael Foot won the leadership election and the party subsequently lurched to the left. In January 1981, three leading social democrats, Shirley Williams, David Owen and William Rodgers, together with Roy Jenkins, a former Cabinet Minister, left the party and promulgated their Limehouse Declaration, establishing the Council for Social Democracy and promising to set up a new party before Easter 1981. Having withdrawn from the protective shell of the Labour party, it became necessary for the Social Democrats to make some ideological justification of their position and it fell to their most experienced politicians to do so. Roy Jenkins had already set out the stall in the 1979 Dimbleby Lecture in which he appealed to all non-fundamentalist socialists and progressives to recognise certain realities of modern politics. He took as his starting-point the ossification of the British party system and the deleterious effects, especially on the economy, of adversarian politics. He argued that the two great parties were coalitions but that no real community of interests existed within them any longer. All that remained was the original structure – locked, as it were, in ice. He argued for the building up, through a proportional electoral system, of 'living' coalitions. He dismissed the counter-arguments that such coalitions could not provide the effective and coherent government which the first-past-the-post system (however unfairly) tended to produce: 'Do we really believe that we have been more effectively and coherently governed over the past two decades than have the Germans … ?' Jenkins argued that Britain suffered from an inability to adapt consistently, together with too great a capacity to change inconsistently. 'The paradox is that we need more change accompanied by more stability of direction.' To this end it was necessary to 'harness the innovating stimulus' of the free market and yet avoid the 'brutality of untrammeled distribution of rewards' or indeed the indifference to unemployment. Jenkins clearly saw a role for state intervention, but his social democratic state was to be important, not omnipotent – it 'must know its place'. As well, market forces would be used, but were clearly insufficient left to themselves.

It was important, wherever possible, to devolve decision-making, giving parents a voice in the school system, patients a voice in the health system, residents a voice in neighbourhood councils, and so on. Social Democrats would be unequivocally committed to end the class system but had no wish to replace it with a brash meritocracy. Above all Jenkins believed it to be necessary to involve in politics at a variety of levels the considerable number of people alienated from the business of government; only their engagement offered a guarantee against extremism of right or left. The three ex-Labour ministers, Owen[13], Rodgers[14] and Williams[15], wrote at length along lines similar to those of Jenkins. Their principal concern, too, was to re-establish a sense of community involvement in politics. 'A true democracy', Owen claimed, 'will mean a progressive shift of power from Westminster out to the regions, to the county and town halls, to communities, neighbourhoods, patients, tenants and parents.'[16] Like Owen, Williams found the British economy dominated by over-large corporations. Wherever possible she argued for 'the need to strengthen the structure of self-government at lower levels'.[17] Most of the nation's problems, wrote Williams, are better tackled by involving 'the community'.

The rise and rise of the Alliance

Given the ideological thrust of Liberalism it soon becomes apparent that the SDP had more in common with modern Liberals than the hastily contrived alliance of the 1980s might suggest. More important to Alliance strategy was the fact that both parties were firmly committed to electoral reform. The constitutional impact of electoral reform would be likely to produce coalition or minority government and to weaken party domination, with voting in the House less easily controlled by the whips and with backbenchers consequently seeing their parliamentary careers more in terms of active membership of committees than of party loyalty. Parliament, as a consequence, would become a much more important body and its select committee system far more competent in terms of scrutinising government policy and eventually perhaps of actually helping to shape policy. With a weakened party system and a strengthened committee system, the pressure for more open government would be much more difficult to resist and a change in the nature of the relationship between backbenchers and the civil service might well ensue, thus affording better protection for the individual citizen (another traditional liberal aim). In short, given time, a proportionately representative House of Commons could revolutionise British parliamentary practice.

The ideological rationale for the Alliance was strongly reinforced by electoral self-interest. Since their first major postwar by-electoral triumph at Torrington in 1958, the Liberals secured an average of 23.3 per cent in by-elections during Conservative governments, yet they managed only 14.6 per cent under Labour governments.[18] By and large the Liberals simply could not win enough working-class votes to make a sustained challenge to the major parties. No wonder the Liberals supported the idea of alliance with the SDP. It might enable Steel to fulfil the vision he had inherited from his mentor and former party leader Jo Grimond: a non-socialist realignment of the centre-left. For more than six months in 1981–82, popular support for the Alliance registered over 40 per cent continuously. However, the Labour MPs who joined the SDP were, with few exceptions, defeated by Labour at the general election of 1983. The replacement of Roy Jenkins as SDP leader by David Owen in 1983, however, introduced a rivalry between the leaders, which made the possibility of greater unity less likely. For the Liberals the Alliance initially brought the expectation of additional working-class support – but not enough, it transpired, to make a major breakthrough in terms of seats won. Nevertheless, it was a close-run thing: in 1983, though ineptly led, divided and generally unpopular, Labour held on to its heartland – just about. The Alliance (26.4 per cent) failed to overtake

Labour (27.0 per cent) in public support, though it came agonisingly close. Worse, it returned only 23 MPs in contrast to Labour's 209.[19] David Steel's lengthy 'sabbatical' from political life immediately after that election told its own story.

The Alliance: decline and fall

By 1987 two developments were beginning to shape the Alliance. At ground level most though not all Liberal and SDP local groups were cooperating fully and acting more or less as a united party. Joint open selection of candidates took place in seventy-eight constituencies and, in a further sixty allocated to the SDP, Liberals were permitted to share in the selection process. At the leadership level precisely the opposite happened. Owen's position was becoming increasingly clear; he firmly opposed the growing local cooperation as 'merger by the back door' and Owen, from start to finish, opposed merger. From the first, Owen's preferred strategy had been an electoral pact with the Liberals with one prime objective: electoral reform. Thereafter there would be simply no need for the parties to merge. By the time of the general election, far from announcing a new kind of politics, the Alliance partners were bickering. Meanwhile, under Kinnock, Labour had won back most of its defecting voters, so that far from bringing to the Alliance cause numbers of disenchanted working-class voters, the SDP could be characterised as a predominantly middle-class Home Counties party: it had more members in the borough of Camden than in all of Yorkshire.

Bearing this in mind, it is not surprising that the Alliance election campaign of 1987 was a comparative failure. In securing 23 per cent of votes cast and returning twenty-two MPs, the Alliance did less well than in 1983. More significant than the results, though, was the obvious failure of the 'dual leadership' strategy. After all, the Alliance claimed to be offering the voters something new – partnership. And partnership proved to be a hostage which fortune seized with both hands. It is fruitless to ponder whether a single leader would have proved a greater electoral asset. Given the deep divisions, to call for a single leader would have been to whistle down the wind.

Steel's call for merger discussions immediately after the election came like a bolt from the pink. The Alliance had failed; its support had slumped in working-class seats, and so the original rationale for two parties in tandem had collapsed. Henceforth they would be competing for middle-class votes unless they combined. When they took place, however, the merger negotiations proved to be such a charade of ineptitude that David Steel felt obliged to resign as Liberal leader. The first merger document was immediately rejected by the Liberals and was disowned by its architect – 'as dead as John Cleese's parrot', said Steel. A fresh team of negotiators was rapidly assembled and a new, less radical document was prepared. Together with a proposed constitution, it was put to both parties for a final decision. At a special meeting held in Blackpool in 1988 the Liberal party voted for merger by a huge majority (2099 to 285). At Sheffield a week later the SDP council also voted massively in favour (273 to 28, with 49 abstentions). The merger proposals were finally put to the membership of both parties and were duly endorsed by both, though only 52 per cent of Liberals and 56 per cent of Social Democrats bothered to vote.[20] Finally in March 1988, almost nine months after the election, the Liberal and Social Democratic parties merged to form the Social and Liberal Democrats (SLD).

The Owenite SDP lived on, however, causing considerable confusion in the public mind and splitting the already diminished third-party vote. The SDP showed itself to be capable of taking sufficient votes to deprive the SLD of the sorely needed stimulus of electoral success. At Richmond in Yorkshire, a by-election in 1988 allowed the Conservatives to hold on to the seat, though their majority was reduced from 19,000 to 2,000. The combined votes of the two 'third parties' (the SDP was in second place) was hugely greater than the Conservative vote and a young William Hague was the beneficiary of their inability to combine. He was the last Conservative candidate to win a parliamentary by-election for a decade. Support for the SDP began to decline thereafter and when, in 1990, the party was overtaken in a by-election by the Monster Raving Loony party, Owen wound the party up, ending a remarkable episode in British politics.[21]

In the meantime the SLD had become engaged in a leadership contest. By the closing date only two candidates, the Liberal MP for Yeovil, Paddy Ashdown, and the Liberal deputy leader Alan Beith, had declared themselves. No former SDP candidate stood. The election campaign was a relatively quiet affair that Ashdown won decisively. His first major test as leader was the European elections of 1989; they were disastrous. The SLD received only 6 per cent of the vote whereas the Green party won 15 per cent. The party was demoralised and near bankruptcy. Ashdown had to turn around the fortunes of this seriously ailing party before the next election and one step was to rename the party the Liberal Democrats. (Polls revealed that some three-quarters of the population got the party's name wrong when asked.)[22] At the Conservative party conference in 1990 Mrs Thatcher likened the party to (another!) dead parrot. One week later the Liberal Democrats took Eastbourne from the Tories, overturning a majority of 17,000. Within a month Mrs Thatcher's premiership came to an end while the parrot went on to another famous victory, at Ribble Valley, the thirteenth-safest Tory seat. By the time of the general election the party was in good fettle. The 1992 general election result (20 seats won) could hardly be represented as a triumph but it was hardly a failure either. After the general election, however, the party gained four stunningly successful by-election victories at the expense of the Conservatives and benefited from the defection of Conservative MP Emma Nicholson.

Ashdown built on this foundation. The Liberal Democrats enjoyed unexampled success in the years of Tory decline. In 1993 the party won at least a share of power in twenty-eight of the thirty-six English county councils and made substantial gains in the districts. Their gains in Scotland and Wales were far less impressive: the main beneficiaries of the Tory decline here (apart, obviously, from Labour) were the Nationalists. However, across the United Kingdom as a whole the Liberal Democrats had become the second party of local government, with more councillors than the Conservatives and controlling four times as many councils. In the European elections of 1994, too, the party had enjoyed its first successes, winning two seats and coming close in five others. Parliamentary by-elections in winnable seats boosted morale and the additional four seats, together with two Tory defections, gave the parliamentary party twenty-six members, more than at any time since the heady days of the Alliance in the early 1980s. Party membership had passed the symbolically important 100,000 and party finances were on a relatively sound footing. Although opinion polls consistently showed a national decline of around two per cent in support, party strategists (who had already opted for robust targeting of winnable seats in 1992) targeted for the next election in a manner described by Butler and Kavanagh as ruthless.[23] Regions and constituencies with poor prospects saw a migration of resources for even their basic functions towards targeted regions and seats.[24] Most of headquarters' support in the forthcoming election was to be concentrated on fifty seats, of which twenty-nine had full-time agents; only one other seat had a full-time agent. All in all, and for very good reasons, the party approached the 1997 election in good heart.

The Liberal Democrats and the end of equidistance

In 1995 party leader Ashdown announced that his party would not be prepared to prop up a minority Conservative government after the next election, thus heralding the demise of the traditional stance of equi-distance[25] according to which the Liberal Democrats were no further in policy terms from the Conservatives than from Labour and so in principle could work with whichever of the major parties had secured most seats after an inconclusive election. Ashdown now declared: 'People must know that if they kick the Tories out through the front door, we will not allow them to sneak in through the back door ...' His theme was clearly spelt out: Britain's future success depended upon the defeat of the Major government and '... every vote for the Liberal Democrats is a vote to remove this Conservative government and the policies they stand for'. The concept of equidistance was therefore unambiguously jettisoned. How great a change was this?

The historic function of the Liberal party in the twentieth century, as articulated for example by Lloyd George in the first election of 1910, had never been to hold an equidistant position: it was to provide a non-socialist radical alternative to Conservatism. When, some fifty years later, Jo Grimond was helping to re-establish the Liberals as a major national party, he called not for equidistance but for a realignment of the left much along Lloyd George's lines, adding significantly that he 'didn't give a tinker's cuss' what a realigned party should be called. Later still, after the 1992 election, David Marquand (then a Liberal Democrat) argued that the party should have 'come clean' to the voters: it was a left-of-centre party and should not have masqueraded as an equidistant centre party. (He has subsequently chosen to rejoin a party that is now pleased to be considered a centre party.)[26] The problem for the Liberal Democrats in 1992 was exactly what it had been since 1950: it professed a preponderance of left-of-centre policies but in the main was supported by disgruntled centre and right-of-centre voters. The Liberal Democrats may well have needed then, as they have since, a Labour victory to have any hope of sharing power, but they continue to rely now as then principally on defecting Conservative support for the electoral successes which would provide the basis on which they could bargain with Labour about power.

It is true that in the 1950s agreements had been reached, in Huddersfield and Bolton, through which Liberals and Conservatives allowed each other a free run against Labour opponents; true also that in the 1987 election one of the Alliance leaders, David Owen, made clear his belief that a post-electoral arrangement with Mrs. Thatcher's Conservative party was perfectly plausible: but by and large for the whole of the century the Liberals, the Alliance and the Liberal Democrats were not located equidistantly between the two major parties. In 1974 the Liberals refused to make a post-electoral arrangement with Heath's Conservatives despite their having received most votes at the previous election, though in 1978 they were willing to keep a minority Labour government in office.

Why should Ashdown signal the end of a policy that had never really existed? To abandon the myth of equidistance was, for Ashdown, to signify a change in the ideological or policy stance not of the Liberal Democrats but of the other parties.[27] The party sought to build on this notion of having marked out its independent position by publishing in 1995 the Liberal Democrat Guarantee, which boldly advocated a programme of increased government spending and a measure of public ownership. In the Littleborough and Saddleworth by-election later that year the Labour party denounced the Liberal Democrats as a high-spending, high-taxation party. Indeed, from assuming the leadership Blair had launched 'an all-out assault on the Liberal Democrat party, laying claim to the Liberal tradition of

Keynes and Beveridge'.[28] When the pro-Labour *New Statesman* advised Labour supporters to vote tactically and support the Liberal Democrats, it drew an extraordinary storm of invective on its head from the leadership. However, in the by-election the Liberal Democrats stuck to their guns: taxation was the price of a civilised society, they claimed. And they won.

In abandoning the myth of equidistance the Liberal Democrats signalled a move not towards Labour but to the left;[29] they also suggested that there were no longer fixed referents in modern British politics. By attempting to 'fix' the party's policy referent, however, Ashdown was able at least to retain the prospect of coming to some arrangement with Labour after an inconclusive election without alienating that considerable section of the party which would have opposed any post-election move towards Labour. He was also able to pursue an active policy of engagement with Labour before the 1997 election. One of the fruits of this was the Cook-Maclennan Report on Constitutional Reform that set out the programme which, to some extent anyway, the Labour government subsequently followed. The programme for Scottish and Welsh devolution was agreed (though the Liberal Democrats were far from happy at the narrow range of powers being promised to the Welsh Assembly). Agreed as well were the creation of a new London authority; the establishment of regional Development Agencies in England; proportional representation for the Scottish, Welsh, European and London elections; a Human Rights Bill; a wide-ranging Freedom of Information Bill; and an independent Commission on reform for Westminster elections. This represented a wide legislative programme, all of it traditional Liberal Democrat policy, to which both parties were committed.

Party organisation

The history of Liberal Democrat organisation is necessarily short and recent. Its most noteworthy features are the distinctive federal structure, unlike that of other major parties, and the absolute commitment to participative politics. In practice the Liberal Democrats, following on the much older traditions of the Liberal party itself, declare a positive commitment to enmesh their philosophy of participation within the formal organisational structure of the party. They claim to do this[30] in the following general ways: the tradition of one member one vote for the party leader (later copied more or less by Labour and later still by the Conservatives) and president; the genuinely representative quality of the parliamentary party; the representation of both genders on all decision-making bodies; the use of proportional representation (Single Transferable Vote) in party elections; a commitment to subsidiarity (the taking of decisions at the lowest level consonant with general party efficiency) through decentralisation to the state parties, the regional and local parties. We shall examine the party organisation with this as our general frame of reference.

The party leader

Leaders of major parties can deflect the task of representing the party to other influential and preferably photogenic leaders: thus even as forceful and dynamic a leader as Mrs Thatcher could confidently defer to other party leaders such as Tebbit or Parkinson. Liberal Democrat and formerly Liberal leaders have rarely had that opportunity. It is true the Alliance had two photogenic leaders, but they sometimes found it so hard to agree as to suggest that domination by a single individual is not the worst fate that can befall a party. The leader of the Liberal Democrats is elected by all members of the party, and an election is called when the incumbent seeks it; on the death or incapacity of the leader; if the leader loses his or her parliamentary seat, or resigns or declares the intention to do so; when a majority of members of the parliamentary party passes a vote of no-confidence in the leader; or when the party president receives a requisition calling for an election signed by seventy-five local parties. A leadership election may be called on the first anniversary of a general election and every year thereafter, though so far this has not happened. In short, a Liberal Democrat leader is in the job till death, incapacity, resignation, loss of support, or loss of his or her seat. Until such time, a party leader enjoying a favourable public image has considerably greater influence in the affairs of his or her party than even the leaders of the major parties. Activists have frequently said somewhat archly that the best way to discover their party's policy on an issue is to listen to Ashdown on the television; exactly the same criticism was made of Steel, Thorpe and Grimond in their respective days as leader. It is an interesting paradox that in a party dedicated to maximising participation, leaders from Grimond onwards have had a reputation for dominating their parliamentary colleagues and party structures.

Parliamentary party

The leader of the party is *ipso facto* leader of the parliamentary party, of which everyone who takes the Liberal whip is automatically a member. The parties in both the Commons and the Lords may (and do) appoint in addition chief whips and deputy leaders. The party in the European Parliament consists of only two MEPs, who have joined the 52-strong Liberal Democrat and Reformist group.

In 1994 the Liberal parliamentary party in the House of Commons took a new approach to the organisation of their parliamentary responsibilities.

The party moved away from the idea of individual MPs seeking to shadow Ministers in government departments to a system of shared responsibility within a number of teams, sub-committees of the parliamentary party covering wider areas of parliamentary activity. The intention was to increase the level of flexibility within the parliamentary party and to improve the party's collective effectiveness within the House.

David McKie argued that the modern parliamentary party compares unfavourably with more colourful predecessors, when the Commons was graced with Liberals of genuine public stature such as Jo Grimond, Jeremy Thorpe, David Steel, Clement Freud and Cyril Smith, not to mention David Owen, Roy Jenkins and Shirley Williams in the days of the Alliance. It is almost certainly the consequence of a style of candidate selection which tends to reward local service and hence to produce, in McKie's words, a 'sound but pedestrian parliamentary party'.[31] The parliamentary party suffered its own crisis of discipline when in 1992 David Alton resigned the whip over the issue of abortion. Although he returned to the fold in 1993 he ceased to play any active role in the party's affairs.

Under the Conservative governments the party in the House of Commons sought to establish itself as an independent party of opposition which opposed the government on issues of principle but not 'for the sake of opposition'. This position was frequently derided both by the government and by the opposition, and in no issue-area more than in Europe, where both parties attacked the Liberal Democrats for inconsistency. In fact Europe offers the best example for exploring both the party's consistency and the justice of its claim to operate a policy of 'principled opposition'. The Liberal Democrats earned the government's displeasure when the party supported a Labour amendment to provide that the United Kingdom's representatives on the new consultative committee of the regions should be elected by local authorities and not nominated by government. The government was subsequently defeated, despite support from the Nationalists. The party earned Labour's displeasure when, in November 1992, the government, with Liberal Democrat support, won by three votes a paving motion to proceed with its Bill to legislate on the Maastricht Treaty. Defeat for the government, said Labour, would have led to a dissolution. The Liberal Democrats earned further Labour opprobrium when the party supported the government on the European Communities Finance Bill in 1994. Labour had proposed an amendment not to sanction any increase in the United Kingdom's contribution to the EU budget 'without action by the government to curb fraud and waste in Europe'. Again the Liberal Democrats accused Labour of opportunism and the government secured a comfortable majority of twenty-seven.[32]

Although neither the government nor the opposition would agree, it is possible to discern the consistent application of 'principled opposition' in these three examples. The parliamentary party, it can be argued, followed party policy and not electoral advantage. 'Principled opposition' under the Conservatives grew into 'constructive opposition' under Labour. Ashdown and four of his senior colleagues sat on a Cabinet committee concerned with constitutional reform, and at the end of 1998, formal cooperation between the two parties was extended to issues of European defence and foreign policy. A plan to expand cooperation into the spheres of health and education, however, was dropped. This kind of limited opposition fits the party's traditional rejection of adversarialism, but it has earned the opprobrium of Liberal Democrat backbenchers who feel inhibited about attacking the government. When, for example, the Conservative censure debate on the government's policy of cutting single parents' allowances began in December 1997, there were only three Liberal Democrats in the chamber and, when the vote was finally taken, the party supported Labour.[33] When, on the other hand, Ashdown was openly critical of the government he earned the opprobrium of government frontbenchers, some of whom oppose any kind of inter-party arrangement. With the resignation in 1999 of Ashdown, chief architect of 'constructive opposition', as party leader and the demise in late 1998 of one of its most influential Labour supporters, Mandelson, the whole project of centre-left re-alignment was in the balance.

What of the Liberal Democrat parliamentary party? Before 1997 there were too few MPs to make generalisations, but we can comment on the forty-six who made up the post-1997 parliamentary party. They were slightly older on average than their major opponents (average age forty-five), though 26 per cent were under forty. Just over one in three had gone to public school (one Etonian) and 70 per cent to university. With over one-third having attended Oxbridge colleges, the Liberal Democrats were almost exactly mid-way between the major parties. In occupational terms the party had the highest proportion of professionals (26.1 per cent); it had about half the proportion of teachers (13 per cent) that Labour had, and fewer 'politicals' (17 per cent) than Labour. The party comprised 36.1 per cent business people but had no manual workers. As with Labour, a high proportion of Liberal Democrat MPs (60.9 per cent) had local government experience. In terms of gender there were only three women MPs, but the party had selected 138 women candidates (compared to Labour's 155 and the Conservatives' 68), indicating its traditional commitment to fairer gender representation.

In the House of Lords of the late 1990s, about sixty Peers took the Liberal Whip; some thirty-five to forty of these could be considered active. They met every Thursday with either the leader or deputy leader in the Lords taking the chair. At these meetings the Liberal Democrat Lords might be addressed by the relevant Commons spokesperson. The party in the Lords, additionally, had its own committees, on more conventional lines than those in the Commons, but the entire party in the Lords was supported by only three paid officials, and so Liberal Democrat peers felt there was a limit to what they could accomplish. Short of assistance, cramped for space, they nevertheless concentrated resources on producing their own amendments to legislation rather than simply responding to Labour's amendments.

Every Wednesday a meeting was held between the leader, deputy leaders and whips in both Houses to review the forthcoming legislative programme, to plan their own amendments and their responses to Labour amendments. Further coordinating meetings were held every other week by the leaders in both Houses.

Liberal Democrat party structure

Before the merger of the two parties the Liberals had already moved toward a federal structure, but time did not allow the many problems that emerged to be satisfactorily addressed. The Scottish Liberal party operated in many respects as an autonomous unit but the federal executive of the national party, with prime responsibility for policy and indeed for strategy, was often perceived by the Scots to render federalism more a myth than a reality. The original move for federalism had arisen chiefly in Scotland, though Welsh Liberals were generally supportive. The position of England had always posed a major problem by virtue of its disproportionate size and wealth, and in order to 'square' England the new federal structure that emerged from the merger negotiations incorporated twelve English regional organisations.[34] The merger negotiations establishing the English regions (potentially one of the more contentious issues) proved successful. There has been no renegotiation of regional boundaries, despite the relocation of some local parties into other regions. English regional parties can, if they choose, seek the status, like Scotland and Wales, of state parties. None so far has done so.

In order to belong to the Liberal Democrats it is necessary to belong to a local party or a specified associated organisation. Thirty members may form a local party, provided such an organisation bases itself upon at least one parliamentary constituency. Local parties are directly represented at the twice-yearly federal conference, depending upon membership. Standing Orders provide for consultative sessions at the September conference in which any member may speak, so in theory it is possible for ordinary members to have an input into the party's policy-making procedures.

One of the pivotal groups in the party structure is the federal policy committee (FPC). Its principal tasks are to approve party publications and to make interim policy decisions on topical issues. FPC has the additional function of making detailed policy of the kind needed to implement the broad policy outlines adopted by conference. Its membership reflects its importance: it consists of the party leader, a representative of the parliamentary party, an MP representing the state parties, a Liberal Democrat Peer, the party president, three local councillors, two representatives of the state parties, and fifteen activists elected at the annual conference. The FPC chair is elected by the parliamentary party. FPC prepares election manifestos for general and European elections in consultation with the parliamentary and European parliamentary parties. It has the power to set up policy working groups that have a remit to consult as widely as possible. Most important of the party committees however, is the Federal Executive. FE comprises the party president as chair, the party vice-presidents, the party leader, two MPs, one Peer, two principal local councillors, one representative of each state party, and fourteen members elected by the federal conference, and five non-voting members; the chief whip, the chair of finance and administration, the federal chief executive and a staff representative, and finally the chair of FPC. The FE provides the hub of a system of subordinate committees and subcommittees. It establishes, among others, subcommittees for publicity and broadcasting, campaigning and elections and international relations. The FE also has the power to conduct consultative ballots of all party members but its own views are taken as representative by the leadership. For example, it was from the FE that Ashdown sought endorsement for extending cooperation with Labour in late 1998.

The structure of the two state parties in Scotland and Wales is broadly similar, though the electoral decline of the Welsh party allows much less scope for autonomy. The Scottish party has its own constitution, its own leader and officers and its own policy-making structure. Moreover the Scottish party holds two conferences a year, making it difficult for members to find the time to play much of a part in federal conferences. The Scottish party jealously guards its autonomy and clearly finds it difficult on occasions to subordinate itself to federal (especially as it is often seen as 'English') policy objectives.

The constitution of the English party informs us that the party does not 'as yet' have a structure for determining state party policy and that as a consequence these powers have been vested in the federal party. Another significant difference regarding England is the existence of regional party structures. These parties have the power to make policy on matters that relate exclusively to their region. They can, if they choose, draw up a regional manifesto for use in general elections provided that this manifesto is consistent with federal policy. An added function of the regional parties is to ensure that local organisations conduct themselves in a manner consistent with Liberal Democrat ideology and policy and to take action against any that might not – though in such cases the local party has a right of appeal to the state party against subsequent suspension.

The party's federal structure generates problems. Organisationally though not ideologically, the Scottish Liberal Democrats (SLD) form a party within a party.[35] Liberal Democrats might urge that this is what federalism is all about, but their reasoning is disingenuous. Federations come under self-induced pressure; indeed they sometimes fracture. At the 1994 conference, for example, a major contribution to the uncertainties of the debate on decriminalising cannabis stemmed from the fact that the conference of the SLD had already declared itself to be in favour. We might wonder what sense the voter would have made of Liberal Democrats in Scotland favouring cannabis decriminalisation but English and Welsh Liberal Democrats opposing it. Realists at party headquarters believe that the structure of power and influence within the party has more to do with financial resources than constitutional theories. In addition to the 20 per cent of their subscriptions which headquarters returns to the regions and the states (and the proceeds of their lotteries), the parties, SLD included, need headquarters' funding to survive, and in effect that means funding from the English party. The SLD has its own bureaucracy in Edinburgh, the Welsh party and six of the English regions have offices (two in private houses) but none could be run effectively without federal funds. This, together with its strong national profile, holds the party together.

Policy-making

Policy-making in the Liberal Democrat party represents a rough balance of power between the leadership, the parliamentary party, FPC and the federal conference. FPC exerts the greatest influence, since it decides the membership of the working groups as well as which draft policy proposals and which papers shall be discussed at conference, and also the content of the election manifesto. The parliamentary party is well represented on FPC, though its influence has been described as largely negative: delaying the development of policies it deems to be potentially damaging electorally.[36] The role in policy-formulation of the leader has been enormous, not the least because he chairs FPC. As Duncan Brack explains: Ashdown 'has been able to stamp his ideas so firmly on the party's policy programme because of the respect and admiration he has enjoyed amongst party members'.[37] It is no secret, however, that tensions started to grow between the leader and FPC and more so between the leader and conference (the 1994 debate on decriminalisation of cannabis offering the best example). Nevertheless the party's policy-making processes are relatively democratic in structure and in nature, and it is probably a healthy sign that the leader becomes impatient with the processes of policy formulation and the membership becomes wary of the leader's long-term strategy of forging a closer relationship with Labour. In 1998 the party embarked on a radical review of policy, establishing eight representative commissions, with outside experts, to shape a mid-term manifesto to be agreed by the September conference. Conference was broadly enthusiastic about the outcome.[38]

Candidate selection

Candidate selection in Scotland and Wales is organised through a candidates' committee, which draws up a list of approved candidates for parliamentary and European elections, coordinates procedures for selection and adoption, publishes criteria for the assessment of candidates, trains them and makes rules governing the selection and adoption of candidates. In England it is the regions that operate candidates' committees and provide candidate lists for parliamentary and European elections, and they, in turn, coordinate with the state party. In addition, however, there exists a federal joint candidates' committee, chaired by the chief whip and with state representatives, which meets at least once a year to oversee the operations at state level. The state/regional party has to take account of previous work for party, and of gender, ethnic and age balance in drawing up their lists. Short lists must include at least one member of either sex and 'due regard' is required for ethnic representation. Hustings are arranged for all candidates on the short-list and all who belong to the local party at the closing date for applications are able to vote. Every member receives through the mail a copy of the short-list, with notification of hustings. All who attend the hustings or who submit a request will receive a ballot paper.

Although in the event only three women MPs were elected in 1997, the Liberal Democrats nevertheless had fielded 138. In 1992 they fielded 144 women candidates and in 1987, 105 – on both occasions the highest number by any party.[39] The party was less successful in terms of ethnicity, fielding only a handful of candidates of black or Asian origin in each of the last three elections. Indeed in 1992 the party candidate in Bethnal Green resigned before the election, because of a 'a high level of racism in the party'.[40] It would be fair to conclude that the selection procedures, more explicit in terms of securing fairer gender representation, have been more successful in that direction. Indeed, if we consider the far larger measure of Liberal Democrat representation on local councils, we see that approximately thirty per cent of all Liberal Democrat councillors are women.[41]

Party members

Liberal Democrat activists have traditionally inhabited a paradoxical world in which the party they worked for was unlikely to achieve power nationally and yet offered reasonable prospects locally for power, or power-sharing; in fact a substantial number of the present party membership are local councillors.[42] Nowadays the party has a higher national profile and might find itself in a pivotal position in Westminster before long. It has already decided to share power in the new Edinburgh parliament. Nevertheless, for a long time the explanation of instrumentalism (in the sense of serving one's self-interest or the interest of one's social group or class) through political involvement, was hardly appropriate for Liberal activists. Who are today's Liberal democrat activists? They are, as a party, almost as old as the Conservatives, with 35 per cent over the age of sixty-five.[43] Women form 47 per cent of party membership. The Liberal Democrats are the most highly educated of any group of party activists, with just under a half having studied for a degree. Bennie *et al.* conclude that they are also 'even more middle-class than the Conservatives'; more specifically, since 49 per cent work in the public sector, the authors conclude that the Liberal Democrats are very much the party of 'the public sector middle class'. The party exhibits a high level of activism, similar to that of Labour, and money-raising is an activity which involves and connects party members, both with each other and with the party as an institution.

The attitudes of party members, as measured by Bennie *et al.*, show them to be far less committed to Europe than their leaders, far less enamoured of the idea of coalition government, but strongly supportive of increased government expenditure and indeed of wealth redistribution. In most respects Liberal Democrats are closer by far to Labour activists than to Conservative ones, though they show greater support for the free market. Overall, their attitudes correspond closely with the 'new Liberalism' that we considered at the beginning of this chapter. Although the members were very strongly supportive of the aim of replacing Labour as the main opponent of Conservatism, a majority also supported the idea of forming a coalition with Labour after an indecisive election. Nevertheless a larger majority saw their party as 'a centre party in between the Conservatives and Labour'.

Liberal Democrat voters

The traditional Liberal vote, speaking generally, suffered from a number of disadvantages: it was socially spread, lacking a distinct social base; it was geographically spread, lacking any identifiable heartland; and it was highly volatile, capturing (or failing to capture) the protest vote. The impact of the alliance with the SDP modified this picture only marginally. The Liberal Democrat vote today, however, is not so fragile. As John Curtice tells us,[44] it is distinctly higher among the salariat and the better-educated. It also has a stronger regional base, having established itself firmly through much of the south-west of England and to a lesser extent in rural Scotland. Moreover its strength has grown at the expense of Labour as well as the Conservatives. Curtice predicted in 1995, on the basis of its regional strength, that the party could lose votes nationally in the 1997 election but still win at least thirty-eight parliamentary seats. He was right.

Ideologically speaking, Curtice found that Liberal Democrat voters were increasingly identifying with traditional Labour policy preferences, especially (like the activists) increasing public spending. Curtice concluded that the evidence suggested that the Liberal Democrat party was making 'inroads into Labour's traditional ideological territory'. Additionally, party voters' attitudes were more distinctively aggregated on the liberal/ authoritarian axis than the traditional left/right axis: they were liberals, not centrists.

Finally, the problem of volatility. The party still lacks what Curtice calls social reinforcement. Only 33 per cent (compared with 45 per cent for Labour and 58 per cent for the Conservatives) reported that the person to whom they spoke most often about important matters was a fellow Liberal Democrat. Nevertheless the party has come to dominate the non-Conservative vote in certain parts of the country, and with its substantial strength in local government (especially in those regions) its vote is more stable and more distinctive than it used to be.

Conclusions

In this chapter we have considered not merely the current 'centre' party, the Liberal Democrats, but its previous incarnations, as the Alliance and as the Liberals. We have examined the continuities and discontinuities, showing the thread that bound together the ideologies of 'new' Liberalism and social democracy, both at the end of the nineteenth century and toward the end of the twentieth. But we have concentrated on the Liberal Democrats and considered their development, the party structure and support, and the role that they have played in modern British politics. The last ten years, which have coincided with Ashdown's leadership, have been extraordinarily successful. 'More than any other Liberal leader in living memory', said *The Times*, 'Mr Ashdown shaped the party of his time.'[45] Currently the party has over 5400 local councillors, 100,000 members, forty-six MPs and two MEPs. It has witnessed the securing of some of its most cherished policies: devolution for Scotland and Wales; the prospect of regional government for England (indeed the reality as far as London is concerned); proportional representation for European and Scottish and Welsh elections; the incorporation of the European Convention of Human Rights into British law and the likelihood of legislation on freedom of information – 'Labour measures but Liberal Democrat victories'.[46] The party is also represented on a Cabinet committee, has followed a policy of constructive opposition, and has at least put consensus (as opposed to adversarial) politics on the agenda. Ashdown firmly believes that the Liberal Democrats will be in national government within ten years.[47] The next Liberal Democrat leader, however, may choose not to continue with Ashdown's policy of partnership with Labour, and if the party is to play a part in government we cannot be certain that it will be the part that Ashdown envisages. The Liberal Democrat party, at the end of the twentieth century, looks a more permanent feature of the political landscape than at any time in the preceding fifty years, and yet these remain volatile times. Permanence is as permanence does. The choice of leader, and the ability of that leader to construct a political strategy that the party will find acceptable, are crucial considerations. Ashdown will prove a hard, some have suggested impossible, act to follow.

Notes

1. George Dangerfield, *The Strange Death of Liberal England*, London, McGibbon and Key, 1966.
2. *The Times*, 27 January 1999.
3. Peter Clarke's *Liberals and Social Democrats*, Cambridge, Cambridge University Press, 1978 is the main source for this account of events at the turn of the century. However he was not concerned to make connections with the Alliance party of the 1980s; so the interpretations are my own.
4. It is interesting to note that a half-hearted attempt was made in 1984 to resurrect the Rainbow Circle by right-wing Labour MPs such as Frank Field. This took the form of general debate on the desirability of arriving at some electoral arrangement between Labour and the Alliance with a view to forming an anti-Conservative coalition government.
5. Clarke sets out the principles of social democracy in a chapter entitled 'Liberals and Social Democrats in historical perspective', in Vernon Bogdanor's edited collection, *Liberal Party Politics*, Oxford, Clarendon Press, 1983.
6. See *ibid.*, ch. 4.
7. Michael Meadowcroft, *Liberal Values for a New Decade*, Manchester, North West Community Papers, 1981, p. 6.
8. Jo Grimond, *The Liberal Future*, London, Faber, 1959, p. 15.
9. Elliot Dodds, 'Liberty and Welfare', in *The Unservile State*, London, Allen & Unwin, 1957, p. 33.
10. *Ibid.*, p. 25.
11. In *The Theory and Practice of Community Politics*, The Association of Liberal Councillors, Hebden Bridge, 1981.
12. *Guardian*, 23 February 1979.
13. David Owen, *Face the Future*, London, Cape, 1981.
14. William Rodgers, *The Politics of Change*, London, Secker and Warburg, 1981.
15. Shirley Williams, *Politics is for People*, Harmondsworth, Penguin, 1981.
16. Owen, *Face the Future*, p. 14.
17. Williams, *Politics is for People*, p. 205.
18. See D. T. Studlar, 'By-elections and the Liberal/SDP Alliance', *Teaching Politics*, **13**(1), January 1984, pp. 84–95.
19. David Butler and Dennis Kavanagh, *The British General Election of 1983*, London, Macmillan, 1984, Appendix 1.

20. The voting was, by the Liberal party, 46,376 for, 6,325 against; by the SDP, 18,722 for, 9,929 against.

21. The best account of the history of the SDP is Ivor Crewe and Anthony King, *SDP: The Birth, Life and Death of the Social Democratic Party*, Oxford, Oxford University Press, 1995.

22. See John Stevenson, 'Liberals to Liberal Democrats', in Don MacIver (ed.), *The Liberal Democrats*, London, Prentice Hall/Harvester Wheatsheaf, 1996, pp. 23–39.

23. See David Butler and Dennis Kavanagh, *The British General Election of 1987*, London, Macmillan, 1988.

24. Richard Holme, 'Sausages or Policemen? The role of the Liberal Democrats in the 1997 campaign', paper to the EPOP Conference, 1997.

25. For a full account of the 'equidistance' debate, see Stephen Ingle, 'The Liberal Democrats and Equidistance', *Parliamentary Brief*, 4(2), November 1995.

26. Marquand's vision for the Alliance was fully explored in 'Our Different Vision', *Federal Green Paper* 17, Hebden Bridge, Hebden Royd publications, 1989.

27. This was accepted by a number of Labour activists. 'The Liberal Democrats', said one former Labour mayor after 60 years in that party, 'are now the only centre-left party and I am delighted to become a member'. He was one of four former Labour mayors to do so. *The Times*, 17 December 1997.

28. *Independent*, 29 April 1997.

29. Most commentators agreed that the Liberal Democrat *Guarantee* was to the left of Labour's policy document *New Labour: New Life for Britain*, in which the word 'socialist' was used only once.

30. Liberal Democrat Party, Policy Briefing No. 2, 1994.

31. *Daily Telegraph*, 3 August 1993.

32. *Keesing's UK Record: 1994*, Cambridge, Circa Publications, 1994.

33. Matthew Parris, *The Times*, 5 December 1997.

34. The Constitution of the Liberal Democrat Party, 1993. p. 3.

35. For a full account of the SLD and federalism see Peter Lynch, *Third Party Politics in a Four Party System: The Liberal Democrats in Scotland*, unpublished monograph, 1995.

36. See Duncan Brack, 'Liberal Democrat Policy' in MacIver (ed.), *The Liberal Democrats*, pp. 85–112. For a fuller discussion of the policy-making process see Stephen Ingle, 'Party Organisation' in the same book, pp. 113–33.

37. Brack, 'Liberal Democrat Policy', p. 97.

38. *The Times*, 20 February 1999.

39. Byron Cridle, 'MPs and Candidates', in *The British General Election of 1992*, D. Butler and D. Kavanagh, London, Macmillan, 1992, p. 219.

40. *Ibid.*, p. 120.

41. Women comprise 29.45 per cent of the membership of the ALDC to which over 60 per cent of all Liberal Democrat councillors belong. There is no reason to believe that the proportion of women among all councillors would be different. (Figures provided by ALDC.)

42. Lynn Bennie, John Curtice *et al.*, 'Party Members', in Don MacIver, *The Liberal Democrats*, ch.6.

43. *Ibid.*

44. John Curtice, 'Who votes for the centre now?', in MacIver, *The Liberal Democrats*, pp. 191–204.
45. Editorial, *The Times*, 21 January 1999.
46. *Ibid.*
47. Peter Riddell, *The Times*, 21 January 1999.

CHAPTER NINE

Parties and Change: Riding the Tiger

So far we have considered Britain's major political parties in their own right; we have accepted certain explicit and implicit assumptions about the importance of parties and their role in administering the modern British state. We examined their histories and ideologies, their structures and composition and the nature of their support. We shall now be examining those original assumptions more rigorously in terms of the changing landscape in which parties operate. We shall be considering two areas of change, that of policy-making (what the role of parties is and how that role itself is changing) and that of territory (how accurate generalisations about 'British' parties are in the constituent nations of the United Kingdom and, more immediately, what surprises devolution might hold for parties). Finally we shall attempt to shape some conclusions about the future of the British party system.

Parties, policy and the business of government

The belief that political parties were created to serve a specific purpose in the democratic polity, fulfilling the functions set out in Chapter 1, is popular but quite misconceived. The truth of the matter is that parties existed in Britain in a clearly recognizable form before the advent of mass democracy and so could not have been designed to serve any democratic purpose whatever. Parties have continually adapted to fulfil the changing needs of a developing party system and their only constant feature is their propensity to change.

The major parties are generally held to have represented for more than a century the interests of the great social classes and to articulate those interests in the form of competing ideologies which spawn alternative policies. The sanctioning, by means of a general electoral victory, of one or other ideology provides a mandate for the party concerned to legislate on the basis of its policies. This fundamentally two-party competition presumes that modern party politics provides a framework for policy within which the Civil Service and government agencies will tend to operate. That framework will represent the fruits of a complex interaction between party leaders, 'experts', activists and supporters, supposedly set within the context of the party's ideology. For the victorious party that framework will enclose a viable programme for government. The party defeated at the election will have at its disposal a similar framework from within which it will criticise the government's policies, thus providing accountability and choice.

The preceding chapters have cast considerable doubt upon the nature of this 'complex interaction' between leaders, experts, activists and supporters, and they have questioned the integrity of the ideological context within which these interactions are said to take place. All the same, the realist will want to argue that the two-party model works, despite its imperfections, as it continues to provide what the voters consider to be effective government and genuine choices. But does it? In the first part of this chapter we shall consider the sharp end of party politics, the impact of party politics upon government policy-making.

Does the party system work?

Jack Hayward raises a fundamental objection regarding the effectiveness of the two-party model. He suggests that Britain's economic policies, the most important area of policy, are determined by forces other than those commanded by parties in government. Leaving aside the cultural and international constraints over which governments have little direct influence, Hayward argues:

> the major source of Britain's difficulties is to be located among the non-state actors and ... the efficacy of a subsidiary state intervention cannot be great when industrial firms, banks, and trade unions – who are directly involved in economic activity and decide in a more direct sense than do British governments – are unable to invest, produce, and sell efficiently ... Politicians in power prate and posture, taking the credit and the blame for the diverse fortunes that ensue from the interplay of international forces, without ... usually being genuinely responsible for either the good or the bad results.[1]

Hayward is not suggesting that the party system is a sham, rather that it is not the prime mover in economic policy or, for similar reasons, in any area of major policy. Changes in the complexion of government and changes in the party system are simply not particularly important for Hayward. His argument is not new. It was expressed more colourfully many years before by Bernard Shaw, whose industrialist Andrew Undershaft berates his politician son in the following terms:

> Do you suppose that you and half a dozen amateurs like you, sitting in a row in that foolish gabble shop, can govern Undershaft and Lazarus? No, my friend: you will do what pays us. You will make war when it suits us, and keep peace when it doesn't ... When I want to keep my dividends up, you will discover that my want is a national need. When other people want something to keep my dividends down, you will call out the police and military. And in return you shall have the support and applause of my newspapers, and the delight of imagining that you are a great statesman. Government of your country! Be off with you, my boy, and play with your caucuses and leading articles and historic parties and great leaders and burning questions and the rest of your toys. I am going back to my counting house to pay the piper and call the tune.[2]

Let us consider Shaw's (and to all intents and purposes Hayward's) position that in British democracy all parties play the tune called by major industrial and commercial interests. In the early years of the century, the radical Liberal Hobson[3] wrote about the difficulties involved in Britain's creating an imperial federation with common defence and trade policies. He nevertheless concluded that the economic advantages to British industry and capital were such that an imperial federation would certainly be established. His arguments were accepted and advanced more forcefully by Lenin who, like Hobson and Shaw, believed that British governments played the tunes called by their paymasters. No imperial federation was created and one of the major reasons for that was the replacement in 1906 of a Conservative administration dominated by the protectionist Joseph Chamberlain by a free-trade Liberal administration. Ideology made the difference. It would be a strange society in which powerful economic forces exercised no political influence, but theirs is not the only power and need not be decisive. So much for Shaw's extreme position. We shall have opportunity to consider Hayward's less extreme position as the argument develops, but there need be no initial disagreement about the proposition that party governments are not free agents. However, they are not prisoners of events over which they have no control. Parties – collectively – matter, but do they – individually – make much of a difference?

Richard Rose, in a celebrated work, addresses precisely this problem.[4] He is particularly keen to examine the validity of the claim that 'adversarial' politics produce policy inconsistencies of such a magnitude as to make medium- and long-term planning impossible.[5] He attempts to show that, on the contrary, party politics do not seriously impact upon government policy because policies are shaped by a range of prior considerations; in short, we do not need to worry about adversarial politics because they do not work. 'What parties say', says Rose, 'is not what parties do.' The adversarial argument suggests that the consensus-based politics of the 1950s and 1960s gave way to the ideology-based politics of the 1970s: socialist planning versus market forces, public versus private ownership, high public spending versus low direct taxation and so on. Rose asserts that this division was largely rhetorical. Nothing is new, he tells us. 'Labour and Conservative governments have been complementary parts of a moving consensus; in office in the past, they have not acted upon mutually exclusive ideological principles.'[6] History suggests that in opposition, parties tend to move towards their ideological extreme but when in government they move towards the centre – so parties 'don't matter'. Even the supposedly ideological government of Mrs Thatcher was, according to Rose, predominantly consensual (that is, the House did not divide on principle on the majority of Bills debated).

With Hayward, Rose urges that major developments in the period he studied were simply not much influenced by changes of government: whether we examine economic inputs (matters within the government's own hands, such as setting the minimum lending rate, the level of public sector borrowing and public expenditure) or economic outcomes that are only partially influenced by government (such as inflation, unemployment and economic growth), the conclusions would be much the same: 'the direction of the British economy is primarily influenced by long-term events independent of party and not the movement of parties in and out of office.' What is true for the economy is true for all areas of government activity. Rhetoric does not transform reality, or as Healey explained to the 1982 Labour party conference à propos economic policy, general elections do not change the laws of arithmetic. Other writers have attacked the adversarian thesis on different grounds, suggesting that such major policy changes as take place tend to occur not so much between governments as within them.[7]

There seem to be solid prima facie grounds, then, for rejecting the adversarian thesis, and Rose presses home his objections by means of a detailed analysis of the policies of successive governments. First he examines the party manifesto. For him a party manifesto is 'an exercise in party management', its function being primarily integrative and coordinative and a search for unity within the party, and is particularly important for opposition parties. Nevertheless both the Conservative and Labour governments 'do the majority of things to which they pledge themselves in their opposition manifesto'.[8] At first sight this appears to run counter to the substantive thesis, but not so: manifestos are predominantly non-adversarial.[9] Moreover, manifesto-driven legislation forms only a small part of a government's whole programme. Rose's analysis shows that even the relatively partisan parliaments of the 1970s were characterised more by consensus than by adversarial politics. The sternest opponents of government and opposition policies, as Norton has shown, came from within the party's own ranks.[10] Far from being an adversarial system, then, Britain's is predominantly consensual. Governments owe their position to popular election, and the British electorate tends towards agreement rather than disagreement on major issues. Once in office a party will not push its own ideology too far because of a recognition that this will encourage its opponents to act similarly when they gain office. Prudent self-interest, then, limits controversial changes in the rules of the game. Finally, if these reasons were not sufficient to dispose parties towards consensual politics, the awesome responsibilities of running the state with the assistance of a permanent non-political Civil Service, together with the general constraints upon its freedom of manoeuvre identified by Hayward, would certainly toll the knell for any government seeking to act in a consistently adversarial manner. New ministers will face old problems, and with the same advice as their unsuccessful predecessors.

Turning to Rose's substantive thesis, he tells us that 63 per cent of all government legislation in the 1970s could be defined as consensual. Leaving aside the problem of classification (not to oppose legislation formally – Rose's definition – does indicate consensus), it is misleading not to distinguish between the relative importance of different pieces of legislation. If only one major government Bill could be classified as adversarial, its symbolic importance and practical effects could be such as to make the label 'consensual' palpably inappropriate. Much the same criticism can be levelled at Rose's analysis of manifestos. The majority of manifesto commitments may not be overtly adversarian, but it is straining credulity to insist that most major manifesto commitments could be considered consensual.

Rose, like Hayward, attaches much importance to the restraints which inhibit incoming governments, domestically what he calls 'long-term secular trends' and internationally the state of the world economy and the global political situation. These restraints are certainly important, but to consider them necessarily paralysing is to ignore those occasions when nations have reversed 'long-term secular trends', with considerable repercussions for their economic and political world roles. Government policies may be not as decisive as some politicians would have us believe but it is unrealistic to believe that parties make no impact whatever. With regard to the role of the Civil Service, two factors need to be borne in mind. First is the ability of a party in government to generate a different perspective within the service by influencing key promotions, or by bringing leading figures into the service from outside, or by making use of expert advice from outside the service, all of which are commonly done. According to Peter Hennessy,[11] many permanent secretaries were selected personally by Margaret Thatcher. 'They have been promoted for qualities of style and commitment', said Hugo Young.[12] The second is that Civil Servants regard it as their duty to advise, and to advise from within the framework of known governmental dispositions. For example, Civil Service advice on taxation systems differed in the late 1960s and early 1970s according to the attitudes of successive governments towards joining the EEC. The anti-EEC Labour government was advised of the disadvantages of VAT, the later pro-EEC Conservative government of the disadvantages of purchase tax and SET: each was told what it wanted to hear. It is well known that departments of state prepare themselves for the implications of electoral victory for each of the major parties. Of course they will attempt to dissuade politicians from adopting policies they believe to be unworkable, but they will generally give loyal support to a minister's policies. In short, though these restrictions upon adversarial government are important, they are not conclusive.[13]

Finally we come to Rose's most deep-rooted objection to the adversarial thesis: that it confuses rhetoric with reality, failing to distinguish between what parties say and what they do. Rose asks us to believe that what people say is not part of reality. This makes sense only if it is always and everywhere true that people do not mean what they say. Otherwise how can we be sure? If a man says: 'One day I shall kill you', then our 'reality' would certainly be transformed even if he did not actually do so. Only if we could be certain either that he did not mean it or that he was incapable of carrying out his threat would our 'reality' be unaffected by his 'rhetoric'. If the Labour party announces in its manifesto that it will abolish the House of Lords, are we to assume that it either has no intention to honour its promise or that it simply would not be able to do so for time (or some other) reasons? Not many members of the Upper House would take comfort from that line of argument in 1999. But the substantive point goes beyond that: it is that rhetoric is very much part of reality. In S.H. Beer's words, 'party stances establish the framework of public thinking about policy'.[14]

All in all, although Rose's and Hayward's work leads us to appreciate the limitations within which parties have to work and to recognise the common ground between them, we have nevertheless to conclude that parties do make a difference and that, if we take any note of the influence of what Rose dismisses as rhetoric, then they make a very substantial difference. To quote Beer again, 'parties themselves, backed by research staffs, equipped with nationwide organizations, and enjoying the continuous attention of the mass media, have themselves in great part framed and elicited the very demands to which they then respond.'[15]

A number of other studies have been concerned with the effect upon specific areas of policy of adversarialism and some reach conclusions very different from Rose's. Andrew Gamble elucidates three varieties of the adversarial politics thesis and finds none of them convincing. 'The surprising thing about adversary politics is not that it destroys continuity of policy in some areas, but that it protects a narrow and unreflecting consensus on some of the most important determinants shaping economic policy.'[16] Suddenly adversary politics is exposed as a conspiracy theory, and Gamble is not the only writer to say so. Ashford argues that, 'superficial' adversarial politics notwithstanding, in times of stress an 'élite consensus' emerges which concentrates decision-making within cabinet and the higher levels of the Civil Service, and this consensus acts independently of party ideology or indeed of parliamentary influence.[17]

Gamble develops his own theory further. Political stability demands continuity of policy so the electorate 'can be offered an effective choice between teams of leaders but not between policies'; adversarial two-party party politics, like Bernard Shaw's democracy, is only a game to catch your attention while someone – the government on behalf of capital – is picking your pocket. He concludes: 'If the two parties ever became genuine adversaries the system would cease to be workable.' It is true that real adversaries beat each other over the head. It is also true that we defined the role of political parties in a constitutional democracy as being to contain conflict. But party systems differ, and to call a system adversarial is a more sophisticated and comparative judgement than Gamble will allow. It is hard to imagine many working in the areas of health or education, let alone key economic areas such as membership of the European Monetary Union, who would dispute the claim that party policies differ and that the differences matter. Did Scots and Welsh voters see no differences between the major parties in 1997 when one promised – and delivered – devolution and one did not? And does devolution not matter?

There is, moreover, another dimension to the relationship between party and policy, which might be referred to as contextual. Here the influence of adversarial politics is far more profound, for it shapes the expectations of all the actors in the drama of government and minutely directs the whole production. As was stated earlier, adversarial politics help to shape the reality which parties confront when they come to power. Senior Civil Servants and pressure group leaders clearly have their expectations shaped by the complexion of the government and the likely complexion of future governments. We have only to consider movements on the stock exchange following unexpected by-election results towards the end of a government to understand this. There is strong evidence, then, that adversarial politics influence this contextual dimension too.

Adversarial politics have yet another profound influence on government business. In *Parliament and Health Policy*[18] the authors consider in detail the influence of parliament in the creation and scrutiny of health policy in the period 1970–75. Every major aspect of health policy in that period was considered and, although this had not been the purpose of the study, clear indications of the influence of adversarial politics emerged. The study began by analysing the kind of contributions which backbench MPs might make to policy formulation and scrutiny, and this was done simply by asking a number of backbenchers what they considered to be their most important function. On the basis of their answers backbench functions were categorised as being four-fold. First there was a deputational function (the MP is deputed to protect and further the interests of constituents). Second came the custodial function, where the emphasis is on protecting customary procedures and the constitution. Third was the advocative function (representing certain interests – e.g. tobacco manufacture). Finally was the partisan-ideological or adversarial (offering support to party leaders so long as they pursue party policy). The purpose of these categories was not to label MPs but to attempt to categorise their contributions to debate on the floor of the House and in committee in order to get the measure of the way parliament actually operates.

During the period under scrutiny one major piece of legislation passed through parliament, the reform of the administrative structure of the National Health Service (NHS), the first major overhaul in nearly thirty years. The need for structural reform was not at issue; neither was any major reallocation of resources, nor any major ideological principle. Yet a tabulation of major contributions to the second reading debate on the Reorganisation Bill (measured in column inches of Hansard) shows that adversarial inputs comprised 36 per cent, by far the largest category. The authors conclude: 'For parliament to spend over a third of its time on partisan point-making, with the full knowledge that it would have no effect on the shape of the policy before it, is an over-indulgence.'[19] What was true of the major debate on the floor of the House was true also of committee discussions. In fact the most successful influence upon the government – and it was successful only in detail – was the House of Lords (where, incidentally, similar categorisation indicated that partisan-ideological inputs accounted for only 4 per cent of all contributions). Now, there were major issues at stake in the proposed legislation concerning, especially, accountability in the new structure, but party loyalty 'was the only significant factor in the debate'.

Within five years NHS reorganisation was back on the political agenda: the 1974 reforms were almost universally considered to have been failures. There is much more in the study to tell a similar story; indeed the House seemed only able to perform effectively in the area of detailed scrutiny and only then when, as with the creation of the NHS Commissioner (Ombudsman) and his committee, detailed and often technical discussion precluded adversarial inputs. The authors conclude their study by suggesting:[20]

> This double failure, lack of parliamentary influence and unsuccessful government policies, are not unconnected … If health is any guide, the nature of policy making is becoming increasingly technical and as a result less amenable to [adversarial] presentation. The British model of parliamentary government requires partisan policy inputs, requires policies to be presented as simple alternatives for public choice. Yet in an increasingly complex age, policies are far less amenable to presentation as simple partisan choices, and

policy inputs come increasingly not from parties but from experts within the executive. The procedures for assessing these policies, however, continue to operate as if they *were* partisan-ideological and so remain basically adversarial.

In procedural terms Britain's two major parties enjoy substantial powers. This is a feature which distinguishes Westminster-style systems from others, including the American. As Hayek pointed out, all the 'constraints upon the supreme power that had carefully been built up during the evolution of constitutionally monarchy were successfully dismantled ...'[21] Balfour's procedural reforms in 1902 'completed the structure of a "parliamentary timetable", enabling a government with even a thin majority to railroad measures through the Commons.'[22] Rose is of the view that the consensus nature of British politics prevents that procedural power from being used in an adversarial way. Margaret Thatcher was elected in 1979 on a minority vote. In 1983 her support declined further and remained almost as low in 1987, but this did not prevent her from forcing a radical policy agenda through parliament for which she claimed a mandate. Thatcher governments transformed the structure of the British state, reducing the status of local authorities to little more than agencies of central government, creating new unelected public agencies, privatising major service industries and recasting the structure, functions and traditions of the Civil Service. Thatcher did nothing more than a Labour government in New Zealand did at roughly the same time, but both she and Prime Minister Lange shook their respective constitutions to the foundation. In New Zealand the indirect consequence of Lange's revolution was electoral reform; in Britain Thatcher's revolution led indirectly but palpably to devolution.

The politics of diversity

Had this book been entitled *The English Party System* it would have covered much the same ground – so far. Most textbooks on British politics imagine that the Celtic countries operate a form of party politics which is mildly, and probably temporarily divergent from the English; and after all, the English do make up about 85 per cent of the population of the United Kingdom. Most textbooks on British politics are written in and for England, and their emphasis has traditionally been focused on England. I have tried, in dealing with all three parties, to include a Celtic dimension. It is time now, however, to consider the politics of the Celtic nations in their own right as constituent parts (for the time being at least) of the United Kingdom. It has to be admitted immediately that space precludes anything more than a sketch, and that principally a sketch of Scotland. But events in the Celtic countries are about to change the British political landscape profoundly and it is well that we understand them.

The English habitually use the descriptions 'English' and 'British' more or less interchangeably. When the English soccer or rugby team take the field the anthem which they sing, unlike the other British teams, is not an English anthem, such as 'Jerusalem', but the British one, 'God Save the Queen'. Until comparatively recently few would take the St George flag to sports fixtures – though they do now – and fewer still fly the cross of St. George from public buildings in England. Only in Northern Ireland would one see more union flags. In Wales it is the red dragon that flutters from most flag poles and in Scotland the saltire is everywhere. After the 1992 general election, of which the Scottish National Party had such high hopes, deputy leader Jim Sillars dismissed his compatriots as 'ninety-minute nationalists'. They only cared for their country during a soccer or rugby game. We shall return to this criticism, but it should be made clear that Scotland, Wales and Northern Ireland have retained distinctive cultures and a distinctive identity and these are expressed in many forms, not the least sport.

National identity

Much has been written about the concept of identity recently, and I do not propose to review the debate, since it is not central to our purposes. But identity only becomes a subject for debate when it is in some kind of crisis, when, as Mercer says, 'something assumed to be fixed, coherent and stable is displaced by the experience of doubt and uncertainty'.[23] The English may not have noticed, but it is 'Britishness' that, especially among the young, has become somewhat uncertain. It is a testament to the strength of Scottish and Welsh culture and sense of nationhood that, even after three and five hundred years respectively of constitutional domination by a much larger partner, they have retained their sense of identity. It seems a paradox that when Anglocentric, usually metropolitan culture is at its most pervasive (through the mass media), Celtic cultures should be enjoying their most fertile period for decades. In fact it is not a paradox: the London-based media project their cultural values into the minds of all who watch and many of those who watch are stimulated to resist. And whatever Jim Sillars may think of it, most young men and a growing number of young women watch international sport. For them Wales or Scotland versus England assumes an importance quite beyond the scope of that particular sport. Over twenty years ago one of Scotland's celebrated sports commentators said of an English defeat at the hands of the Scots in Glasgow: 'The poor English. They came expecting a game of football and what they got was a tribal war.' National pride has a visibility in international sport and as George Orwell pointed out some time ago it is not a force for brotherhood and friendship. There is in truth much that the peoples of the United Kingdom have in common but they are not the same. This can be seen in art, in song, in architecture – and in sport. The English need to be more sensitive to these differences.

Brown, McCrone and Patterson, in the timely second edition of *Politics and Society in Scotland*,[24] pose the question: why is the sense of Britishness so weak? In an age which has seen the demise of nationalised industries and services, where the name 'British' was commonly used, there is little that gives a salience to Britishness. The great achievements of the British – the creation of a vast empire, collective heroism and defiance in time of world war, the creation of a National Health Service to name the more obvious – are in the past. But what is not so much written about, despite its importance for a long period of time, is religion. To be more precise, the triumph of Protestantism. That lowland, protestant Scotland saw itself at risk from the Gaelic-speaking Catholics in the north explains much of the impulse for the 1707 Act of Union between England and Scotland. Indeed, the pre-Union Scottish parliament frequently concerned itself with the 'problem' of Irish (i.e. Gaelic) culture and language. Protestantism, which brought most of the United Kingdom together, is no longer the socio-political force it once was.

External pressures too have tended to impact upon the sense of 'Britishness'. Many more people now go overseas for their holidays, and not simple to southern Europe. Although only 6 per cent of Scots, for example, regard themselves as 'Scottish and European',[25] fear or distrust of Europeans is not widespread. The European Union, moreover, offers an impressive safety net for those who might otherwise fear for Scotland 'going it alone'. The European 'them' against the British 'us' is no longer a factor. Increasingly decisions affecting aspects of Scottish life, such as fishing and agriculture, are taken not at Westminster but in Brussels. In addition to the growth in influence of Europe is the pervasive influence of globalisation. Again, we have no need to go further than point out that inward investment to the United Kingdom is generated by companies who make decisions in Tokyo, Seoul or San Francisco. The Scots cannot control them, but neither can the British. It is in the face of these pressures that the perceived need has grown to control at least some aspects of national life, and many of those aspects are part of a Scottish, Welsh or Northern Irish agenda rather than a British one. This can be seen as part of a much larger development of the so-called 'post-industrial society' which rejects bigness wherever possible precisely because it connotes lack of identity.[26]

But does this sense of identity have any political consequences? The *British Election Survey of 1997* showed that 23 per cent of Scots and 13 per cent of Welsh people did not regard themselves as British; a further 38 per cent of Scots and 29 per cent of Welsh regarded themselves as more Scots (or Welsh) than British. However, far more Welsh regarded themselves as equally British or more British than Welsh (51 per cent); the equivalent for Scotland was 35 per cent. As for the English, 46 per cent regarded themselves as equally English and British, suggesting that many simply do not perceive a difference. What the consequences of these differences amount to is a matter for conjecture.[27]

This awareness of a separate identity feeds off fundamental differences in the party systems in each of the Celtic countries. Northern Irish politics, for very obvious reasons, is totally distinctive with a party system dominated by two Unionist parties and two Nationalist parties. Alone of the mainland parties the Conservatives field candidates in some Northern Irish constituencies but with minimal impact. In Scotland and Wales the existence of powerful nationalist parties and the long-term weakness of the Conservatives makes their systems quite different from the English. But the differences are in fact even more profound.

The Scottish party system

Concentrating on Scotland we shall see that even when the party system seems the same there are fundamental differences. In the nineteenth century – after the 1832 Reform Act anyway – the Liberals monopolised Scottish politics for over half a century. As Brown et al. demonstrate, electoral support for the Liberals remained above 50 per cent until the turn of the century. In 1865 it reached an amazing 85 per cent.[28] (The national vote for the Liberals in that year was 60 per cent.) It is important to remember from our twentieth-century perspective that we are not comparing like with like. Nevertheless, in nineteenth-century Scotland the Liberals enjoyed a hegemony unparalleled in England. Liberalism throughout the United Kingdom took up long-term residence in non-conformist and low-church communities. Liberal radicalism appealed to the Scots, as did its emphasis on self-reliance and the improvement of popular education.[29]

It was the Irish Home Rule issue which broke the Liberal party in Scotland and the advent of Labour which destroyed it. In 1906 when Asquith won his towering majority the Liberal vote in Scotland (at 56 per cent) was now nearer the national vote (50 per cent). Its further demise – and much later renewal – more or less mirrored that of the national party. The Liberal Democrat party in modern Scotland holds ten seats but on a smaller proportion of the vote than that enjoyed by the national party. All the generalisations we commonly make about Liberal Democratic under-representation in the first-past-the-post-system have to be stood on their heads as regards Scotland.

The Conservative party in nineteenth-century Scotland enjoyed a measure of success but its association with the landed interest usually worked to its disfavour, and it was unable to take the industrial working-class with it in the way that Disraeli was able to do nationally. However, the party received a substantial bonus in 1886 when the Unionists split from the Liberal party. Hutchison shows how the Unionists' switching their allegiance to the Conservatives allowed the latter to broaden their appeal.[30] Their real strength, however, was to be found in the West of Scotland, and the party played to that strength in the dangerous days of William Carson and the Ulster Volunteers when in 1912 it changed its name to the Scottish Unionist party. Working-class protestant voters gave the Conservatives considerable political strength. As Fry says, 'till 1974 they never got much less than 40 per cent of the vote, and often rather more; afterwards they never got much more than 30 per cent, and often rather less.'[31] The rise of the Scottish National party (SNP) made serious inroads into Conservative support just as protestantism was becoming less politically influential. From 1974 the Conservative vote declined. Almost inexorably. But what really flattened the Conservative party (which had now dropped the Unionist tag) was the advent of Thatcherism. The Scots voted decisively against the Conservatives but they were still ruled by Margaret Thatcher. For most Scots the Thatcherite project of self-reliance seemed a threat to their sense of community – and when she famously declared that this was because there was no such thing as society – their worst fears were justified. More reliant on the state in terms of benefits, housing and jobs, Scotland, like Wales and the North of England, suffered disproportionately as it shrank. But most damaging of all to Scottish Conservatism was the introduction – one year ahead of England – of Thatcher's dreaded 'poll tax'. Scotland perceived itself as a guinea-pig. Although after her departure John Major revived the party's fortunes a little, the blow of 1997 could scarcely have been more crushing – only 12 per cent of the vote and not a single seat. So, too, in Wales – not a single seat. (But not a single seat out of thirty-seven in the old 'People's Republic of Yorkshire' either.) In Scotland today the Conservatives are in total disarray, though in the new Scottish parliament – which they resisted – and its proportional electoral system – which they resisted – the party has regained some visibility and some hope.

Just as the Liberals dominated the nineteenth century so Labour has the twentieth, its rise keeping in step with that of the party nationally; indeed the British Labour party, as we have seen, was to a large extent fashioned by workers' representatives from Scotland and the North of England. But Labour's dominance of Scottish politics, which has some echo in Wales, is quite distinctive from that of England as a whole, though as we have seen Labour is equally dominant in parts of the North of England. We shall have more to say about Labour later but for the moment it is worth observing that even in the disastrous election of 1983 the Labour party in Scotland won forty-one seats (Conservatives twenty-one) on 35 per cent of the vote (Conservatives 28 per cent). Labour in Scotland never suffered the prolonged crisis of confidence that both wracked and then transformed the party in England.

The fourth and most distinctively Scottish of the parties is the SNP. The SNP was founded between the World Wars, though the origins of the movement date back further, to the days of the Scottish Home Rule Association (SHRA) of 1886. But the SHRA had grown as an adjunct to the Liberal party and it declined as the party declined, especially since Labour, interested in building a strong central state, did not pick up the baton of Home Rule. But other groups did pick it up. The Scottish National League, for example, proposed the establishment of a National party and in 1934 the SNP came into being. Though titled 'party' the SNP was, in reality, more of a ginger group, trying to work through the major parties – it epitomised what Brown *et al.* call 'instrumental nationalism'.[32] Although the idea of an independent Scotland did not enjoy a great deal of support, the idea of Home Rule did: in 1949 more than two million people signed a petition calling for Home Rule.

But the SNP beat the drum for Scotland, and the discovery and exploitation of North Sea oil gave that drum much greater resonance. In 1967 Winnie Ewing won a notable by-election at Hamilton, in Labour's heartland. In the 1970 election it secured 11 per cent of the vote and won its first general election seat; by February 1974 its vote had doubled and it won seven seats. In October it secured 30 per cent of the vote and won eleven seats. As we have seen, the Labour government (1974–79) began a long and finally fruitless battle to secure devolution to Scottish and Welsh assemblies, and SNP influence declined. However, under the deft leadership of the egregious Alex Salmond and the hammer of Thatcherism, the party emerged into the 1990s with a brave heart. Salmond skilfully managed to lead his party to campaign for the vote for a Scottish parliament within the United Kingdom, though fundamentalists regarded this as selling independence out. In the general election of 1997 the SNP became Scotland's second party, and in the 1999 elections to the first Scottish parliament since 1707 the SNP became the second largest party (35 seats compared to Labour's 56) and the official opposition.

This brief history has shown the distinctiveness of Scottish culture, and by extension that of the other Celtic countries. We have seen that these cultural differences feed through into political attitudes and we have further seen that the party systems themselves in the Celtic countries are significantly different to England's. Scotland and Wales have four-party systems and the politics of the three UK national parties are distinctive in their Scottish and Welsh settings. A number of those who write about these differences seek to set the records straight, and they also write out of a sense of justified pique that these differences receive such scant attention in so many books on 'British' politics. But they too are guilty of errors of generalisation, referring as Brown *et al.*, for example, frequently do to 'south of the border'. But south of the border lie all sorts of regional differences, and closer examination of many of the 'distinctive' phenomena of Scottish politics shows those to be replicated in parts of England. What is distinctive about Scottish and Welsh politics, however, is what we began with: the indestructable idea of separate identity.

We have concentrated chiefly on Scotland in this discussion, but the differences between the Celtic countries have been acknowledged. The

Welsh party system, superficially very similar to the Scottish, is nevertheless by no means the same. The Welsh National party, Plaid Cymru, for example, though it originated in 1925, was traditionally much more concerned with the Welsh language and culture than it was with competing politically. It was not only more of a ginger group than a party, but a ginger group with a narrow focus. Only when disillusionment with the economic policies of a Labour government at Westminster presented opportunities for evangelising in South Wales in the 1960s did the Plaid make any headway among English-speakers. Even so the party did not gain representation at Westminster until 1974 when it returned two MPs on a Welsh vote of 10.7 per cent.[33] Peter Lynch shows that 'modernisers' within the Plaid sought to commit the party to more progressive socio-economic policies.[34] However, despite the successful creation of a Welsh-language television station S4C (Sianel Pedwar Cymru) and the election as leader of moderniser Dafydd Wigley in 1991, Plaid Cymru's four electoral successes in 1992 and 1997 were each in its Welsh-speaking heartland. Like the SNP the Plaid campaigned for the establishment of the new assembly though (again like the SNP) its policy goal is independence within Europe. On a turnout of only 46 per cent Labour, against all expectations, did not gain an overall majority and Plaid Cymru, like the SNP, became the largest party of opposition, breaking through in English-speaking areas for the first time.

The impact of devolution

The impact of devolution in terms of the governance of the United Kingdom, though profoundly important, is not the focus of our attention here. We are concerned with its likely impact upon the British party system. The Edinburgh parliament and the Welsh assembly has been elected by means of an additional-members system similar to the German and New Zealand systems. In 1996 New Zealand which, like Scotland, had hitherto operated a first-past-the-post electoral system, held its first proportional election. The traditional two-party system, already fracturing under the promise of electoral change, gave way to a five-party system with no single party in a position to govern alone. It took eight weeks to form a government, and the 'kingmaker' in the process was the leader of New Zealand First (NZF) which commanded only 13 per cent support in the election. Within little more than a year NZF had disbanded and the left-wing Alliance party (an amalgam of smaller parties) also disintegrated. With the next election less than a year away, due to be held in November 1999, the system seems to be returning to a two-party format. The capacity for small parties to survive, indeed thrive, in a proportional system seems to pose a threat in New Zealand. In Scotland the fissures within Labour, between New and Old, pro-Union and pro-independence could lead to schisms;

indeed each of the national parties could find tensions between the national and the Scottish leadership.[35] There is scope for division too within the SNP, between those who find that the devolved system gives them sufficient scope and those who wish to bring the system to its knees so that independence becomes the obvious option.

The Scottish Labour party experienced major difficulties in preparing for the Edinburgh parliament. Labour's espousal of devolution was openly portrayed as a policy to 'head off' independence and to derail the SNP. Labour expected a rousing endorsement of its hegemony after enacting the legislation. What happened in contrast was the explosion of a series of scandals involving West of Scotland Labour MPs[36] and West of Scotland Labour councils and, equally damaging, major squabbles within the party concerning the selection procedures for Labour's constituency and list candidates[37]. In the event, Labour was able to form a government only through a coalition with the Liberal Democrats. At the root of the latter was the firmly-held belief, echoed in Wales over the selection of Alan Michael as leader of the Welsh Labour party, that the party leadership in London was seeking to control the Scottish and Welsh parties. But this is simply pre-prandial nibbles; the main course will appear when the Edinburgh parliament is in operation. Because Labour is part of a governing coalition with the Scottish Liberal Democrats, the party's agenda for Scotland will be hammered out within a Scottish context, with its coalition partner, and not at Millbank Towers. Even if the national leadership had secured just the kind of party representation it might wish for – New Labour to a person (it did not) – and even if the party had won the right to govern alone and with a majority (it did not), Scottish Labour will begin to act independently of the national leadership. This is the whole thrust of the 'new' politics in Scotland. Scots, including those in the Labour party, want to manage their own affairs; they no more want to be controlled by Millbank Towers than they did by a Conservative government at Westminster.[38]

What is true of Labour is true also of the Conservatives. When he was Secretary of State for Scotland, Michael Forsyth attacked the SNP not because it was anti-British but because it was not sufficiently pro-Scottish.[39] William Hague gave his seal of approval to an autonomous Conservative party in Scotland with the right to draw up its own manifesto. David McLetchie, the leader of the Scottish Tories – the only party to have fought 1997 opposed to devolution – replied by saying: 'The Scottish parliament is for keeps but the jury is out on the United Kingdom.'[40] It was Disraeli who had urged that the Tory party, if it was not a national party, was nothing. Scottish Tories seem to be redefining 'the nation'. 'We are the Tartan Tories', McLetchie concluded, 'Scotland's other national party'.

For their part the Liberal Democrats, as we have seen, have for some time been a federal party to a degree that their competitors have not. Although one might conclude that the impact of devolution on the party will be correspondingly less, the dynamics of devolution will almost certainly put the federal party under greater strain. The focus of the Scottish Liberal Democrats will be increasingly on Edinburgh and this will clearly have repercussions for the party nationally.

All in all, the phrase 'we are all nationalists now' seems to sum up the changes that have taken place, especially in Scotland. The impact of devolution on the British party system, then, is likely to be substantial; yet the parties themselves – or at least Labour and the Liberal Democrats – seemed quite unaware of this as the legislation went through Westminster. Happy as the schoolboys in Thomas Gray's 'Elegy':

> No sense have they of ills to come
> Nor care beyond today.

Parties and the future

Parties are facing dramatic changes. The nature of party government itself is unlikely to remain unaffected. Parties are less popular than hitherto, and new social movements more popular. Klingemann and Fuchs tell us that across Europe 'there is a clear increase in non-institutionalised participation and a clear decline in attachment to political parties'.[41] These authors are optimistic about the future for parties but they stress that a more politically aware electorate is turning increasingly to more clearly focused or single-issue groups which by-pass elections and parties and thereby tend to erode 'the legitimacy of the competitive party system'.[42] What also tends to erode the legitimacy of the party system is the fact alluded to earlier in this chapter that policy nowadays tends to be of a more technical and long-term nature and not so easily amenable to adversarial presentation. A good example of such policy is that regarding genetically modified foods. It is hardly to be conceived that there is a distinctively ideological Conservative or a Labour policy regarding these foods. But, crucially, governments are required to make decisions and oppositions are required to hold them to account.

Tony Blair seems to be responding to the changing nature of party politics. Cynics believe that his policy of inclusiveness is designed to perpetuate Labour in office. We have seen how he has reshaped his party policy-making machinery so that it can be driven from the centre. He has attempted much the same task with government policy, with the re-vamping of the Prime Minister's and Cabinet Offices, the appointment of the Cabinet Enforcer and so on. Officially this is to promote what No. 10 calls 'joined-up thinking'[43] but it is buttressed by an unprecedented attention to media presentation, both made possible by additional numbers of special advisers. These now number some sixty, and cost the taxpayer an additional £1.5 million.[44]

Blair's stated intention, like Ashdown's, is to 'detribalise' British politics.

Soon after its election, the government sought the help of Sir David Simon, chairman of BP, to assist with its European policy, Martin Taylor of Barclays to advise on social service reform, and Howard Davies, deputy governor of the Bank of England, to supervise financial services.[45] Blair was not the first Prime Minister to harbour the ambition to be more than just a party leader. Lloyd George was similarly motivated, Winston Churchill intended to form a government of 'men of good will of any party and no party', Edward Heath proposed a national coalition. Policies considered by the Blair government shortly after its coming into power signalled, for some commentators, the down-grading of ideology (for example the partial privatisation of London Transport or the possible introduction of 'hotel' charges in NHS hospitals). Since then Chris Patten was given the task of chairing the commission to consider the future of the Royal Ulster Constabulary, and both Michael Heseltine and Kenneth Clarke have been invited to Downing Street to discuss EMU entry. Some critics have noted that Blair's public pronouncements are essentially non-partisan. They amount, says one, to the statement: 'being a good person is important. Vote Labour'.[46]

If Blair is attempting to build a centre and left-of-centre coalition to dominate British politics for the next century as the Conservatives dominated the last one, some might feel that electoral reform would provide a useful tool. In appointing a commission under Lord Jenkins to consider electoral reform, and with that commission recommending a system known to be acceptable to the Labour leadership, one might have imagined that the leadership would clasp the proposed reform to its bosom. But it has not. Indeed the Jenkins report, much awaited and much commented upon, seems to have been sunk without trace.[47] Many critics thought that Ashdown's decision to resign as Liberal Democrat leader was the result of this lack of movement.

Is it defensible to introduce electoral reform for Scotland, Wales, London and Europe but not for Westminster? Logically perhaps not, but politically the reverse can be argued. There will be so much political change in the next few years that reform in so central an aspect of the nation's affairs would be unwise. To many the coalition government (formal or informal) that might emerge would signal the end of adversarialism in policy-making and bring British party politics not kicking, not screaming into the modern world. It would bring an end to so-called 'elective dictatorship' – governments elected by a minority of voters declaring that they had a mandate to do whatever they chose. It would prevent short-termism in policy-making. It would prevent the kind of mismanagement of politics discussed earlier in this chapter in the field of health. It might do all of these things, though if New Zealand experience is any guide, it might not. In 1996 the decision of who was to govern New Zealand and on what terms was decided not by the representatives of a minority of some 40 per cent of voters but by the representatives of a minority of 13 per cent of the voters.

It is true that the post-reform House of Representatives was more truly representative of the nation than any previous parliament, but that was the only major success of the reform. Electoral reform has always been seen by supporters such as Lord Jenkins as the one agent of certain transformation, but surely he is wrong. All three of Britain's major parties have been transformed within the existing system. The alliances which comprised them have changed almost completely. Jenkins believed this could not happen. The Liberal Democrats have secured forty-six seats at Westminster partly through tactical voting. Jenkins believed this could not happen. With the constitutional changes promoted by the Blair government, decentralisation and pluralism have been given a massive fillip. Jenkins believed this could not happen.

But there are other arguments against reform. As Roy Hattersley has noted, when Blair speaks of an end to tribal politics he means divorce from 'the ideals which inspired the Labour party from Keir Hardy to John Smith'.[48] More generally, Matthew Parris reminds us that those who 'cry "beyond Party" from below, and leaders who cry "beyond Party" from above, [forget] those who inhabit the gulf between them, the tens of thousands of men and women from door-knockers to councillors who owe their status and often their income to party; and it is upon such men and women that Blair's (and Ashdown's) career rests'.[49]

And still others. Fuchs and Klingemann assure us that a system's legitimacy rests on two factors: its performance and the extent to which it reflects the underlying values and norms of the people. Parties, they argue, are crucial to both. They further suggest that with the demise of the Soviet system, state performance is more important than underlying values, which are no longer seen to be under threat. If parties are important then we should remember that, according to Schmitt and Holmberg, 'political conflicts are the raison d'être, the breath of life, for political parties. Without conflict parties languish ... the ideological distinctiveness of parties is the single most powerful predictor of flourishing partisanship'.[50] Partisanship, they continue, contributes directly to the stability of party systems and indirectly to the stability of the state. 'That is what is at stake when partisanship fades away.' It is true that Daniel Bell wrote forty years ago about the decline of unifying values[51] and that, more recently, Inglehart has seen traditional party loyalties giving way to 'post-materialist' loyalties, to social movements that is, such as feminism, environmentalism and the like,[52] but it is also true that in the United Kingdom the work of Seyd and Whiteley, to which we have frequently had cause to refer, has been instrumental in re-awakening politicians in both major parties to the importance of vibrant party organisations, and the importance of ideology to that vibrancy. Social movements may come and go; the party system is part of the democratic structure of the state, and party activists are not very likely to heed the call to mobilise to fight party 'X' because 'party "X" is just like us'.

This is not to argue that we need adversarial procedures to dominate the legislative and scrutinising processes of government. We are promised reform of the House of Lords, a Freedom of Information Act and procedural reform in the Commons. These changes will impact substantially upon the adversarial excesses which have done so much to earn public opprobrium; they may lead, who knows, to better government. If so, then the last of Jenkins' arguments for electoral reform will have been met.

We need parties, then, and we need parties to change and develop with the times. British parties over the last twenty years have undergone greater changes than at any time in the last seventy years. In the first edition of this book, I quoted from a speech made by Lloyd George on the hustings in Cardiff during the 1910 election. He warned that because it was perceived as a class party, the Labour party would drive the middle classes into the arms of the Conservatives. 'You are not going to make socialists in a hurry out of the farmers and traders and professional men in this country, but you may scare them into reaction ... if they are threatened then they will surely sulk and harden into downright Toryism. What gain will that be for labour?' It took the Labour party almost a century to learn that lesson and it has been a century dominated by the Conservatives. There is every reason to believe that the parties of the centre and centre left (even if we cannot be certain which is which!) can be as dominant in the next century – though as ever nothing is certain. I suggested at the outset that Britain has only rarely been a genuinely two-party system, and went on to argue that in many respects the nation suffered the consequences of operating as if it *were* (adversarial government policy) without reaping the benefits (regularly alternating governments). If the Liberal Democrats can sustain their current strength nationally they would in practice be creating a three-party system. This would transform British politics by introducing majority government, by limiting the procedural excesses of adversarialism and yet retaining the invigoration of ideology. British parties generally need to walk the fine (but not *awfully* fine) line between adversarialism and 'post-ideological' politics. This task will be made the harder by the additional need to retain a sense of unity and national cohesion in the face of devolution. Parties can only accomplish both of these tasks by retaining a strong sense of identity. We tend to assume that ideology is the key to party identity, but this is only partly true. Partisanship, a feeling of belonging, is actually the key. That feeling of belonging is most often expressed in ideology but actually it is prior to ideology and more fundamental. In Chapter 1 we considered Barker's argument that the essence of party in the British context was not so much ideology as the emergence of a leadership which could retain allegiance. Party, he said, represented a response to deep human instincts – the stimulus of leadership and the warmth of communal action. So long as parties retain that sense of commitment and belonging, it will be expressed in some form of ideology. Devolution will bring a greater degree of pluralism to the British party system and a powerful third party will change the way the system operates. But we still need our parties to fight each other even if – or perhaps precisely because (as Andrew Gamble tells us) – it's not a real fight … but they *must* agree to stop at dinner time.

Notes

1. In A.M. Gamble and S.A. Walkland, *The British Party System and Economic Policy 1945–83*, Oxford, Oxford University Press, 1984.
2. George Bernard Shaw, *Major Barbara*, Harmondsworth, Penguin, 1960, p. 124. (The play was first performed in 1905.)
3. J.A. Hobson, *The Crisis of Liberalism: New Issues of Democracy*, London, King, 1909.
4. Richard Rose, *Do Parties Make a Difference?* 2nd edn, London, Macmillan, 1984.
5. S.E. Finer also advances this argument in *Adversary Politics and Electoral Reform*, London, Wigram, 1975.
6. Rose, *Do Parties Make a Difference?*, p. xxvii.
7. Lord McCarthy, the former trade union leader, for example, counted four changes in policy during the Labour government of 1964–70, four changes of policy during the 1970–74 Conservative government and five changes of policy during the 1974–79 Labour government in the field of incomes policy alone.
8. Rose, *Do Parties Make a Difference?*, p. 65.
9. What they represent is not so much parties contradicting each other as parties 'talking past' each other. He explains: 'A systematic analysis of the 1970 and 1974 manifestos shows that slightly more than half (57 per cent) of all manifesto pledges are nonpartisan.'
10. Philip Norton, *Dissension in the House of Commons 1945–74*, London, Macmillan, 1975, and *Dissension in the House of Commons 1974–79*, Oxford, Oxford University Press, 1980.
11. See Peter Hennessy, *Cabinet*, Oxford, Blackwell, 1986.
12. Hugo Young, 'The strong-arm tactics that politicised Whitehall', *Guardian*, 17 July 1986.
13. Sir Leo Pliatsky, 'Ministers and Officials', *London Review of Books*, vol. 10, July 1980.
14. S.H. Beer, *Modern British Politics*, London, Faber, 1965, p. 347.
15. *Ibid.*, p. 347.
16. Gamble and Walkland, *The British Party System and Economic Policy*, p. 171.
17. Douglas Ashford, *Politics and Policy in Britain – The Limits of Consensus*, Oxford, Blackwell, 1981.
18. Stephen Ingle and Philip Tether, *Parliament and Health Policy, The Role of the MPs 1970–75*, Farnborough, Gower, 1981.
19. *Ibid.*, p. 143.
20. *Ibid.*, p. 155.
21. Friedrich Hayek, *Law, Legislation and Liberty*, vol. 3, *The Political Order of a Free People*, London, Routledge & Kegan Paul, 1979, pp. 2–3.

22. Bruce Lenman, *The Eclipse of Parliament*, London, Edward Arnold, 1992, pp. 18–19.
23. K. Mercer, 'Welcome to the Jungle; Identity and Diversity in Post-Modern Politics', in J. Rutherford (ed.), *Identity, Community, Culture and Difference*, London, Lawrence & Wishart, 1990, pp. 43–71.
24. Alice Brown, David McCone and Lindsay Patterson, *Politics and Society in Scotland*, 2nd edn, London, Macmillan, 1997, p. 214.
25. Scottish Election Survey 1977, quoted *ibid.*, p. 221.
26. L. Niethammer, *Has History Come to an End?*, London, Verso, 1992. p. 36.
27. Not all nations are or seek to be states, for example. See Eric Hobsbawm, *Nations and Nationalism since 1790*, Cambridge, Cambridge University Press, 1990.
28. Brown *et al.*, *Politics and Society in Scotland*, pp. 128–32.
29. One of the best historical accounts of Scottish party politics is I.G.C. Hutchison, *A Political History of Scotland; Parties, Elections and Issues*, Edinburgh, John Donald, 1986. See also M. Fry, *Patronage and Principle: A Political History of Modern Scotland*, Aberdeen, Aberdeen University Press, 1987.
30. Hutchison, *A Political History of Scotland; Parties, Elections and Issues*, p. 207.
31. Fry, *Patronage and Principle*, p. 252.
32. Brown *et al.*, *Politics and Society in Scotland*, p. 148. Jack Brand has written about this in some detail in 'SNP Members: The way of the faithful', in Pippa Norris and Ivor Crewe (eds), *British Elections and Parties Yearbook*, New York, Harvester Wheatsheaf, 1992.
33. See Alan Butt Phillip, *The Welsh Question: Nationalism in Welsh Politics 1945–70*, Cardiff, University of Wales Press, 1975.
34. Peter Lynch, 'From Red to Green: The Political Strategy of Plaid Cymru in the 1980s and 90s', *Regional and Federal Studies*, **5**(2), 1995, pp. 197–210.
35. Even in 1992, for example, when Ashdown had suggested that his party would vote against a Queen's Speech by an incoming Labour government with a small majority which did not include a commitment to electoral reform, even if it proposed devolution. Scottish Liberal Democrats were adamant that they would never support such a stratagem.
36. These scandals filled the pages of the Scottish press for months. They involved, for example, the suicide of Paisley South MP Gordon McMaster and the alleged involvement of Tommy Graham MP in a 'hate campaign' aimed at McMaster. They involved a long-running bribery charge against Scotland's first Asian MP, Mohammad Sarwar. They involved corruption charges against a number of local councillors in the West of Scotland. They involved accusations of vote-rigging, intimidation, nepotism, religious favouritism among a number of local councils.
37. The leadership's attempt to prevent some of the more dubious figures within the party's local government activists from securing nomination is caught up with an obvious desire on the part of some in Millbank and some in the Glasgow office to rid themselves of 'Old Labour' names. The inability of the long-serving Falkirk West MP Dennis Canavan to secure constituency or list nomination was seen by many Scots of all persuasions to be scandalous.
38. An ICM poll only one year after Labour came to power showed that only 28 per cent of Scots believed that Labour was mainly a Scottish party. *The Times*, 16 July 1998.

39. For example, *The Scottish Identity*, Williamson Memorial Lecture, published by the University of Stirling, 1996.
40. Magnus Linklater in the *The Times*, 4 February 1999.
41. Hans-Dieter Klingemann and Dieter Fuchs, *Citizens and the State*, Oxford, Oxford University Press, 1995, p. 429.
42. *Ibid.*, p. 431.
43. Mary Ann Sieghart, *The Times*, 2 July 1998.
44. *The Times*, 7 July 1998.
45. *Independent*, 21 May 1997.
46. Alain de Botton, *Daily Telegraph*, 12 October 1998.
47. An edited version of the report is to be found in *The Times*, 30 October 1998.
48. *Scotland on Sunday*, 15 November 1998.
49. *The Times*, 23 January 1998.
50. Hermann Schmitt and Sören Holmberg, 'Political Parties in Decline?', in Klingemann and Fuchs, *Citizens and the State*, p. 123.
51. Daniel Bell, *The End of Ideology: On the Exhaustion of Political Ideas in the Fifties*, 2nd edn, New York, Free Press, 1968, pp. 22–23.
52. Ronald Inglehart, 'The Changing Structure of Political Cleavages in Western Society', in R.J. Dalton, *Electoral Change in Advanced Industrial Societies: Dealignment or Realignment?*, Princeton, Princeton University Press, 1984.

Bibliography

Abrams M. *et al.*, *Must Labour Lose?*, Harmondsworth, Penguin, 1960.

Anderson, Bruce, *John Major*, London, Fourth Estate, 1991.

Andrews, David, 'Capital mobility and state autonomy: towards a structural theory of international monetary relations', *International Studies Quarterly*, **38**(2), p. 193.

Ashford, Douglas, *Politics and Policy in Britain – The Limits of Consensus*, Oxford, Blackwell, 1981.

Aspinall, A., 'English Party Organisation in the Early Nineteenth Century', *English Historical Review*, **41**, 1926, pp. 389-411.

Attlee, C.R., *The Labour Party in Perspective*, London, Odhams Press, 1937.

Bailey, S.D. (ed.), *The British Party System*, London, Hansard Society, 1952.

Baker, D., and Fountain, I., 'Eton Gent or Essex Man?' in Ludlam, S. and Smith, M.J., *Contemporary British Conservatism*, London, Macmillan, 1996, pp. 86-97.

Ball, Alan R., *British Political Parties*, London, Macmillan, 1981.

Ball, Stuart and Seldon, Anthony (eds), *The Heath Government 1970-74*, London, Longman, 1996.

Barker, Ernest, *Reflections on Government*, London, Oxford University Press, 1967.

Barker, Rodney, *Studies in Opposition*, London, Macmillan, 1971.

Beer, M., *A History of British Socialism*, London, Bell and Sons, 1920.

Beer, Samuel, *Modern British Politics*, London, Faber, 1965.

Beer, Samuel, *Britain against Itself: The Political Contradictions of Collectivism*, London, Faber and Faber, 1982.

Bell, Daniel, *The End of Ideology: On the Exhaustion of Political Ideas in the Fifties*, 2nd edn, New York, Free Press, 1968.

Benewick, R. *et al.*, *Knowledge and Belief in Politics*, London, Allen & Unwin, 1973.

Benn, Tony, *Parliament, People and Power, Agenda for a Free Society*, London, Verso, 1992.

Bennie, Lynn, Curtice, John, *et al.*, 'Party Members', in MacIver, Don (ed.), *The Liberal Democrats*, London, Prentice Hall/Harvester Wheatsheaf, pp. 135-55.

Berkeley, H., *The Myth That Will Not Die*, London, Croom Helm, 1978.

Berki, R.N., *Socialism*, London, Dent, 1975.

Berrington, H.B., *Backbench Opinion in the House of Commons 1944-55*, London, Pergamon Press, 1963.

Blake, Robert, *The Conservative Party from Peel to Churchill*, London, Eyre and Spottiswoode, 1972.

Blumler, Jay, 'The Modern Publicity Process', in Ferguson, M. (ed.), *Public Communications: The New Imperatives*, London, Sage, 1990.

Bogdanor, Vernon, *Liberal Party Politics*, Oxford, Clarendon Press, 1983.

Brack, D., 'Liberal Democrat Policy', in MacIver, Don (ed.), *The Liberal Democrats*, London, Prentice Hall/Harvester Wheatsheaf, 1996, pp. 85–111 .

Brady, Frank (ed.), *Boswell's Life of Johnson*, London, Signet Classics, 1968.

Brand, C.F., *The British Labour Party*, London, Oxford University Press, 1995.

Brand, Jack, *The Power of Parliamentary Parties*, Oxford, Clarendon Press, 1992.

Brown, Alice, McCrone, David and Patterson, Lindsay, *Politics and Society in Scotland*, 2nd edn, London, Macmillan, 1997.

Bulmer Thomas, Ivor, *The Party System in Great Britain*, London, Phoenix House, 1953.

Burch, Martin and Moran, Michael, 'The Changing British Elite', *Parliamentary Affairs*, **38**(1), Winter 1985, pp. 1–15.

Burke, Edmund, 'Thoughts on the Causes of the Present Discontents', in *The Works of Edmund Burke*, vol. 11, 1815–27.

Butler, D. and Kavanagh D., *The British General Election of 1983*, London, Macmillan, 1984.

Butler, D. and Kavanagh D., *The British General Election of 1987*, London, Macmillan, 1988.

Butler, D. and Kavanagh, D., *The British General Election of 1992*, London, Macmillan, 1992.

Butler D. and Kavanagh D., *The British General Election of 1997*, London, Macmillan, 1997, p. 49.

Butler D. and Pinto-Duschinsky, M., 'The Conservative Elite 1918–78: does unrepresentativeness matter?' in Layton-Henry, Z., (ed.), *Conservative Party Politics*, London, Macmillan, 1980.

Butler, D. and Stokes, D., *Political Change in Britain*, 2nd edn, London, Macmillan, 1974.

Butler, R.A., *The Art of the Possible*, Harmondsworth, Penguin, 1973.

Butt Phillip, Alan, *The Welsh Question: Nationalism in Welsh Politics 1945–70*, Cardiff, University of Wales Press, 1975.

Cannon, J., *The Fox/North Coalition*, London, Cambridge University Press, 1969.

Cecil, Lord Hugh, *Conservatism*, London, Home University Library, 1912.

Chesterton, G.K., *Return of Don Quixote*, London, Chatto& Windus, 1917.

Clarke, Peter, *Liberals and Social Democrats*, Cambridge, Cambridge University Press, 1978

Clarke, Peter, 'The Keynesian Consensus and its enemies', in Marquand, David and Seldon, Anthony (eds), *The Ideas that Shaped Post-War Britain*, London, Fontana Press, 1996, pp. 67–88.

Coates, D., *The Labour Party and the Struggle for Socialism*, Cambridge, Cambridge University Press, 1975.

Coates, K. and Topham, T., *Trade Unions in Britain*, Nottingham, Spokesman Press, 1980.

Cole, Margaret, *The Story of Fabian Socialism*, London, Heinemann, 1961.

Cornford, James, 'The Transformation of Conservatism in the late nineteenth century', in *Victorian Studies*, **VII**(1), September 1963, pp. 35-66.

Cowley, Philip, 'Just William? A supplementary analysis of the 1997 Conservative leadership contest', *Talking Politics*, **10**(1), Autumn 1997, pp. 91-5.

Cowley, Philip and Norton, Philip, *Blair's Bastards: Discontent within the Parliamentary Labour Party*, Hull, Centre for Legislative Studies, 1996.

Crewe, I., Barrington, B. and Alt, J., 'Partisan Dealignment in Great Britain 1964-74', *British Journal of Political Science*, **7**(2), April 1977.

Crewe, I., and Sarlvik, B., 'Popular attitudes and electoral strategy', in Layton-Henry, Z. (ed.), *Conservative Party Politics*, London, Macmillan, 1980, pp. 244-75.

Crewe, Ivor and King, Anthony, *SDP: The Birth, Life and Death of the Social Democratic Party*, Oxford, Oxford University Press, 1995.

Critchley, J., *Some of Us: People who did well under Thatcher*, London, John Murray, 1992.

Crosland, Anthony, *The Future of Socialism*, London, Cape, 1956.

Crossman, Richard, *New Fabian Essays*, London, Turnstile Press, 1953.

Curtice, John, 'Who votes for the centre now?', in MacIver, Don (ed.), *The Liberal Democrats*, London, Prentice Hall/Harvester Wheatsheaf, 1996, pp. 191-204.

Curtice, John and Stead, Michael, 'The results analysed', in Butler, D. and Kavanagh, D., *The British General Election of 1997*, London, Macmillan, 1997.

Dangerfield, George, *The Strange Death of Liberal England*, London, McGibbon and Key, 1966.

Dennis, N. and Halsey, A.H., *English Ethical Socialism*, Oxford, Clarendon Press, 1988, p. 4.

Desai, Radhike, *Intellectuals and Socialism*, London, Lawrence and Wishart, 1994.

Disraeli, Benjamin, *Sybil*, Harmondsworth, Penguin, 1980.

Dodds, Elliot, 'Liberty and Welfare', in Watson, George (ed.), *The Unservile State*, London, Allen and Unwin, 1957.

Downs, J., *An Economic Theory of Democracy*, New York, Harper Rowe, 1957.

Drucker, H.M. (ed.), Multi-Party Britain, London, Macmillan, 1979.

Epstein, L.D., *Political Parties in Western Democracies*, London, Pall Mall, 1967.

Fairness at Work, Government White Paper, London, Cm. 3968, May 1998.

Faucher, Florence, 'Is there room for democratic debate at British Labour party conferences?', a paper presented to the PSA annual conference, Nottingham, 1999.

Feiling, K., *The Second Tory Party*, London, Macmillan, 1938.

Feuchtwanger, E.J., 'J.E. Gorst and the Central Organisation of the Conservative Party (1870-82)', *Bulletin of the Institute of Historical Research*, **33**, 1959.

Feuchtwanger, E.J., *Disraeli, Democracy and the Conservative Party*, Oxford, Oxford University Press, 1968.

Finer, S.E., *Adversary Politics and Electoral Reform*, London, Wigram, 1975.

Finer, S.E., Berrington, H.B. and Bartholemew, D.J., *Backbench Opinion in the House of Commons 1955-59*, London, Pergamon, 1961.

Fisher, Justin, *British Political Parties*, London, Prentice Hall/Harvester Wheatsheaf, 1996.

Fisher, Justin, 'Party Finance', in Norton, Philip (ed.), *The Conservative Party*, Prentice Hall/Harvester Wheatsheaf, 1996, pp. 157-69.

Fisher, Sir Nigel, *The Tory Leaders*, London, Weidenfeld & Nicolson, 1977.

Forsyth, Michael, *The Scottish Identity*, Williamson Memorial Lecture, published by the University of Stirling, 1996.

Friedman, Milton, *Capitalism and Freedom*, Chicago, Chicago University Press, 1962.

Fry, M., *Patronage and Principle: A Political History of Modern Scotland*, Aberdeen, Aberdeen University Press, 1987.

Fukuyama, Francis, *The End of History and the Last Man*, London, Penguin, 1993.

Gamble, Andrew, *The Free Economy and the Strong State*, London, Macmillan, 1988.

Gamble, Andrew, 'The Conservative Party', in H.M. Drucker (ed.), *Multi-Party Britain*, London, Macmillan, 1970, p. 40.

Gamble, Andrew, 'The Legacy of Thatcherism', in M. Perryman, (ed.), *The Blair Agenda*, London, Lawrence & Wishart, 1996.

Gamble, A.M. and Walkland, S.A., *The British Party System and Economic Policy 1945–83*, Oxford, Oxford University Press, 1984.

Gash, N., 'From the origins to Sir Robert Peel', in R.A. Butler (ed.), *The Conservatives*, London, Allen and Unwin, 1977, p. 125.

George, Henry, *Progress and Poverty*, printed in London, Manchester and Glasgow, 1882.

Giddens, Anthony, *The Third Way: The Renewal of Social Democracy*, Oxford, Polity Press, 1998.

Giddens, Anthony, 'The Future of the Welfare State', in Michael Novak, *Is There a Third Way?*, London, Institute of Economic Affairs, 1998, pp. 25-9.

Gilmour, Ian, *The Body Politic*, (rev. edn), London, Hutchison, 1971.

Gilmour, Ian, *Dancing with Dogma*, London, Simon and Shuster, 1992.

Gilmour, Ian, *Inside Right*, London, Hutchinson, 1977.

Gilmour, Ian and Garnett, Margaret, *Whatever Happened to the Tories*, London, Fourth Estate, 1998.

Goodhart, Philip, *The 1922*, London, Macmillan, 1973.

Goss, S., *Local Labour and Local Government*, Edinburgh, Edinburgh University Press, 1988.

Gramsci, Antonio, *Selections from Prison Notebooks*, London, Lawrence & Wishart, 1971.

Grimond, Jo, *The Liberal Future*, London, Faber, 1959.

Guttsman, W.J., *The British Political Elite*, London, MacGibbon and Kee, 1963.

Haldane, R. B., *An Autobiography*, London, Hodder & Stoughton, 1929, p. 330.

Hanham, H.J., *Elections and Party Management*, Longmans Green, London, 1959.

Harrison, Brian, *The Transformation of British Politics 1860-1995*, Oxford University Press, 1996.

Harrison, Martin, *Trade Unions and the Labour Party since 1945*, London, Allen & Unwin, 1960.

Haxey, S., *Tory MP*, London, Gollancz, 1939.

Hayek, Friedrich, *Law, Legislation and Liberty*, vol. 3, *The Political Order of a Free People*, London, Routledge & Kegan Paul, 1979.

Hearnshaw, F.J.C., (ed.), *Social and Political Ideas in the Age of Reaction*, London, Harrap, 1932.

Heath, A. and MacDonald, S., 'Socialist change and the future of the Left', *Political Quarterly*, **58**(4), October–December 1987, pp. 364-77.

Hennessy, Peter, *Cabinet*, Oxford, Blackwell, 1986.

Hennessy, Peter and Seldon, Anthony (eds), *Ruling Performance: British Government from Attlee to Thatcher*, Oxford, Blackwell, 1987.

Hobsbawm, Eric, *Nations and Nationalism since 1790*, Cambridge, Cambridge University Press, 1990.

Hobson, J.A., *The Crisis of Liberalism: New Issues of Democracy*, London, King, 1909.

Hogg, Quintin, *The Conservative Case*, Harmondsworth, Penguin, 1959.

Holme, Richard, 'Sausages or policemen? The role of the Liberal Democrats in the 1997 campaign'. Paper to the EPOP Conference, 1997.

Holmes, Martin, 'The Conservative Party and Europe: From Major to Hague', *The Political Quarterly*, **69**(2), June 1988, pp. 133–47.

Holthsam, G. and Hughes, R., 'The State of Social Democracy in Britain', in Cuperus, R. and Kandel, J. (eds), *European Social Democracy*, Amsterdam, Friedrich Ebert Stiftung, 1998.

Howell, Chris, 'From New Labour to No Labour? The Blair Government in Britain'. Paper delivered to the APSA conference, Boston, 1998.

Hume, David, *History of Great Britain*, vol. II, London, 1824.

Hunt, A. (ed.), *Marxism and Democracy*, London, Lawrence & Wishart, 1980.

Hutchison, I.G.C., *A Political History of Scotland; Parties, Elections and Issues*, Edinburgh, John Donald, 1986.

Hutton, Will, *The State We're In*, London, Jonathan Cape, 1995.

Hutton, Will, *et al.*, *Stakeholding and its Critics*, London, Institute of Economic Affairs, 1997.

Ingle, Stephen 'The Emergence of Multi-Party Politics', in Hayward J. and Norton P. (eds), *The Political Science of British Politics*, Brighton, Wheatsheaf, 1986, pp. 105–19.

Ingle, Stephen, 'Party Organisation', in *The Liberal Democrats*, MacIver, Don (ed.), London, Prentice Hall/Harvester Wheatsheaf, 1996, pp. 113–33.

Ingle, Stephen, 'The Liberal Democrats and Equidistance', *Parliamentary Brief*, **4**(2), November 1995.

Ingle, Stephen, 'William Morris and Bernard Shaw', in Parekh, B.C., *The Concept of Socialism*, London, Croom Helm, 1975, pp. 73–83.

Ingle, Stephen and Tether, Philip, *Parliament and Health Policy, The Role of the MPs 1970–75*, Farnborough, Gower, 1981.

Inglehart, Ronald, 'The Changing Structure of Political Cleavages in Western Society', in Dalton, R.J., *Electoral Change in Advanced Industrial Societies: Dealignment or Realignment?*, Princeton, Princeton University Press, 1984.

Interim and Final Report of The Committee on Party Organisation, London, National Union of Conservative and Unionist Associations, 1949.

James, R.R., *The British Revolution 1886–1939*, London, Methuen, 1978.

Janosik, E.G., *Constituency Labour Parties in Britain*, London, Pall Mall Press for the Foreign Policy Research Institute, 1968.

Jones, Bill, 'Clause Four and Blair's Brilliant Campaign', *Talking Politics*, **8**(1), 1995.

Jones, Harriet and Kandiah, Michael (eds), *The Myth of Consensus: New Views on British History 1945–1964*, Basingstoke, Macmillan, 1996.

Jowell, R., Witherspoon, S. and Brooks, L. (eds), *British Social Attitudes*, Aldershot, Gower, 1988.

Judge, David, *The Parliamentary State*, London, Sage, 1993.

Katz, R.S. and Mair, P., *How Parties Organise: Change and Adaptation in Party Organisations in Western Democracies*, London, Sage, 1994.

Kavanagh, Dennis (ed.), The Politics of the Labour Party, London, Allen & Unwin, 1982.

Kelly, J., *Conservative Party Conferences*, Manchester, Manchester University Press, 1989.

Kinnock, Neil, *Making Our Way*, Oxford, Blackwell, 1986.

Klingemann, Hans-Dieter and Fuchs, Dieter, *Citizens and the State*, Oxford, Oxford University Press, 1995.

Kramnick, Isaac (ed.), *Is Britain Dying?* London, Cornell University Press, 1979.

Labour Party Year Book 1984-5, London, Walworth Road, 1985.

Layton-Henry, Z. (ed.), *Conservative Party Politics*, London, Macmillan, 1980.

Leach, Robert, *British Political Ideologies*, London, Prentice Hall, 1996.

Lenman, Bruce, *The Eclipse of Parliament*, London, Edward Arnold, 1992.

Leopold, John, 'Trade Unions, Political Fund Ballots and the Labour party', *British Journal of Industrial Relations*, **35**(1), March 1997, pp. 23-38.

Letwin, Shirley Robin, *The Anatomy of Thatcherism*, London, Fontana Books, 1992.

Lijphart, A., *Democracies, Patterns of Majoritarian and Consensus Government in Twenty-One Countries*, New Haven, Yale University Press, 1984.

Ludlam, S. and Smith, M.J., *Contemporary British Conservatism*, London, Macmillan, 1996.

Lyman, R.W., *The First Labour Government, 1924*, London, Chapman and Hall, 1957.

Lynch, Peter, 'From Red to Green: The Political Strategy of Plaid Cymru in the 1980s and 90s', *Regional and Federal Studies*, **5**(2), 1995, pp. 197-210.

Lynch, Peter, 'Preparing for devolution: the Scottish Conservatives after the 1997 electoral wipeout', *Regional Studies*, forthcoming, pp. 1-14.

Lynch, Peter, *Third Party Politics in a Four Party System: the Liberal Democrats in Scotland*, unpublished monograph, 1995.

Macaulay, T.B., *History of England*, New York, Harper and Brothers, 1861.

Madison, James, *The Federalist* (1787), New York, Modern Library, 1941.

Mair, Peter, *Party Systems: Change, approaches and interpretations*, Oxford, Clarendon, 1997.

Mandelson, Peter and Liddle, Roger, *The Blair Revolution*, London, Faber & Faber, 1996.

Maor, Moshe, *Political Parties and Party Systems*, London, Routledge, 1997.

Marquand, David, 'The Blair Paradox', *Prospect,* May 1998, pp. 19-24.

Marquand, David and Seldon, Anthony (eds), *The Ideas that Shaped Post-War Britain,* London, Fontana, 1996.

Marqusee, Mike, 'New Labour and its Discontents', *New Left Review*, No. 224, 1997, pp. 127-42.

Marx, Karl and Engels, Friedrich, *Manifesto of the Communist Party*, Moscow, Progress Publishers, 1952.

Maude, Angus, 'Party paleontology', *Spectator*, 15 March 1963.

McKenzie, R.T., *British Political Parties*, London, Heinemann, 1955.

McKenzie, R.T., 'Power in the party: intra-party democracy', in Kavanagh, Dennis (ed.), *The Politics of the Labour Party*, London, Allen & Unwin, 1982.

McKenzie, R.T. and Silver, A., *Angels in Marble*, London, Heinemann, 1968.

McKibbins, R., *The Evolution of the Labour Party 1916–24*, London, Oxford University Press, 1977.

Meadowcroft, Michael, *Liberal Values for a New Decade*, Manchester, North West Community Papers, 1981.

Mellors, Colin, *The British MP*, Farnborough, Saxon House, 1978.

Mercer, K., 'Welcome to the Jungle; Identity and Diversity in Post-Modern Politics', in J. Rutherford (ed.), *Identity, Community, Culture and Difference*, London, Lawrence & Wishart, 1990, pp. 43–71.

Minkin, L., *The Labour Party Conference*, London, Allen Lane, 1978.

Minkin, L., *The Contentious Alliance*, Edinburgh, Edinburgh University Press, 1991.

Mitchell, Austin, *Four Years in the Death of the Labour Party*, London, Methuen, 1984.

Morris, William, *News from Nowhere*, London, Lawrence & Wishart, 1973.

Morton, A.L. (ed.), *The Political Writings of William Morris*, London, Lawrence & Wishart, 1973.

Niethammer, L., *Has History Come to an End?*, London, Verso, 1992.

Norris, Pippa, 'New Labour, New Politicians?', in Norris, Pippa and Evans, Geoffrey, *A Critical Election: British Parties and Voters in Long-Term Perspective*, London, Sage, 1999.

Norris, Pippa and Crewe, Ivor (eds), *British Elections and Parties Yearbook*, New York, Harvester Wheatsheaf, 1992.

Norton, Philip, *Dissension in the House of Commons 1945–74*, London, Macmillan, 1975.

Norton, Philip, *Dissension in the House of Commons 1974–79*, Oxford, Oxford University Press, 1980.

Norton, Philip, *Does Parliament Matter?* London, Harvester Wheatsheaf, 1993.

Norton, Philip, *The Conservative Party*, Prentice Hall/Harvester Wheatsheaf, 1996.

Norton, Philip, 'The Conservative Party: "In Office but not in Power"', in King, Anthony *et al.*, *New Labour Triumphs: Britain at the Polls*, Chatham NJ, Chatham House, 1998, pp. 75–112.

Norton, Philip and Aughey, Arthur, *Conservatives and Conservatism*, London, Temple Smith, 1981.

Nutting, Anthony, *No End of a Lesson*, London, Constable, 1967.

Oakshott, Michael, *Rationalism in Politics*, London, Methuen, 1962.

O'Gorman, Frank, *The Emergence of the British Two-Party System 1760–1832*, London, Edward Arnold, 1982.

Olson, Moncur, 'A Theory of the Incentives Facing Political Organisations: Neocorporatism and the Hegemonist State', *International Political Science Review*, **7**, 1986, pp. 165–89.

Orwell, George, *The Road to Wigan Pier*, Harmondsworth, Penguin, 1963.

Ostrogorski, M., *Democracy and the Organisation of Political Parties*, London, Macmillan, 1902.

O'Sullivan, N.K., *Conservatism*, London, Dent, 1976, p. 24.

Owen, David, *Face the Future*, London, Cape, 1981.

Perryman, M. (eds), *The Blair Agenda*, London, Lawrence & Wishart, 1996.

Pinto-Duschinsky, M., *British Political Finance 1830–1980*, Washington DC, American Enterprise Institute, 1981.

Pinto-Duschinky, M., 'Central Office and "power" in The Conservative Party', *Political Studies*, **20**(1), March 1972.

Pliatsky, Sir Leo, 'Ministers and Officials', *London Review of Books*, **10**, July, 1980.

Plucknett, T.F.T., *Taswell Langmead's Constitutional History*, 10th edn, London, Sweet and Maxwell, 1946.

Poirier, P. P. , *Advent of the Labour Party*, London, Allen & Unwin, 1958.

Powell, Enoch, 'Conservatism and Social Problems', *Swinton Journal*, Autumn 1968.

Pugh, M., *The Making of Modern British Politics 1879–1939*, Blackwell, Oxford, 1982.

Quinton, Anthony, *The Politics of Imperfection*, London, Faber & Faber, 1978.

Radice, G. and Pollard, S., *More Southern Discomfort*, London, Fabian Society, 1993.

Rallings, Collin and Thrasher, Michael, 'The 1998 local election results and democracy', *Talking Politics*, **11**(1), Autumn 1998, pp. 37–42.

Ramsden, J., *An Appetite for Power*, London, HarperCollins, 1998.

Ramsden, J., *The Making of Conservative Party Policy*, London, Longman, 1980.

Report of the Enquiry into the Export of Defence Equipment and Dual-Use Goods to Iraq and Related Questions, HC 15, London, HMSO, 1996.

Roberts, G.K., *Political Parties and Pressure Groups in Britain*, London, Weidenfeld & Nicolson, 1970.

Roberts, K., Cook, F. and Semeonoff, E., *The Fragmenting Class Struggle*, London, Heinemann, 1977.

Rogers, William, *The Politics of Change*, London, Secker and Warburg, 1981.

Rose, Richard, *Politics in England*, London, Faber, 1965.

Rose, Richard, *The Problem of Party Government*, London, Pelican, 1976.

Rose, Richard, *Do Parties Make a Difference?* 2nd edn, London, Macmillan, 1984.

Rose, Richard, 'Voting Behaviour in Britain 1945–74', in his *Studies in British Politics*, 3rd edn, London, Macmillan 1976.

Ross, J.F.S., *Parliamentary Representation*, London, Eyre and Spottiswood, 1948.

Roth, Andrew, *Parliamentary Profiles*, London, Parliamentary Profiles Services, 1984.

Rush, Michael, 'The Selectorate Revisited: selecting party candidates in the 1980s', *Teaching Politics*, **15**(1), January 1986, pp. 99–114.

Rutherford, Jonathan (ed.), *Identity, Community, Culture and Difference*, London, Lawrence & Wishart, 1990.

Sartori, G., *Parties and Party Systems: A Framework for Analysis*, Cambridge, Cambridge University Press, 1976.

Saville, J., 'The ideology of labourism', in R. Benewick *et al.*, *Knowledge and Belief in Politics*, London, Allen & Unwin, 1973.

Schmitt, Hermann and Holmberg, Sören, 'Political Parties in Decline?', in Klingemann, Hans-Dieter and Fuchs, Dieter, *Citizens and the State*, Oxford, Oxford University Press, 1995.

Schoen, D.E., *Enoch Powell and the Powellites*, London, Macmillan, 1977.

Schumann, H.G., 'The problem of Conservatism', in *Journal of Contemporary History*, **13**(4), October 1978.

Schumpeter, Joseph, *Capitalism, Socialism and Democracy*, London, George Allen & Unwin, 1976.

Scruton, Roger, *The Meaning of Conservatism*, Harmondsworth, Penguin, 1980.

Scruton, Roger (ed.), *Conservative Thinkers*, London, Claridge Press, 1988.

Seldon, Anthony, (ed.), *How Tory Governments Fall*, London, Fontana Press, 1996.

Seldon, Anthony and Ball, Stuart, *Conservative Century: The Conservative Party Since 1900*, Oxford, Oxford University Press, 1994.

Seyd, Patrick, 'New Parties, New Politics? A Case Study of the Labour Party', *Party Politics*, no. 4, 1999 forthcoming.

Seyd, Patrick and Whiteley, Paul, *Labour's Grass Roots*, Oxford, Clarendon Press, 1992.

Shaw, G.B., *Everybody's Political What's What*, London, Constable, 1944.

Shaw, G.B., *Major Barbara*, Harmondsworth, Penguin, 1960.

Shaw, G.B., *Prefaces By Bernard Shaw*, London, Odhams Press, 1938.

Shaw, Eric, *Discipline and Discord in the Labour Party*, Manchester, Manchester University Press, 1988.

Shaw, Eric, *The Labour Party Since 1945*, Oxford, Blackwell, 1996.

Shaw, Eric, 'A better way to make policy', *New Socialist*, December 1989/January 1990, pp. 30-3.

Shaw, Eric, 'The Determinants of the Programmatic Transformation of the British Labour Party'. Paper given at the APSA conference in Boston, 1998.

Shell, D. and Beamish D., *The House of Lords at Work*, Oxford, Oxford University Press, 1993.

Stevenson, John, 'Liberals to Liberal Democrats', in *The Liberal Democrats*, MacIver, Don (ed.), London, Prentice Hall/Harvester Wheatsheaf, 1996, pp. 23-39.

Strachey, John, 'Tasks and Achievements of British Labour', in Crossman, R.H.S., *New Fabian Essays*, London, Turnstyle Press, 1953.

Studlar, D.T., 'By-elections and the Liberal/SDP Alliance', *Teaching Politics*, **13**(1), January 1984, pp. 84-95.

Tether, Philip, *Conservative Clubs*, unpublished PhD thesis, University of Hull, 1990.

Tether, Philip, 'Conservative Clubs: A neglected aspect in Conservative Organisation', *Hull Papers in Politics*, no. 42, 1988.

Tether, Philip, 'Kingston upon Hull Conservative Party: a case study of a Tory party in decline', *Hull Papers in Politics*, no.19, December 1980.

Tether, Philip, 'Members and Organisation', in Norton, Philip, *The Conservative Party*, Prentice Hall/Harvester Wheatsheaf, 1996.

Tether, Philip, 'The Party in the country: development and influence', in Norton, Philip, *The Conservative Party*, Prentice Hall/Harvester Wheatsheaf, 1996.

Thomas, D., 'The New Tories', *New Society*, 2 February 1984.

Tressell, Robert, *The Ragged Trousered Philanthropists*, St Albans, Panther Books, 1965.

Turner, J.E., *Labour's Doorstop Politics in London*, London, Macmillan, 1978.

Uttley, T.E., 'The significance of Mrs Thatcher', in M. Cowling (ed.), *Conservative Essays*, London, Cassell, 1978.

Wagar, W. (ed.), *H.G. Wells: Journalism and Prophecy*, London, Bodley Head, 1965.

Walker, Peter, *Ascent of Britain*, London, Sidgwick & Jackson, 1977.

Ward, J.T., 'Derby and Disraeli', in D. Southgate (ed.), *Conservative Leadership 1832-1932*, London, Macmillan, 1974.

Ware, Alan, *Political Parties and Party Systems*, Oxford University Press, 1996.

Webb, Sydney and Beatrice, *Soviet Communism: A New Civilisation?* London, WEA, 1935.

Wells, H.G., *The New Machiavelli*, Harmondsworth, Penguin, 1970.

Whiteley, Paul, *The Labour Party in Crisis*, London, Methuen, 1983.

Whiteley, Paul, 'Declining local membership and electoral support', in Kavanagh, Dennis, *The Politics of the Labour Party*, London, Allen & Unwin, 1982.

Whiteley, P., Seyd, P. and Richardson, J., *True Blues: The Politics of Conservative Party Membership*, Oxford, Oxford University Press, 1994.

Wickam-Jones, Mark, *Economic strategy and the Labour Party*, Basingstoke, Macmillan, 1996

Wilkes, Stephen, 'Conservative Government and the Economy', *Political Studies*, **45**(4), 1997.

Willetts, David, 'Conservative Renewal', *The Political Quarterly*, **69**(2), June 1998, pp. 110-18.

Williams, Francis, *A Prime Minister Remembers*, London, Heinemann, 1961, p. 535.

Williams, P.M., *Hugh Gaitskell: A Political Biography*, London, Cape, 1979.

Williams, Shirley, *Politics is for People*, Harmondsworth, Penguin, 1981.

Williamson, H.R., 'The Seventeenth Century', in Bailey, S.D. (ed.), *The British Party System*, London, Hansard Society, 1952.

Young, Hugo, *One of Us: A Biography of Margaret Thatcher*, London, Pan, 1990.

Index